Sweden: Choices for Economic
and Social Policy in the 1980s

Sweden:
Choices for Economic and Social Policy in the 1980s

Edited by
BENGT RYDÉN
and
VILLY BERGSTRÖM

London
GEORGE ALLEN & UNWIN
Boston   Sydney

George Allen & Unwin (Publishers) Ltd,
40 Museum Street, London WC1A 1LU, UK

George Allen & Unwin (Publishers) Ltd,
Park Lane, Hemel Hempstead, Herts HP2 4TE, UK

Allen & Unwin Inc.,
9 Winchester Terrace, Winchester, Mass 01890, USA

George Allen & Unwin Australia Pty Ltd,
8 Napier Street, North Sydney, NSW 2060, Australia

First published in 1982

An earlier version of this book was published in Swedish as Vägal i
Svensk Politik: Ekonomi och samhälle på 80-talet *by Studieförbundet*
Näringsliv och Samhälle.

British Library Cataloguing in Publication Data

   Sweden: choices for economic and social policy in the 1980s.
1.   Sweden — Economic conditions — 1945-
I.   Rydén, Bengt II. Bergström, Villy
III.   Vägval i Svensk politik. *English*
330.9485'058   HC375
ISBN 0-04-339027-7

Set in 10 on 11 point Times by Alan Sutton Ltd, Gloucester
and printed in Great Britain by Biddles Ltd, Guildford, Surrey

Contents

The Authors

VILLY BERGSTRÖM is a professor of economics at Uppsala University, currently engaged in research on capital formation and industrial growth at the Swedish Work Life Centre. He wrote *Kapitalbildning och industriell demokrati* (Capital Accumulation and Industrial Democracy) in 1973. From 1975 to 1977 he was a member of the Economic Policy Group of the Studieförbundet Näringsliv och Samhälle (SNS) (Business & Social Research Institute).

BENGT RYDÉN is a doctor of economics and managing director of the SNS. His dissertation *Mergers in Swedish Industry* appeared in 1972. In 1979 he was editor and author of *Mot en ny konsumentpolitik* (Toward a New Consumer Policy). In 1980 he prepared a government report on industrial policy. He set up the SNS Economic Policy Group in 1974 and has since acted as its chairman.

GUY DE FARAMOND, a Frenchman of Swedish descent, used to work in Sweden as a correspondent for French newspapers. He is now on the staff of a new French daily, *Forum International*, in Paris.

MICHAEL HARRINGTON is an American social critic and political analyst, best known for his book *The Other America*, published in 1963. This study of poverty in the United States had a broad political impact and triggered a number of social reforms. In 1980 he wrote *Decade of Decision*. He is chairman of the Democratic Socialist Organising Committee.

ANDREW MARTIN is a social scientist at the Massachusetts Institute of Technology; formerly at Harvard University, where he specialised in research on Swedish affairs.

HANS L. ZETTERBERG, a former professor of sociology at Columbia University and Ohio State University, is currently managing director of SIFO (Swedish Institute of Public Research), an opinion-polling institute. He is also associate professor at Umeå University.

JÖRGEN WESTERSTÅHL is professor of political science at Göteborg University and author of *Objektiv nyhetsförmedling* (Objective News Presentation), published in 1971).

STAFFAN BURENSTAM-LINDER is professor of economics at the Stockholm School of Economics. He was minister of trade in the three-party coalition governments of 1976–8 and 1979–81. In 1969 he published *Den rastlösa välfärdsmänniskan* (trans., *The Harried Leisure Class*, 1970).

LARS NABSETH is professor of economics and managing director of the Federation of Swedish Industries. He chaired a government Commission on the Ordinary Steel Industry in 1977. His previous works include *Löneökningars verkningar inom industrin* (Effects of Wage Raises in Industry), 1961, and *The Diffusion of New Industrial Processes* (with G. F. Ray, 1974).

JAN WALLANDER has a PhD in economics and is president of the board of Svenska Handelsbanken. His *I huvudet på en kapitalist* (Inside the Head of a Capitalist) was published in 1974.

GÖRAN BORG, a professor of mathematics, was formerly head of the Royal Institute of Technology in Stockholm. He is at present attached to the SNS Technological and Industrial Policy Group.

BENGT-ARNE VEDIN has a PhD in technology and is currently attached to the SNS, where he directs the research project Innovationsklimatet i Sverige (The Innovative Environment in Sweden). Among his recent works are *Media Futura, Corporate Culture for Innovation, Creativity Management, Radical Product Innovation* and *Innovation Organization*.

ERIK DAHMÉN is professor of economics at the Stockholm School of Economics. Among his earlier works are *Svensk industrial företagarverksamhet* (Swedish Industrial Enterprise), published in 1950, and the 1969 SNS publication *Sätt pris på miljön* (Put a Price on Environment).

WALTER KORPI is a professor of social policy at the Institute for Social Research, Stockholm University. His past publications include *Arbetarklassen i välfärdskapitalismen* (trans., *The Working Class in Welfare Capitalism*, 1978) which received the C. Wright Mills award of 1978.

BO SÖDERSTEN, a professor of economics at Lund University, wrote *Internationell ekonomi* (trans., *International Economics*, 1970) in 1969. Since 1979 he has been a member of parliament.

LARS BERGMAN is a doctor of economics and devotes special interest to energy questions. In 1978–9 he worked at the Institute for Applied Systems Analysis in Vienna and is now at the Stockholm School of Economics.

KARL-GÖRAN MÄLER is professor of economics at the Stockholm School of Economics. His speciality is the economics of resources and environment.

KARL-OLOF FAXÉN is assistant professor of economics and head of the research department of the Swedish Employers' Confederation.

BENGT-CHRISTER YSANDER is an assistant professor of economics. In 1978 he was a member of the SNS Economic Policy Group. He is currently attached to the Industrial Institute for Economic and Social Research, Stockholm.

ERIK LUNDBERG is professor emeritus at the Stockholm School of Economics. Among his books are *Business Cycle and Economic Policy*, a 1955 SNS publication, and *Svensk finanspolitik* (Swedish Fiscal Policy), 1971. Since 1974 he has been a consultant to the government of Portugal. He has been a member of the SNS Economic Policy Group since it was set up in 1974.

OLOF PALME is chairman of the Social Democratic Workers' Party. He was prime minister from 1969 to 1976.

Introduction

The start of a new decade should be a time for reflection. As the era of the 1970s gives way to the 1980s we would be well advised to look back and try to understand why the past decade was so plagued by disillusionments, disquiet and pessimism. Can we derive lessons from the 1970s that will reverse this trend in the 1980s? Which political directions should Sweden move in if we are to shape a better society over the next decade? What are the limits on our freedom of action, and which mistakes can we avoid making?

These are the questions taken up in the fifteen essays that comprise this book. Qualified writers from the worlds of research, politics and public debate have been invited to present their views on a variety of problems both economic and political in nature. Our aim is to transcend the increasingly shortsighted perspective typical of big-time politics and to focus rather on some important matters of principle that are too often left aside in the rush to solve day-to-day problems.

Although contributors span a wide spectrum of political opinion they were selected not as representatives of ideological tendencies but as experts in the particular fields under discussion. None the less most of the essays here necessarily reflect, implicitly or explicitly, the opinions and values of their authors. If the results are not always sufficiently balanced or objective, it is the editors, not the authors, who should be held responsible.

The range of topics covered in this book obviously represents a subjective choice and is by no means complete. Yet the questions discussed here are all fundamental to the economic and social life of our country. When it comes to such issues as political democracy; wages, prices and taxes; energy supplies; the ownership of enterprises; and the functioning of the mixed economy, the decisions we make in the 1980s will be crucial to the whole future development of Swedish society.

These are political options worthy of careful analysis, serious debate and thorough consideration for many years to come.

BENGT RYDÉN

Note

The contributions to the Swedish edition of this book were completed during the first months of 1979. Corrections and additions for the English edition were made later in 1980 and 1981. The translation into English is by Peter Landelius.

1
Sweden in the 1980s: How Gloomy Are the Prospects?

BENGT RYDÉN and VILLY BERGSTRÖM

Expected and Unexpected Events of the 1970s

The 1970s turned out to be a decade full of political and economic drama. Who could have predicted ten years ago – after the stable developments of the 1960s that the Western world was entering a period of weak economic growth and industrial stagnation and that it would be plagued by the worst unemployment and inflation of the last fifty years? Who could believe in a breakdown of the international monetary system? Who foresaw the oil crisis and the halt of nuclear power in a number of countries? Who could imagine that industrialisation and the growth of exports would begin to gather momentum in a number of poor developing countries and that a structural crisis would hit the Western world with threats of bankruptcy for the very companies which had been the backbone of Swedish industry?

But at the same time much of what happened in the 1970s has been without surprises. This is the case with large sectors of technological and industrial development (computerisation, automation, communication, and so on). It is the case with the democratisation of working life, increasing the power of the unions and diminishing that of corporate owners. It is also the case with the expansion of the public sector. Predicted events also include the shift towards more public regulation and participation in industry. It has meant increased importance for everything we refer to when talking of the quality of life – a better environment, more leisure, increased possibilities for making the decisions that affect one's life. But it has also meant continued centralisation, bureaucratisation, intensified efficiency and a sense of alienation in the individual facing large private and public bureaucracies.

The prognosis industry has a bearish market right now. It is harder than ever to hit the bull's eye. The 1970s have left behind a series of wrecked prognoses and the many breaks in trend have led to mistaken forecasts having serious consequences for corporations and authorities. However, any decision with long-term implications must be based on some idea about the future. The question is how well founded that idea is. Despite the turbulence of the 1970s, society is a sluggish machine and responds slowly even to forceful shifts of the helm. One can arrive at a well-founded opinion of what will happen in the 1980s. It is possible to discern signals, indications and tendencies which tell us something about the future.

Our purpose in this book is not to present a complete picture of the politics and economy of Sweden in the 1980s. The book is strictly limited to what we see as most important and most problematic. Concrete solutions are discussed by several of the authors. Our choice of problem areas in the present essay, as well as for the book as a whole, is determined by a common frame of reference – values, lines of interest, and knowledge. But not even within that framework can we offer a complete inventory of the problems, just a collection of examples.

Growing Demands – Stagnating Production

As in previous years, increasing demands have been made in the 1970s on the productive capacity of our society, but external economic disturbances and a decreased adaptability have weakened that capacity. The demands for an increase in material living standards and growing public activities (health care, education, housing and so on) have continued incessantly, just as in the golden 1960s, while demands for a higher quality of life (leisure, time-related wages, a job in the town where one lives) have been added or become more accentuated. During the 1970s as a whole we have tried to take more out of the productive apparatus – here we include the public sector – than it has been able to produce. This has contributed to inflationary pressures, deficits in Sweden's external balance (4 per cent of GNP) and a historically enormous government budget deficit (10 per cent of GNP). 'The society of increasing demands' can be seen as the result of attitudes created in the younger generations by an uninterrupted increase in the standard of living in the 1950s and 1960s. But political competition, with a new instability and a weakened government power, have also contributed.

Changes in the Public Sector

A factor of direct relevance to this question has been the size, direction and financing of the public sector. It was possible to take that factor lightly as long as the public sector was small in proportion to the economy as a whole. Currently the production of public services accounts for over 30 per cent of GNP and it is growing faster than other sectors of the economy. The efficiency of the production of public services has therefore become a fundamental macroeconomic issue.

We believe that it will be necessary to try out a system that informs citizens of the real cost of production and consumption of different public services better than the current system does. It can be done by means of cost-related fees when this is compatible with other social goals. Other methods are also conceivable, for instance, publicly announced 'shadow prices'. Both fees and shadow prices must be combined with a freedom of choice for the consumer which exposes public producers to competition. Changes in this direction will probably be necessary lest the citizens' feeling of social solidarity and their will to sacrifice for the community be weakened. This need not lead to either increased income gaps or a shrinking production of public services.

A New Swedish Model?

The incompatibility between demands on society and its productive capacity are also closely related to wage formation. A decisive question is whether the Swedish model of wage formation through free negotiation has played itself out. Freedom becomes an illusion when the contracting parties actually negotiate on the rate of inflation and the level of unemployment rather than on real wage increases, and when collective agreements cannot be concluded without important personal tax reductions.

Unless important changes occur in the conditions fundamental to Sweden's very centralised wage formation process (primarily the rate of inflation but also marginal income taxes), it seems to us inevitable that the roles of unions, employers and government authorities in wage formation must change and that the contracting parties as a consequence will gradually shift to other tasks. Such a development is accelerated by weak economic growth, since that means that there is not much in real terms to negotiate about for labour as a group. The reduction of Sweden's economic imbalances by industrial recovery will need growing company profits and a slow development of nominal and real wages. Continued social compromise and balance in the labour market will presumably need reforms which more than at present draw wage-earners into the decision-making process of private industry with regard to investment and structural change, so that the redistribution of resources from consumption to capital formation is accepted as just and equitable. 'The power over the enterprise' must be given increased legitimacy.

The solution of all these very difficult problems calls for a new Swedish 'historical compromise' between labour and capital, unions and employers, left and right – a compromise of the same meaning and importance as that of the late 1930s ('The Saltsjöbaden Agreement').

The Weakening of Government Power

A palpable change which took place in the early 1970s in Sweden was the adoption of a new Constitution, and it had a clear political significance: the chances for the Social Democrats to govern alone for long periods have declined. The unique characteristic of Swedish democracy that enabled an often strong one-party cabinet to direct social development has disappeared. Up until this time Sweden was governed by unwritten but agreed-upon rules that changed the letter of the Constitution of 1809. This Constitution gave the biggest party a large and extended overrepresentation in the two-chamber system. The reform of the Constitution has increased democracy – the direct and proportional effect of popular will on the composition of the Riksdag – but also entailed a weakening of government power. That is a clear result of the political developments of the 1970s.

Other political changes of the decade point in the same direction, namely, the decline in class-related voting and the greater mobility of the electorate. During the 1970s as many as 10 per cent of the electorate have been seen to switch their sympathies between the socialist bloc and the bourgeois bloc on the basis of their opinion on single issues or persons. This, too, weakens the power of government: a greater risk of losing in the near future shortens a government's horizon.

If we combine these observations with the fact that the period of electoral mandate is now only three years the prospect for a strong, economically sound and farsighted (although perhaps unpopular in the short run) policy is less likely from now on. In the 1950s and 1960s the Social Democratic government knew that it was very likely to bear the main responsibility of governing the country for a long time ahead. This awareness forced it to plan its economic policies in a long-term perspective and put severe restraint on what the electorate could be offered in terms of reforms. Under the present Constitution no party seems to be able to count on – or have to fear – being in government for any long and uninterrupted period, at least not while the balance of forces between the two blocs swings within the interval we have been used to during the postwar period.

Another phenomenon which tends to strengthen our argument is the new watershed of Swedish politics which has appeared in the last decade and seems primarily to divide the bourgeois parties into two camps: on the one hand the mild degree of populism which expresses itself in a negative attitude to modern industrial society, big cities, the power of big centralised unions, big business, and so forth, represented chiefly by the Centre Party, which has grown out of the class-based Farmers' Party; on the other hand, the 'old capitalist right, represented by the conservatives. There is some tendency to this division in the Socialist camp as well.

These tendencies may not, however, last in times of dwindling economic growth. Struggle over limited resources may restore the classical front between labour and capital. The 'green wave' may turn out to have been a phenomenon of prosperity, ending maybe in the active anti-nuclear campaign before the referendum in March 1980. The labour market conflict in May 1980 showed that trade unions had no difficulties in mobilising the rank and file. Under the surface, class-consciousness seems to have survived a long period of labour market co-operation and relaxation.

Withering Authority and Increasing Intolerance

Parallel to the political tendencies mentioned, general respect for politicians has diminished. It is difficult to say whether this is a deep-seated tendency in the sense that it is true of people in general more than before. Maybe the dissolution of class feeling and class voting is related to a weakening of the reputation of politicians. But it seems evident that the attitude of the media towards politicians is much less respectful than previously. Proposals and statements made by politicians and parties are judged less with regard to their content; they are instead often related to a kind of tactical game and to the fluctuating results of opinion polls. At times journalists are given to interpretations of the decisions and gambits of the parties in terms of conspiracy, while at the same time the editorial pages lament the growing public disdain for politicians. The way the media treat the nuclear issue is an example of this.

Altogether one is justified in talking of the withering of authority as regards the relationship between the public, the media and the politicians. This tendency has its counterparts in other central areas of social life. One problem which projects a sinister shadow over the future is the decline of the youth culture and schools. Hardly anyone will deny nowadays that schools are in a serious crisis. One of the most tragic trends is the penetration of the abuse of alcohol even into the subteens age group. Concomitant with a dissolution of norms within schools there seems to have developed a strong uniformity of norms among teenagers with regard to habits, clothing and attitudes which strongly affect those who fall outside the accepted pattern. In its worst form intolerance is sharpened into racism, and this at a time when schools do much more than before to stress democratic values, tolerance and solidarity.

In the grown-up world we have the same tendency towards intolerance – not least with regard to immigrants – and a declining social spirit. The latter tendency expresses itself through increasing tax evasion and welfare cheating, both of which are estimated to be much more widespread than before.

A Bleak Economic Future

There are further grounds for pessimism as one looks at future trends in the Swedish economy. Like all industrialised countries, Sweden has been hit by the energy crisis and its consequences. Prospects for the future supply of energy are dim. There is a risk that the energy problem will entail such international complications and internal crises in the 1980s that everything else we have pointed to is reduced to relatively minor status. But even if there turns out to be no direct limitation of the supply of energy energy prices will rise.

The referendum on nuclear power in March 1980 resulted in a vast majority in favour of the use of the twelve nuclear power plants that are built or under construction. The dominant political issues in Sweden since August 1976 have disappeared overnight. The result is of course a relief for our energy supply. But still much of Sweden's export industry is in primary products such as iron ore, pulp, paper and steel. These industries were developed because they had a competitive advantage due to cheap energy in hydroelectrical power. It was possible to continue the low-cost energy policy throughout the 1960s despite the fact that by then the greater part of energy came from imported oil. Owing to the new energy situation in the world Sweden's basic industries are bound to suffer from a continuous decline in competitiveness as energy prices in Sweden catch up with those in competing countries and as new capacity in these same sectors is being built up in low-cost countries. Our conditions for growth will not deteriorate drastically – but they will deteriorate enough to make the redistribution of income between sectors of the economy and between groups of citizens considerably more difficult than before.

On top of the general decline in the conditions of growth for industrial countries which follows from the scarcity of energy, the strongly export-oriented Swedish economy has been hit by long stagnation – not even in 1980 did industrial production reach the previous peak of 1974 – and a slump in investment. Sweden dropped out of line with international costs in 1975–6, which worsened our structural crisis into a general crisis of profitability. We are living in the aftermath of the cost crisis, particularly in the sense that industrial capital formation and expansion have still not picked up in a sustained manner.

The general lockout and strike on the labour market in May 1980 – the greatest labour market conflict since 1909 – shows that the road back to external balance by spurred industrial investment and increased production will be long and lead to social conflicts. The end result has to be a greater share of capital in production and this has to be reached by stagnating real wages and booming profits. A strong bourgeois government may have difficulties in achieving this. A weak three-party bourgeois coalition government is certain to have great difficulties. The parliamentary election in September 1979 resulted in a tiny majority for the three non-socialist parties. Those parties restored the coalition government that had been wrecked by the nuclear power issue and was followed by a minority Liberal government in the autumn of 1978. Until now the government has constantly pushed the problems ahead and – with the exception of the devaluation round of 1977 and the savings plan of October 1980 – done virtually nothing to stall the adverse development. The structural deficit of the balance of payments is worsening every year, now amounting to 4 per cent of GNP or some 15 per cent of exports.

Thus we enter the 1980s in the wake of a period of weakening government power, with vast financial needs to cover the budget deficit, with too small an industrial sector and a strong need for structural change in the economy, while there is much to indicate that mobility is tending to decline in the labour market.

The Positive Side of the Coin

We have pictured a sombre but quite reasonable summary of Sweden's political and economic situation at the beginning of the 1980s. But one can also give another image of the situation, stressing aspects whereby the balance is considerably redressed, especially as compared to many other industrialised countries.

The Swedish political party structure has resisted the stresses of the 1970s. By contrast to that of Norway and Denmark, there have not arisen any parties which have more or less placed themselves outside the community of values with regard to welfare policies. No political party has voiced any animosity against aliens. Not even the tax revolt has had a very explosive effect in the most heavily tax-burdened nation of the world – at least not explicitly. The Centre Party has swept up, in a mild form, the nostalgic and anti-intellectual attitude to modern industrial society that has had malign expression in our neighbouring countries. The Swedish Communist Party subscribes to the ideas of Eurocommunism, has freed itself from foreign ties and works within the pattern of parliamentary democracy. None of the Riksdag parties has broken away from the old community ethic of the welfare state, built on, tolerance and respect for the opinions of others within a strongly compressed framework of values.

Even the economy offers the elements of an alternative image. The steel and shipbuilding crisis, as well as that of the forestry sector, was met with comprehensive government measures to prevent an uncontrolled restructuring which would have had devastating effects on employment. The bitter class confrontation produced by the industrial crisis in England, France and Italy has so far been avoided in Sweden. The wage agreement for 1978–9 after a series of currency devaluations shows the kind of social responsibility on the part of the unions we have been used to from the 1950s and 1960s. The malign events on the labour market in the spring of 1980 were partly a result of a clear attempt at redistributing incomes from blue-collar workers to white-collar workers and capital-owners, partly a result of the sheer incompetence of government and labour market mediators at handling labour market disputes.

The international economic crisis of the 1970s touched the average Swedish consumer relatively mildly. Open unemployment never rose above 2·5 per cent. It is only the jobless young people, unable to enter the labour market, who have been hard hit socially – and that is serious enough. Overall, however, Swedish society and the Swedish economy – the welfare state – have proved enormously strong against the instability and crises of the 1970s. But the question whether that strength will get us through the problems of the 1980s as well remains unanswered. We know that the strains and difficulties will be great. We know less about how old solutions, combined with the many institutional innovations of the 1970s, such as 'industrial and institutional democracy', will be able to cope with those strains while conserving the spirit of consensus and social solidarity.

2
Sweden Seen from the Outside

GUY DE FARAMOND, MICHAEL HARRINGTON and ANDREW MARTIN

> This chapter takes the form of a conversation about
> Sweden, with Villy Bergström as moderator, between
> three foreigners with a good knowledge of the country.
> Michael Harrington is an American politician and
> social critic with a social democratic orientation,
> Andrew Martin is an American political scientist. Guy
> de Faramond is a French journalist. Martin and
> Faramond have lived in Sweden for long periods.

Bergström: If you look at Sweden's social development since the
Second World War and if you were to pick out a few tendencies
– some that you regard as very positive and some that you
consider more doubtful or negative – what would you pick out?
I would like to stress that this discussion should be a blunt and
critical review of Swedish society.

Harrington: I have a difficulty there since I am very positive about
Sweden. The number one positive thing, I think, in particular
from an American point of view, would be that the question of
full employment was placed at the absolute centre of the
political agenda and that so much policy has been developed
around that, in contrast with the enormous social costs of an
unemployment rate in the United States that consistently runs
several times higher than in Sweden. From my point of view the
superiority of Swedish social democracy to American liberalism
is right there, and even recently I noticed that after the Social
Democrats were voted out of power the bourgeois parties have
nevertheless been following basically socialist lines of policy
and development. I have heard about the present development
in the steel industry, where the part which I like is the idea of
subsidising an unprofitable production for a period of time on
the grounds that that is a better way to handle the problem than

to disemploy people who would be thrown out into the streets.

As far as my criticism of Swedish society is concerned – and I really have difficulties coming up with any, not that it is perfect but from an American point of view it is so much better than the United States – I would say that two things strike me and I suspect that they are related. In my very brief visit to Sweden I was struck by the degree to which society still remains a class society in terms of manners, restaurants, and so on. That is to say, there has been a floor placed on society, there has been, in terms of the absolute living standard of everyone, a tremendous advance made, but nevertheless there still seems to be class society.

Related to that was the decision which may now be reaching its limits: the decision to leave the private sector intact, to leave private corporations in control of the overwhelming majority of the economy and to place on top of a private economic structure a very shrewd and imaginative social structure, either requiring the private sector to be much more social than it normally would be or to redistribute income – by tax policy – out of the private sector into social programmes. I understand all the arguments in favour of that: Sweden's special position as a rather small country, an export-oriented economy which must remain competitive in the world market, and so on. But I now wonder if that possibility is not running out. My feeling is – and this is impressionistic – that Swedish social democracy will now have to move somewhat in the direction of socialising investment as well as consumption. Gunnar Myrdal said at a meeting when he was over here in the United States, 'We socialised consumption but not production'. I am now wondering if the socialisation of consumption, within the framework of a private corporate-dominated economy, does not run into the structural limitations of the private corporate-dominated economy. That is one of the reasons why I am fascinated by what I have been able to learn about the Meidner Plan, which strikes me as not simply a move in the direction of a redistribution of wealth as against income, but also, at least potentially, as a move in the direction of the democratisation of investment policy. I think this is necessary in all advanced capitalist economies.

Martin: I just want to add a couple of points. There are the kinds of things that we from this side admire so much, such as the priority placed on full employment and the ingenuity with which various techniques are invented to achieve it. That comes first. Then you try to meet other priorities consistently with that. For example, there is the way the Social Democrats have tried to deal with inflation. They have not only refused to do so by unemployment but have also avoided resort to methods likely to undermine the ties between the Social Democratic Party and the unions on which its strength depends. Instead of imposing an incomes policy the way the British Labour Party did at times, they have sought alternatives such as the so-called active labour market policy together with cost-reducing structural change. This was an ingenious and, for a long time, apparently successful way of trying to reconcile the different kinds of policy goals while also preserving the cohesion of the labour movement on which the achievement of the goals depends.

Yet it has also had its costs, such as the intensification of mobility, forcing workers to move to new jobs. More and more the negative effects of this were not fully compensated. What has now happened is a backlash against it. That seems to me an illustration of precisely what Mike was saying about the attempt to superimpose the strong state on capitalism and trying to set the parameters within which capitalism develops. The attempt does not seem to have prevented structural change from taking place essentially in directions and at a pace determined by capitalist investment decisions.

Harrington: I want to add one thing to Andy's point about the problems of the strong state superimposed. I think that Sweden is probably more successful than any other country doing that and I suspect that there are historical-cultural reasons for that success. One of the jokes I sometimes make in this country is that I think that the best solution we could have to America's problems would be to import about 250 million Swedes. I am quite serious. I think that there are values in Swedish culture as regards co-operation and solidarity that certainly don't transfer here. I remember being in France during an election in 1969 or 1970, a presidential election, and I think Mittérand was running on a programme of Swedish socialism for France. One of the questions I always had in my mind was: 'Will Swedish socialism work without Swedes?'

Faramond: I agree completely with both Andy and Mike when they say that full employment has been the most important element in Swedish politics in the postwar period. Even in the latest crisis the government has tried to keep up employment at all costs. The money that went into the Labour Market Board (AMS) and all AMS efforts, including retraining programmes and grants to employees who moved to other places and other jobs – all this was very positive indeed. The number of people who go through AMS programmes and then actually find new jobs is very high compared with similar activities in other countries. Employment is extremely important in Swedish economic policy.

As regards negative points of view I find one important tendency: a lack of self-criticism among the Social Democrats.

Bergström: Do you refer to the period right now when the Social Democrats are out of office?

Faramond: Not only now but also the whole time when they held office. In the whole postwar period there has been a very noticeable lack of self-criticism; especially after the 1976 elections they ought to have applied some real thinking to the economic policy they had pursued and to the social development they have called forth. They should have used this period for thoroughly criticising themselves – but they haven't.

But let me return to the positive factors. As a foreigner, or semi-foreigner, I should like to underline a couple of things. One is the excellent way in which legislation is prepared in Sweden. A very penetrating discussion takes place before the laws are made, with opportunities for various organisations to submit their opinion and also discussions in the press and among the people. In due course a Bill is then presented in parliament that everybody knows is practical and applicable. Look at the procedure in France! Here numerous laws are made that are never implemented, simply because they can't be. They are theoretical constructions without anything to do with reality. In France *députés* and senators lose a tremendous amount of time and energy on legislation that can never be applied. One French politician who has studied the Swedish system is most impressed by it. He says that France is a graveyard of non-implemented laws.

Bergström: The next question is very broad and bears upon what we have been talking about. Over the years I would say that Swedish social democracy has been working along two lines. One is to strengthen industrialism, gather the fruits of large-scale industry, mechanisation, and so on, and the other to use the fruits to build the welfare state. As Andy pointed out, this has meant a lot of mobility on the part of the working class. As a result, new suburbs grew up without the roots that the traditional society had. Maybe in this process the spirit of community or solidarity was lost. There are signs that this has really happened. Looking at society now I am very much concerned about what has been going on in the last five to ten years. There is a deterioration of life style among teenagers, for instance, teenagers' behaviour towards the older generation, and schools have great difficulties. Alcoholism is increasing, crime rates are going up. My broad question is: the Social Democrats lost the last election after having run the country for forty-four years; what has been lacking in social democratic policy over the years to allow this development and to result in a loss, after having had the opportunity to shape society for such a long time?

Harrington: From my point of view I would not place too much emphasis on the loss of the election. Indeed – although obviously, were I Swedish, I would have voted for the Social Democratic Party – I don't think that it is the worst thing that has happened. Forty-four years *is* a long time to be in power continuously, and some of my friends in the Swedish Social Democratic Party have even said that they have found that an interregnum (and I suspect that it is only an interregnum) is a very useful thing in terms of thinking and having more time, not always being responsible for society.

Secondly, let me suggest, regarding the general problem, a sweeping solution, so sweeping that it might be worthless. You are talking, obviously, about problems that are common to all advanced capitalist societies. It is happening here; I think perhaps one of the most striking things about the deterioration of New York City is the deterioration of public amenity and civility. Just the nastiness of it seems to increase on subways and streets. The lack of basic human concern which stops people walking the streets in peace, to put it at its simplest level. I think that in part this has to do with the sociological trends that exist in Sweden and here. Here it is because of the unplanned workings of a market subsidised by the federal government in which the plan follows the spontaneous priorities of profit. In Sweden the mobility comes more from planning, but you get – again I think Sweden is better – some of the same problems. As soon as you get economies of scale and modern industry you get a certain kind of alienation.

But I should like to suggest another factor, although I don't know how this fits into Swedish society. I think that the decline in religious faith is a major factor in all Western societies. The death of God as a social factor, the decline in religion in the Hegelian sense of representing the spontaneous consciousness of the community, that which binds the community together, providing a kind of collective unconscious in terms of values, images, and so on, all this is now disappearing; and I wonder if what you are describing is not a problem of the emergence of agnostic or atheist societies, which I personally regard as unavoidable. I think that the death of God is universal. I am not downplaying the problem – nor would I – and by the way I think there are policies that can try to reverse some of the sociological and economic causes of this. For example, right now I am studying the Bedford-Stuyvesant restoration. It was an attempt in a black slum in New York which has some remarkably good and beautiful brownstone houses. Rather than bulldozing and putting up housing projects the aim was to try to use a variety of incentives to the private sector to restore an old neighbourhood, and it had a certain amount of success. I don't think it will work everywhere. I think its success in this case largely due to unique factors, for example, that it was sponsored by Robert Kennedy, it was patronised by the old bourgeoisie for reasons of its own. I don't think it is repeatable in the South Bronx. What I am saying is that social thinkers and planners should adopt policies which seek community and should regard a lot of moving around and a lot of that kind of disruption and a lot of newness as a social cost that ought to be avoided.

The next point is that probably the first country that came up against this – and there is literature on this – was Britain with its new towns, the famous problems that the planners encountered when they put a population down in the middle of something that was totally new even though better structurally than where its occupants came from.

Martin: In so many ways there has been an erosion of the norms of traditional society, of the pre-industrial pattern of authority, values, and so on. But there has also been an erosion of the norms of capitalist society as well, particularly the increasing constraints on freedom of economic decisions in the last few years. There has been a replacement of the market as far as many aspects of society are concerned, such as housing, and partly even labour itself. Such changes establish new values of social solidarity in place of capitalist as well as traditional values. The social democratic labour movement has been the central driving force in bringing about these changes, and what has made it possible are the political resources provided by a social movement in which the values of solidarity already exist. Paradoxically, however, the way in which those political resources have been mobilised and concentrated may itself erode the values embodied in the movement. The social democratic movement has put great emphasis on maximising effectiveness – effectiveness in managing the economy and in mobilising its political resources. It has achieved both kinds of effectiveness by a high degree of organisational centralisation – in the party, the state and the unions. But this seems to undermine the movement's character as a movement whose cohesion depends as much on its values as its organisation. So what seems to happen is that a very valuable resource for replacing both traditional and capitalist values is eroded. The potential for an alternative normative system and culture is thereby destroyed, or at least weakened. Maybe this is why the social changes achieved by social democracy have not really created a new society even though they have replaced much of traditional and capitalist values.

Bergström: At one point in time, I think in the 1930s, there was a fight in the labour movement over whether working-class youth should be let into the ordinary school system or whether the movement should build its own school system with its own values. You know which line won. Let me add one thing to your answers and see if you want to comment on it. When I lived for longer periods in the United States I always thought that the higher crime rate and the social evils that you have to a larger extent than in Sweden had to do with the much greater competitiveness of this society, on all levels and in all activities, at the workplace, in schools, at the universities. Swedes are very sheltered, we don't live in a highly competitive situation, and yet we are getting more and more of the social evils that I thought would at least partly be explained in terms of 'losing' due to hopeless handicaps in the race.

Harrington: It could be at a certain point of time, but not necessarily at all. Norman Thomas, who ran for president on the Socialist Party ticket six times, was a Protestant minister in the Harlem section of New York as a young man. It was a poor white neighbourhood, mainly Italian then. He told me that there used to be a lot of crime but that it was 'functional crime': people without a coat stole a coat from people with coats. That is understandable – it is a redistribution – but what really began to frighten Thomas in the last years of his life was the appearance of totally irrational and unmotivated crime, and my reaction to that has to do with the breakdown of a culture. I think it is often related to social structure. One of the things in America that I think has reinforced the voids where God used to exist in this culture is that at the same time God stopped existing. He was a good explanation for miseries. At the same time wrath began to overwhelm society, ingenuity seemed to become perverse, and in a sense the experience of living in New York City and watching it disintegrate tends to reinforce all the theories of alienation.

Martin: Religion was certainly a source of norms and integration of the community, not only through its content but also the organisational effect that religion ordinarily had in the local community, with the church part of the life of the locality where people lived. It was directly experienced. The destruction of this kind of community would probably have happened anyway in Sweden, as elsewhere, as a result of purely capitalist development as well as development influenced by the social democratic movement. The difference the movement might have been expected to make is to provide alternative norms and cohesion in ways that can be directly experienced. But it has perhaps lost its potential for that, even in the trade unions where it has probably been greatest.

Harrington: Related to what I was saying before when I was talking about social movement is a marvellous phrase that a British sociologist came up with in *The Affluent Worker.*[1] The phrase is 'instrumental collectivism' and the distinction is between the collectivism of a social movement inspired by an ideal counter-culture, the way social democracy was in its historical origins and the collectivism which is a practical collectivism: 'I want to get more money, I want to have good social security, pensions, and so on'. There is a huge difference between the two.

Faramond: Frankly I believe that Swedes have concentrated too heavily on developing an industrial society and neglected some of the social consequences of that policy. On the other hand my opinion of Swedish politics is that when problems are dis-covered politicians try to put things right and create a new common interest. The feature characteristic of Sweden is precisely that problems are attacked at an early stage. I have seen that when living in Sweden, seen how measures were taken before problems became too great, with sharp social tensions as a result. But Sweden does suffer from a dreadful anonymity, an indifference to one's neighbour, that is the most disagreeable thing about Sweden. Mike and Andy may not be aware of that since they have never lived there as long.

Bergström: But surely that is an odd statement, a paradox? I agree with you that when it comes to people's attitudes to one another there exists a lack of contact ability – perhaps due to shyness – but at the same time there is an extremely well-developed anonymous solidarity in Sweden. The fact that a majority of Swedes allow 50 per cent of their income to go to the government and that we have a social security system that does not allow people to fall back into the proletariat stage and go to the dogs, as often happens to a higher degree in other countries, and that a substantial share of consumption, bigger than in other countries, is channelled to collective sectors in order to establish a real levelling – all this indicates a tendency that contradicts your description at the more personal and individual level. Isn't this awkwardness and inability of ours to establish contact with others due to the fact that Swedes have only recently moved into towns or cities, only recently becoming urbanised?

Faramond: That is quite correct. Sweden became industrialised very late and has in three generations achieved what the great industrial countries did in six or seven generations. Sweden is a very young industrial nation and that is probably an important element in the explanation. The *civilité* that has developed in European cities and perhaps in the United States has not yet had time to take shape in Sweden, I mean the way people are polite to each other and are used to living close to each other. Swedes haven't had time to adapt to the changes in society. Everything has happened too fast. However, this may not be a matter for government, state, community and union but something that everybody must become aware of and which must unfold in society as a whole.

On the credit side should also be added the fact that Sweden has managed to check the expansion of its larger cities. Slums have not developed despite very large shifts in the population. These shifts have taken place in socially acceptable forms. A certain social deterioration has of course occurred, but it is nothing compared with the wretched conditions in the big cities of other industrial countries. Attempts have been made to halt centralisation – one example is that government administration units have moved to other cities – but I am a trifle shocked by the relative brutality of the procedure. The brusqueness was quite remarkable for Swedish conditions.

Bergström: I think that Sweden has been a much more authoritarian society than Americans can imagine. Looking back twenty-five years, I can even remember it myself: class structure was based on family background, income and education and all these things went together. If you belonged to an old bourgeois family you had a good education, high income, and so on. There was an authoritarian structure to society which has broken down very rapidly – in ten years. At the same time respect, let us say, for education has gone and income has been enormously equalised, though not wealth. At the same time there has been a dissolving of old working-class communities where people kept track of each other and everybody knew one another. It is a process that has been very fast and nothing else has taken its place. You may be right that secularisation is part of it. Maybe you exaggerated it a little as regards Sweden, but of course it is part of it.

Martin: I guess what I was suggesting is that it is a consequence of the particular way of achieving the equalisation – through large political organisations, a strong state, a strong society, as Erlander put it. Maybe the result is that the egalitarianism takes an individualistic form, so that as far as the individual experience goes it induces instrumental rather than solidaristic collectivism.

Bergström: I want to go on to more specific things after these broad questions and I would like to talk a little about the 1950s, which was said to be a very dull decade in Sweden. We had a coalition government with the Farmers' Party and Tage Erlander was prime minister at the time. He was said to be a practical man, not too interested in ideology. I think, though, that is unfair. He taught Swedes to accept a level of taxation that is enormous compared with most other countries, he taught them to realise that you have to pay a lot of income tax and keep down private consumption to have a decent society and a welfare state. I heard him talk once to a student group in Uppsala after the 1960 elections and the main platform in that campaign had been the introduction of a sales tax in order to increase public resources. It is quite remarkable that over 65 per cent of GNP goes through the budget of the public sector.

In order to look at it from an individualistic point of view, let us say from that of an individual employer, we might take an example. An employer wants to pay an employee 100 dollars more a year. It costs him about 140 dollars with all payroll taxes and if you as an employee get 100 dollars more you keep 30 dollars after tax if you belong to the middle-class income bracket. Consequently you have a marginal tax rate of 110 over 140, which is 80 per cent. And if you add to that what happens to families in the normal bracket, let us say between 50,000 and 80,000 crowns, if you add to the taxes the loss of family allowances, fees to nursery schools that increase with income, you will find that a family within these normal brackets cannot influence its own personal disposable income. This may be nice when income drops but not so nice when it goes up. Now my question is: do you think that this has gone too far, that it creates problems, or do you think that it is mainly a positive thing, this equalisation of personal income?

Harrington: I think that the dangers of that trend are much smaller than those of the contrary, the trend of the United States. I really think that the question is pragmatic. Let me explain what I mean by that. President Carter announced in his first year in office that he wanted to reduce federal government spending to 21 per cent of GNP: including transfers, the whole federal sphere. It was fluctuating between 18·5 and 22·5 and at that moment was rather high partly because of the very great social costs of chronic joblessness which is reflected in the federal payments for food stamps, for special extensions of the employment compensation, loans to the states, and so on. So Carter said 21 per cent. I have been arguing for some time that this is the sheerest platonism. Why 21 per cent? On what tablet handed down from the almighty is marked 21 per cent? Why not 24, why not 16, why not 32? My point is that there is no right percentage. The argument is what is happening in society and how – assuming that you have a dynamic society whose total resources are growing – do you want to spend the increments? Do you want to spend the increments on social consumption, on leisure, reduced working time, or on individual consumption?

One of the things that struck me about Sweden in my very brief experience there – but I often read about it – is that by and large the things that the Swedish taxpayer receives for those very high taxes are good. The problem in the United States is that most taxpayers feel that the goods and services they receive are not good. I decline to answer what is right for Sweden. Actually I don't know. But I am just saying that methodologically I don't think that there is anything inherently wrong in the government taking 65 per cent of income for social spending if that increases the quality of life, the freedom of society, and so on, if it is part of a solidaristic incomes programme. It may well be that Sweden has now run up to a certain limit; it could be that you now want for a variety of reasons to increase individual consumption. It is the platonism of Carter that I think ought to be avoided at all costs.

Martin: Again it seems to me that we are dealing with a fundamental dilemma of social democracy. In a lot of ways it is an attempt to replace market performance or wealth as the basis for people's access to resources by some kind of a needs principle, some kind of conception of what a just distribution is. Yet the legitimacy of the capitalist market principle is not really challenged, at the same time that social policy and the taxes to support it are legitimated by the alternative principle of social justice. This seems to produce a kind of contradiction in a social democratic society. On the one hand you are telling people that they are really entitled to the differences resulting from their participation in the production process. But on the other hand you say that the distribution that results isn't just, so the differences should be taxed away. The capitalist market principle is still available as a weapon with which to attack such redistributive taxes, making it easy for people to complain that they are not allowed to keep what is rightfully theirs and that this deprives them of the incentive to work or innovate.

One thing that has struck me is how wage policy has moved some way beyond this. But it has not gone all the way. I don't mean the solidaristic wage policy itself but its implications for the traditional role of wages in allocating labour. That is, instead of relying on differences in wages in different firms to induce workers to move from one firm to another, much greater emphasis is placed on information, which is one of the functions the labour market scheme is supposed to perform. It is really a non-market mechanism that replaces a market mechanism. If you work in a firm that cannot afford equal pay for equal work and the firm collapses, the Labour Market

Board is going to help you shift to another job, and from the point of view of the whole society this moves labour to where its productivity is greater. But the shift is brought about partly by specific information about the new job rather than a wage difference, so information, or one form of information, is substituted for the price system, or another form of information which is not about specific jobs but depends instead on unequal pay. Still, there are differences in pay for different work so the old system has been partially eroded although a completely new system has not been created in place of it.

Faramond: It is obvious that the levelling of income is more advanced in Sweden than perhaps in any other Western country and that there is less competition in Sweden than in France and the United States. Yet I don't think we ought to disregard competition. Social valuations of professions and status still remain, and that is human nature. I don't think we should underestimate the fact that the old competitive mentality still exists in Swedish society.

Bergström: I can see a paradox here. A dispassionate comparison between Sweden and the United States shows Sweden to be very advanced as regards social and economic levelling of income and wealth. But even so Sweden has perhaps in a certain subjective sense a tighter class structure than the United States. The old upper classes had a background in the nobility and the civil service. They supplied the civil service with officials and had a monopoly of education, culture and social status, income and wealth. That structure was so firmly rooted and has survived a substantial levelling in income and wealth so well that the values of the old class society are passed on from one generation to another. Are you also of the opinion that in spite of all objectively measurable levelling, Sweden is still a class society when it comes to values and style of life?

Faramond: There is no doubt about that. To my mind social democracy has underrated the difficulties of changing this kind of social structure rapidly. Many sons and daughters of workers have gone to university but have had trouble achieving the results they aspired to. Students with a bourgeois background find studying easier, they are used to books, they have learnt to express themselves clearly and well, they understand a more sophisticated usage, and all this has become very powerful and hard to break. To have grown up in an upper-class environment obviously facilitates higher studies compared with a working-class background. Actually, I don't believe that special structures have been so profoundly affected by levelling measures as some people like to think.

But let me sum up: there is no doubt in my mind that things

have gone too far here, and the Social Democrats have realised that too. They were forced to change tax legislation time and time again; for instance, the rule that nobody will have to pay more than 85 per cent marginal tax, and now even the Social Democrats have begun to talk about tax reforms. At least in the economic system we now have there must be some economic encouragement for a private individual to work more if that system is to function. Tax ethics are said to deteriorate in Sweden, which is a pity, for Sweden used to have a very high moral standard in that field. In my opinion taxation has gone too far. It is much too tempting and immensely remunerative to evade taxes with today's marginal tax rates.

Bergström: What if you compare with France?

Faramond: Of course it is even worse in France. A very large sector of the population are not wage-earners and have all the opportunities in the world to evade taxes. It is a matter of a stereotyped assessment between enterprises and authorities and in the cases where hundreds of thousands of small businessmen accept that assessment one knows that is is far short of their actual income. It is estimated in France that the national budget is reduced by one quarter owing to tax evasion.

Bergström: This very far-reaching redistribution of personal income goes with a rather easy taxation of capital income as in most capitalist countries, especially capital gains income. Much of personal capital income among very high-income earners is transferred to capital gains income but, on the other hand, with a tough redistribution of personal income practically no new wealth could be created. You cannot get new capitalists coming up from the income-receiving class, the working class. And at the same time social democracy has been greatly dependent on capitalism to deliver all the goods and has been encouraging it. This means that the traditional owners have been strengthened and they haven't been challenged by new ones coming up. Lack of mobility on the capital formation side is created by this heavy equalisation of personal income and leeway for capital income.

Harrington: I thought for a long time that it applied to the United States rather than Sweden, but I now think that it applies to the whole capitalist world, no matter how left-wing the welfare state gets. The key capitalist feature of the welfare state that keeps the bourgeoisie in power is capitalist control over investment. We see it so vividly with Carter. He campaigned on a rather populist platform – full employment for labour, for blacks, and so on – but he was not elected for five minutes before he started chasing after the leaders of American business to get their support and to do so by adopting large parts of the programme which he had defeated in political combat. I think that that is a fact of life everywhere. This is why the discussion of the Meidner Plan, the idea of an alternate mode, is so important. I view the Meidner Plan not simply as an egalitarian device but as a device that proposes to move in the direction of socialised investment and to create out of the working class, so to speak, a collective investor, understanding that a competition among workers to see who could become a private entrepreneurial investor is out of the question to 99·99 per cent. I think that is a profoundly important point and that is what I meant when I said earlier that it seems to me that the Swedish social democratic welfare policies are coming up against structural limitations.

Martin: I find this a perplexing kind of problem, even within the framework of the Meidner Plan. It seems really necessary to have continuing structural change, with the creation of new firms and new enterprises, to stay afloat in a world of competition since you are so dependent on international trade. Perhaps the problem could be eased by reducing some of that dependence. I don't know to what extent such options exist, but autarchy is presumably out. So then some structural change is unavoidable. But how can it be brought about by some alternative to capitalism? Within the framework of the Meidner Plan I have difficulty in seeing where the functional equivalent of capitalism for the creation of new firms is. Of course the Meidner Plan does not reach far enough down to affect the small firms. But it doesn't seem wise to rely on individual enterprise to be a creative force in the economy if the enterprise is going to be taken over if it should prove successful enough to fall within the scheme. This is another instance of a contradiction between two principles: profit-motivated competition and a kind of selective investment planning. The contradiction may become intolerable beyond a certain point, which may have now been reached. But if you really want to use the planning approach on a sufficient scale to replace the functions performed by capitalism, there has to be a lot more institutional invention. I guess that kind of invention began when the Social Democratic Party first tried to deal with such questions in 1967–8 with the new industrial policy, setting up the new agencies like the Investment Bank, the State Enterprise Holding Corporation, and so on. Selective investment planning would not be an impossible thing to achieve, I think, but it requires much more than has been done. If you are going to develop new kinds of economic institutions to replace the ones that have been eroded you have to meet this challenge. Otherwise the only alternative may be to go back and give up some of the gains or go down, deteriorate, in a kind of British situation.

Harrington: When one talks about social ownership it is certainly not necessary to talk about a single enterprise in an industry or something like that, on the lines of Daniel Deleon: everything organised in a vertical trust. There is a place for partial socialisation in societies in a world which is still profit- and corporate-dominated. But the tendency of that profit and corporate domination is to co-opt any partial socialisation. The process is seen in the United States in the Tennessee Valley Authority. It has more and more adapted to business norms and criteria and its environmental record has probably been worse than private utilities, and so on. To deal with this problem of innovation socialist thinking should be in terms of a variety of publicly owned enterprises with some incentives and some punishment, but the punishment should never be disasters, never in the area of necessities but in the area of luxuries. I think it is at least worth thinking about.

I thought for a long time that certainly in some areas of luxury goods the best way to handle them is to have a market, that the market is an absolutely terrific device for handling certain problems like styles. So long as income is roughly equal and the market is not wrecked by oligopolies it is a great idea. I wonder if a market in the sense of different social enterprises having a limited competition might not begin to answer this.

Finally, the obvious problem, that you see in Yugoslavia, is where you get a collective capitalism in the social enterprises which does not want to invest any of its profits in the under-developed parts of Yugoslavia and which wants to invest in the developed parts which behave exactly like a private capitalist, only it is composed of 5,000 people in a works council.

Bergström: That is an interesting answer you give to these questions. I don't think we can pursue them too far, otherwise we would be stuck in economic systems. But I would like to ask something else. Looking at the Swedish managerial class would you say that it is a very co-operative and quiet class of managers, or is it only that they haven't much political influence in the sense that they can stop reforms by starting political propaganda openly? Would you say that the Swedish managerial class has accommodated itself to a situation where the labour movement delivers labour market peace in exchange for egalitarian social reforms? What I am struck by is how socially oriented many of them are in Sweden compared with what I have seen in the United States. Do you have any impressions of that?

Harrington: Let me answer as far as it concerns America. In America one of the things that I have never been able to answer and that I find very puzzling right now is: American business feels itself to be beleaguered, challenged, the captive of all kinds of liberal and left-wing planners in the state, and I can't understand how they don't realise that they have all the power. And so I think there are large non-economical elements that enter into the formation of this kind of consciousness. The American managers are a very puzzling group of people. Henry Ford received insufficient support for a meeting to complain in general about the terrible regulations, and so on, yet all this applies after one year of a Democratic president doing everything he could to follow the corporate programmes.

Bergström: Big Swedish corporate leaders go to the United States, they meet their counterparts and they go to France and all over. The very big Swedish corporations are multinational and if you take the biggest ones, Volvo, ASEA, Electrolux, their managers are paid, after tax, never more than 25,000 dollars a year, mostly between 15 and 25,000. That is nothing compared with what they would get in America, and they do have an international labour market. Maybe they see some positive things in social democracy, things they have learnt to appreciate after all these years?

Faramond: I don't think it should be viewed that way. They still have a tremendous income and they can afford a summer house and a yacht, and I should think that one reaches a saturation point in consumption. They can consume as much as they can reasonably wish and ask for *and* build up a fortune. They are certainly richly compensated in Sweden. Apart from that, some of their consumption is paid for by the company, such as travelling, and so on.

Martin: My impression is that on the whole Villy is right. There is an enormous difference in the constraints under which Swedish business operates. I am puzzled by the same thing. American managers are so parochial that they don't understand. European businessmen apparently understand the difference, they come to Sweden and invest to get away from unions. The other thing is that in Sweden I have been impressed by a considerable difference among businessmen in terms of their accommodation to having to confront a strong labour movement. Some Swedish businessmen think it is fine and see advantages in this. They seem to have a kind of managerial orientation: the labour movement has always been interested in efficiency, we are interested in efficiency, so we all get 25,000 dollars and are running a terrific show here. You find the epitome of managerial capitalism but you also find some who are not yet reconciled, and I get the feeling that now some Swedish businessmen are seeing their opportunity finally to

drive back this beast. I think some may feel a greater urgency
now than a few years ago, precisely because of the changes that
have come about in employment security, increasingly
narrowing the options, the increase in power of the unions in
the workplace, the increasing pressures of various kinds so that
they feel more and more constrained, that they can't be good
managers any more. Now the Meidner funds idea comes along
and threatens the authority structure. It isn't that their
ownership status is threatened but the authority and autonomy
that property institutions give, as if they are going to become
employees of unions or something. I suspect they feel that this
has been going too far and that it is high time it got stopped,
otherwise we shall go down the drain.

Bergström: Tnere is a strong movement now in Sweden for
industrial democracy and also for the Meidner ideas. These two
things reinforce each other. Industrial democracy gives workers
on the shop floor a lot of control so that they can even close a
shop if it is dangerous to work there and so that they also have
positions on the managerial board. Do you believe that this
could be a substitute for the old social control that has been lost
and bring back something of the spirit of the labour movement
that was lost through centralisation over the years? I don't
know how closely you have been following developments, but
they are very definite.

Harrington: My feeling is that for European socialism in general
one of the most exciting things that has happened for years has
been the emergence in France of the autogestion movement,
what Mittérand sometimes calls Mediterranean socialism, with
a greater anarchist emphasis on the communitarianism of the
workplace. Even Anthony Crosland, who is a friend of mine
although obviously we have considerable differences of
opinions on social theory, said last time I saw him in London in
1973 that he thought that industrial democracy was a coming
issue, which I found interesting since Crosland is normally
thought of as being to the right of the centre of the Labour
Party. It is tremendously important and at the same time I
think there are limits and that one has to be careful. A
capitalist economy and technology is structured to minimise
participation. It is designed that way. There is an excellent
book by an American Marxist who died recently, Harry
Braverman.[2] It is called *Labor and Monopoly Capital* and it
makes the point that the history of capitalist technology is not a
technological history but a social, political and economic
history, in which the expropriation of the skill of the artisan and
the expropriation of any part of the decision-making process of
the individual worker arises not out of a technological

imperative but out of a view of work in society. The author of *Labor and Monopoly Capital* makes the point which I very much agree with, that if you take a, so to speak, capitalist technology designed to create a great mass of sheep and a few innovative managers and then say, 'Everybody now has the right to participate', where the possibility of serious participation is quite limited, I think that is better than non-participation but that one has to . . . What I am saying is that industrial democracy arrives at rather radical demands, whereas some people think that it is an easy way.

In America this came about when Elton Mayo and the founders of industrial psychology discovered that a happy worker is a more productive worker; and so you got the whole view on the part of American management, which was to give the sense but not the reality of participation to the worker, leading to things such as suggestion boxes, company baseball teams, bowling teams, newspapers, all that kind of stuff. It is very good but I think it is a more radical demand than some of its proponents are aware of. Finally, and again the American comparison is striking, the American labour movement with almost no exceptions is hostile to any idea of industrial democracy. One of the reasons has to do with the high unemployment economy. The view of most American trade unions is that industrial democracy and participation are code words for more production with fewer workers. They have understood the Elton Mayo quest, so that when the Department of Health, Education and Welfare about three or four years ago came out with a report on work in America, focusing on dissatisfactions of work, particularly among people in industrial work, interestingly enough those who downgraded the significance of that the most were the unions, including by the way not simply the more conservative trade unions but also many of the socialist trade unions. I think that if it is properly understood it might give socialism back its soul, but . . .

Bergström: Swedish trade unions have also been very reluctant on this point. In the 1920s the first labour government set up two government commissions, one about socialisation, the other headed by Wigforss about industrial democracy. Practically nothing was done between that commission in the early 1920s and, I would say, the late 1960s. In the late 1970s Palme was talking about the third stage of democracy: first, political democracy, then came social democracy with respect to the welfare state and now we are about to enter the third stage, economic democracy. But I wonder if there aren't many problems here that we should touch upon, for instance, the pretension of the labour movement in Sweden now, not only to speak for labour as a productive force but also for consumers. Some people – even socialists – say that labour tries to get too much power here. To give a concrete example: labour unions and the labour movement now try to block the opening of shopping centres on Sundays. Obviously it is a nuisance for members in the retail workers' union to work on Sundays, but they also pretend it is better for the consumer to ban open stores on Sundays. And the same development is taking place in bureaucracy. One might speak of industrial democratisation there, too, or rather institutional democracy. In that field labour is not constrained, as in business, by the market, the rate of profit and demand. What you can see so far is a tendency to use the new power to create better working conditions, often disregarding the customers of bureaucracy. I could give you examples of that. There is a tendency to use the new power to make it more comfortable so that you can work less and the burden be taken over by those who apply to an agency or a bureau for help. We may now be in a transition period, in the process of having given more power to labour, but so far labour may not have to take the consequences of these decisions. We have to find some means there to transfer responsibility and sanctions along with the new power.

Harrington: That is an interesting point. Ralph Nader has been very critical of the trade union movement for not being at all concerned with the products and he has criticised the automobile union, the UAW, which is certainly one of the most progressive in the United States, on the grounds that it was turning out a shoddy product, unsafe, and so on, and that it is the proper function of the producers of goods or services to be concerned about the quality of the goods or service. And yet I see the problem that you raise. It becomes most acute in some of the service areas; I have seen that in education. I belong to the American Federation of Teachers and in the crisis in the City University of New York there were layoffs; in some cases even tenured faculty members were laid off. The union's position, which I disagreed with, has been that you should have city-wide seniority in the City University so that if a political scientist is dropped at Queens College, he can go to any political science department in the entire city and push somebody out. What this implies is that college professors are semi-skilled production workers and that you can replace any of them with any other without a further thought, whereas the fact is that one political scientist is an expert in American society and another is an expert in African society and that they are not interchangeable.

On principle I want workers to be concerned with the quality of their products. One of the most horrible things that capitalism did to working people was to make them totally indifferent and even ignorant of what they were producing. One thing that socialism should try to recapture is some sense of workmanship. On the other hand, when you get out of that generalisation into the problems of bureaucracies exercising the choice and creativity it is not easy. Yet I don't want to give up the ideal, and that poses the problems you raise.

Faramond: So far a kind of equilibrium has prevailed in Sweden with the Social Democrats holding the political power and the capital-owners the economic power. On the whole it has worked well, but I wonder if a disequilibrium won't set in now that the capital-owners will be kept much more in check by the unions. I can't make any comparisons with French capitalists for even though France has a very large nationalised sector the capitalist-entrepreneurs enjoy a great deal of freedom. Here when the economy is going to the dogs the hard rule of kicking the workers out is enforced, and that is all there is to it. The confrontation between wage-earners and capital-owners is much sharper and the debate is carried on more in terms of class struggle here than in Sweden. The difference between France and Sweden – where social democracy has been very successful – is that politicians try to solve problems before the situation becomes so acute that a confrontation is inescapable. Sweden has tried to handle structural crises and meet them before strong social tensions arise. The steel industry in Lorraine and other areas with large steelworks is on its way to being stamped out completely. Nothing is done, while in Sweden the authorities have quickly taken measures to restructure the steel industry and reduce it while minimising the social consequences. The French textile industry is in the same predicament. In Sweden you have had and still have the same problem. A crisis is now emerging in the Vosges. Nothing has been prepared, nothing is done to alleviate the effects. French capitalism is simply less restrained than Swedish capitalism.

Martin: I would like to add a couple of things. One really has to do with another dimension of democracy in everyday life, in addition to industrial democracy, and that is somewhat related to your point about bureaucracies, that when bureaucracies become internally democratic they may be even less responsive to their clients. When you think of people in their roles as consumers it is perhaps better to speak of them as users not only of products but also of services, including local government, housing, and so on. It seems to me that on the whole, historically and certainly particularly in the last few years, when there have been major moves in the direction of industrial democracy these moves have been due to a sensitivity to the needs of people for some degree of control over their own lives, primarily in their roles as producers. There has been less sensitivity to people's needs in their role as users. I don't want to go too far here because you have a lot of legislation designed to protect consumers from bad products, shoddy products, and so on, so there is information and good consumer protection in that sense. But that is not the same thing as the kind of control that comes with industrial democracy. There, at least ideally, the aim is for workers in the place where they actually work to be able to have a voice in its design, in their relations with authority, in how work is allocated, and so on. They should really have a kind of power to affect conditions in their own immediate situation. That is the aim. But now think about people as users, say, of the services provided by the bureaucracy, or of housing where people live in the local communities, or in relation to their schools. What kind of control do they have? Consider local government and the amalgamation of local governments and the growth of larger and fewer units where increasingly people are faced with representatives elected by larger and larger constituencies, with representatives becoming more inaccessible. The services on which people are dependent are organised by large bureaucracies. They may seem very efficient from the point of view of the governments whose policies are being carried out. They may even be getting more democratic internally, so the people at the bottom of the ladder inside the bureaucracies have more say in how they work. But the actual users of their services, the clients, are individuals outside the bureaucracies. They are not organised so as to have much say in how they live, as individual tenants facing not only the highly centralised managements of housing but also the highly centralised tenants' association. Dissatisfaction with this kind of situation has emerged in the various *byalag* and tenants' movements and the like. We have a great deal more of that in the United States, unofficial grass roots protest organisations. On the whole while the labour movement has tried to find scope for a person in his productive role to participate in decisions that affect him, the movement does not seem to have been very imaginative in developing scope for people to have a say in how their immediate neighbourhoods look, how they are run and the services they get. Perhaps this is especially true of welfare recipients. There seems to be at best a technocratic or paternalistic attitude: these are sick or unfortunate people, they need help. But the idea that sick or poor people themselves should have some kind of organised voice on how they are taken care of, how hospital routines are determined, when they get woken up, what they get fed – all that kind of thing seems to be unthinkable.

Bergström: That has to do, I think, with lingering traces of the old class society. You face a bureaucracy and you keep your mouth shut, you don't try to challenge the bureaucracy: that is authority. There is probably much more of that still operative in Sweden, whatever has happened in the field of democrat- isation, and so on. Much more so than in the United States, so I think that your points are perfectly well taken from a United States point of view. The labour movement never encouraged this kind of activity.

Martin: And was sometimes dismayed. I think of the famous story of the elms when people had to go up in the trees and the government authorities thought it was a terrible travesty of democracy – as if the government got elected with a mandate to cut down elms! Once you get an elected representative he does not seem to be directly accountable in some institution- alised way. He always has a tremendous opportunity to decide on his own or at least as a member of a small elite. But accountability can't be confined in this way to just a limited choice among candidates once every few years. That is the real travesty of democracy.

Bergström: The articulation of political will is only through limited channels: trade unions, political parties, and so on. What you have in mind is the system of personal elections which gives the elected person a more personal relationship with his constituency.

Martin: There again is the ambiguity that we were talking about. In effect you get both capitalist and labour organisations tending to be concentrated in powerful central organisations, but the more that this happens, the more the elites at the top deal simply with each other. I don't think that the American representative system which would decompose parties would be a solution. That would probably be worse than the disease. It does seem that some means must be found to decentralise in the living-place, to diffuse, decentralise, distribute, decon- centrate in the living-place just as is being done in industry; to identify certain kinds of decisions that can be taken in a decentralised way; to exert some kind of influence on how the living environment is designed, from architectural and engineering considerations downwards, just as in the design of the workplace.

It is almost natural that the labour movement, built as a movement by producers, should be more sensitive to producer role needs, yet it is very vulnerable politically in so far as it is insensitive to these other kinds of needs, and some new kinds of social invention are called for.

Faramond: As regards elms, election systems and bureaucracy, let me say that France takes an intermediate position between Sweden and the United States. In most cases the voter knows his *député* and can address himself to him. He has certain hours that are at his constituency's disposal, he can arrange things and there is much more personal contact. People vote for him rather than for his party. I believe that each country has the system that is best suited to its special character and that the Swedish system suits the Swedes.

The incredible thing about Sweden is that the parties have remained intact, that they haven't broken up and that there has not arisen any Poujadism in Sweden. You have been spared what happened in Norway and Denmark. The Poujadist tendency in Sweden has taken a much more acceptable form by the Centre Party assuming that role, which has taken much more malignant forms in neighbouring countries.

Social democracy has proved remarkably rigid and insensitive to new ideas, such as local citizens' groups, and so on. It has to do with what I said earlier about Social Democrats not having been humble enough and prepared to criticise themselves. On the other hand I have found that Swedish bureaucracy works very smoothly compared with ours. French bureaucracy is very unwieldy. Letters aren't answered and if you go to a government office you have to wait for hours and still perhaps not see the person you want to see. Swedish bureaucracy is relaxed in quite a different manner and a number of things can be arranged over the telephone which would be impossible in France.

Let me say also that there is an obvious risk with industrial democracy: that wage-earners don't receive the proper training and preparation that would enable them to discuss the really important issues concerning the management of the enterprise. Instead there may be a tendency to discuss trivialities that the employees feel they really know about and the result will be a bureaucracy which paralyses the company when it might otherwise have been a cohesive force making the firm grow and everybody working for the same goal. I believe the problem now is that only 10–15 per cent of workers take an active part in union work and this trend must be broken if industrial democracy is to be meaningful. People on the shop floor must be brought into the democratisation process, also the big issues where they can decide about company investment. So far this has not happened in Sweden, or at least only to a very small extent.

Bergström: But wage-earners do take part in decisions already today, for instance, about how much money should be allocated to funds for the working environment calculated on the 1974 profits; and the unions took a very active part when the new big nationalised steel company was created. To some extent the wage-earners' influence is making itself felt.

Faramond: I think that the unions are likely to become more active thanks to the new labour legislation and that they will really do their utmost to extend the influence to all members. Working groups for various purposes should be formed in the firms and that way people should be drawn into the decision process.

Let me add that Palme often speaks of the three steps: the step to political democracy, then the realisation of all social reforms and then the step to economic democracy. A fourth step seems to me to be neglected in Sweden, the step to cultural democracy. Culture must be spread in a much better way than now. People must learn to enjoy literature, music and art, and from an early age too. Even though there is more talk in Sweden about cultural democracy than elsewhere, I don't think there is enough said or done. The Cultural Council, for instance, ought to be decentralised. Now it appears to be very bureaucratic and centralised.

Bergström: What is your view of the fact that Sweden has got a new constitution? It means that there will no longer be very long periods of labour government. That there were in the past had to do with the fact that there was a two-chamber parliament with one chamber depending on election results as much as twelve years old. And also the fact that the bourgeois parties won in 1976 makes them a plausible alternative in the future. There won't be very long periods of labour rule, the governments will alternate like in any other Western society. What do you think that will mean to society as a whole and to the labour movement? Will it move to the right or to the left as a result of this?

Harrington: Let me focus on where I feel I have some reason to speak. In the first place, one of the striking things that the defeat of the socialists in Sweden demonstrates is the irreversibility of much of what they accomplished, even supposing that alternations will take place in the foreseeable future. It is not going to affect the basic and fundamental structure of Swedish social and economic policy. Secondly, if my analysis is right, applying not only to Sweden but applying very definitely to Sweden, all welfare states in this period are facing structural problems that require them to take a much more active role in investment decisions and investment benefits – the two go together. And if one argues further, as I do, that industrial democracy is a very important dimension in what Palme is talking about – something extremely real, trying to change one of the most fundamental inequities and iniquities of capitalism historically – then I think that the Swedish social democratic movement has got a couple of very basic structural items on its agenda and the fact that it might go into and out of power does not change its task of organising a new consensus and working it out. These things are very problematic. It is much easier to identify the problem and specify in broad terms the direction of the solution than actually to structure the solutions so that they work, but I think the socialists in Sweden have a tremendous job ahead. It still seems to me that in Sweden innovation and imagination and creativity are almost a monopoly of the social democratic movement. The bourgeois parties are just tagging behind and really in their year or so in power have offered nothing new whatsoever. I find this break to be a very good experience for the Social Democratic Party and Swedish society if it recharges that imagination. My feeling is that political problems are by no means insuperable. I would even argue that forty-four years in power generally is probably too long, although I would have been for the party in every term of it.

Martin: Perhaps I can follow up on what I was saying in connection with the other question. It is quite possible that some of the very kinds of discontent that we have been talking about concerning centralisation – tendencies to perhaps an excessive bureaucratisation, and so on – that the reaction to this will take the form of greater reliance on individualistic solutions. And the more that people find a remedy in individualistic solutions the more they are likely to give political support to the non-socialist parties. This, even more than the constitutional changes, is what is likely to bring about alternation in government, or at least make it likely to happen. Then under those circumstances it may be that the constituency for welfare state solutions rather than individualistic ones may erode, and more and more the welfare state will become reduced. Instead of being a universal system on which everybody relies it will become more and more a welfare state for a smaller and smaller number, more and more a welfare state for the poor, while the rest of society relies more on individualistic solutions.

I think this is what happened in Britain. Mike mentioned Crosland and what he wrote about the welfare state and full employment being irreversible, implying that these are permanent achievements. I don't know if this is so. In the British case at least it was possible for this to become eroded over time, partly because economic change doesn't stop; it poses new problems, so there have to be new solutions. New issues arise, creating situations in which there are new choices. For example, the pension fund was set up on a universalistic basis, but in future years when more and more people require pension payments and benefits begin to catch up with payments the issue may come up about whether it might be, so to speak, more efficient to concentrate the higher benefits on relatively poor people and let more and more people rely increasingly on private pension systems. This would erode the national pension system and it would also erode the capital formation aspect of the pension system. But if the bourgeois government is in power they might prefer this on the ground that it is better to allow a multiplicity of private pension funds to flourish, because it means that more saving is again channelled into the private sector by private financial institutions and that from a capital market efficiency point of view this is better. They may also argue from an anti-bureaucratic view that this gives people more choice. I don't know whether this is so or not, but it seems to me that you could conceive of such institutional changes occurring when issues arise again in the future. More generally, the assumption that the welfare state and full employment is a permanent achievement implies that the economic basis for this can be preserved, and I think this is by no means a certainty.

Bergström: Certainly with drastic economic changes like the crisis tendencies which we have now and which they have had in England, the options become much wider. I don't believe in irreversibility either, I think you are perfectly right there.

Martin: One possibility seems to me to be that of stalemate, because in periods when bourgeois governments are in power they may choose certain economic policy mixes that the unions find unacceptable, and the government can enforce those policy mixes. On the other hand it may be that the unions will then refuse to co-operate on wages, or try to compensate by increasing wage demands. They may not be able to enforce those wage demands, but there may be more social strife, more difficult wage negotiations, perhaps more strikes, and so on. There may be an even greater difficulty on the part of the central union federations, union leaderships, to maintain cohesion within the unions. Again, a kind of British scenario which could certainly make impossible the maintenance of the welfare state.

Faramond: In my opinion it is quite natural that 'the other half' of Sweden will rule the country now and then. The Swedish political system has always allowed great co-operation across the party lines. The opposition has been involved in the decision process, but to my way of thinking it is a healthy thing that political power will alternate more between the two blocs in the future. However, the three-year period that was introduced is a great mistake. It can't continue. No government can carry out its programme in three years.

Unlike Andy I don't believe there is any risk that social welfare will be disrupted and that progress will be less rapid than before. All industrial countries are facing enormous problems and the new industrial countries that are emerging will begin to compete. The rich countries will run into immense difficulties of adjustment and economists will probably be much more powerful and influential in the future.

The most dramatic problem right now is of course unemployment. It is a tragedy that society can't offer work, above all to its young people, and there must be a radical change. We are back where we started: Sweden has an advantageous and enormously ambitious employment policy, and it is quite obvious that the bourgeois government is trying to carry out social democratic policy and to be equally ambitious.

Notes: Chapter 2

1 John H. Goldthorpe, David Lockwood, Frank Bechhoffer and Jennifer Platt, *The Affluent Worker in the Class Structure* (Cambridge, Cambridge University Press, 1969).
2 Henry Braverman, *Labour and Monopoly Capital. The Degradation of Work in the Twentieth Century* (New York, Monthly Review Press, 1974).

3

The Political Values of the 1980s

HANS L. ZETTERBERG

The Party Structure

The party structure in Sweden has been very stable all through the twentieth century. It can be illustrated by a kind of triangular figure resting on one of its angles (see Figure 3.1). A Swede who fell asleep in 1920 and woke up in 1980 would not have any difficulty in recognising the parties although all of them except the Social Democrats have changed their names. At the upper end of the triangle is the left–right scale. Here is the struggle for control of work, means of production and economic surplus. We find Communists and Social Democrats to the left, Liberals at the centre, and Conservatives to the right. It speaks well for Swedish

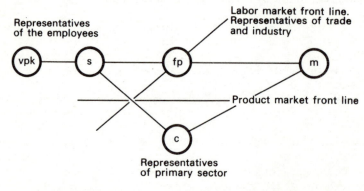

c =	Center Party (previously Agrarian Union)	m =	'Moderate Party of Unity', Conservative
fp =	'People's Party', Liberal	s =	Social Democratic Workers Party
vpk =	'Communist Party of the Left'		

Figure 3.1 *The political party structure in Sweden.*

politics of the twentieth century that no fascist party has occupied a permanent place in the party pattern.

At the lower end of the triangle we find the Centre Party which traditionally has represented the primary sector. Its front line against the others has been the product market, primarily the food market. The Centre Party has struggled for subsidies for its producers and for price guarantees. It is significant that Centrist Nils G. Åsling, when minister of industry in the three-party coalition of 1976–8, had no ideological difficulties with increasing enormous state support not only to agriculture and forestry but also to the other sectors of industry. It is possible that the Centre Party will develop into a more general party for subsidies with national autarchy as its political platform.

The Swedish party structure is thus devised to solve the left/right problems and producer/consumer problems. Other questions, such as abortions and religious education, can lead to the creation of new parties with no place in the established system (for example, KDS = Christian Democratic Union). Foreign political loyalties among Communists lead to pro-Soviet (APK = Communist Workers' Party) and pro-Chinese (SKP = Swedish Communist Party) splinter factions which strongly criticise the Eurocommunist VPK. In this essay we can ignore the small extra-parliamentary parties that have arisen outside of the main front lines of Swedish politics. The minimum rule (4 per cent of the votes) for parliamentary representation contributes to making the small parties politically powerless.

The social position of the parties (see Figure 3.1) has led to a number of simple tenets for Swedish politics:

• The Conservatives get the influence they want if they can keep sound economic development in the forefront of the debate;
• the Centre Party get the influence they want if they can keep the interests of needy regions and industries in the forefront of the debate;
• the Social Democrats get the influence they want if they can keep the interests of wage-earners in the forefront of the debate.

There is no such basic tenet for the Liberals – and according to the triangle in Figure 3.1 there cannot be. The Liberals should have the best chances of influence when questions of interior policy *other* than economic development, employee welfare and help to needy industries and regions are at the forefront of debate.

The traditional way of solving cross-line political questions – that is, those that do not come into the left/right or producer/consumer patterns – has been to seek a balance between cross-line interests in the choice of party political nominees. For instance, the major parties have long been eager to include one or two teetotallers and one or two practising Christians among their candidates (this has usually led to an overrepresentation of these particular interests in the Riksdag). In the 1970s it became customary to offer women more or less formal quotas in nominations so as to accommodate the constantly more pressing urge for equality. In so doing, the fundamental party structure has been able to survive and function in spite of the existence of cross-line questions. However, it is evident that the party structure in Sweden can be maintained only if cross-line questions do not become too numerous or too cumbersome. The question of nuclear power in the 1970s has been a far greater strain on the political system than on private industry.

It is of course possible that the Danish experience of party fragmentation will repeat itself in Sweden. We know that the sympathisers of every political party are more conservative than their Riksdag representatives and party officials. If the latter grow too insensitive to their most conservative voters, the risk of party fractures increases. However, the tolerance for different groups of interests within parties seems to be rather large. Anti-system parties had no chance in Sweden as long as there was an untested bourgeois alternative. The failure of the bourgeois alternative in the shape of the three-party government of 1976–8 was caused to such a degree by a single issue – nuclear power – that many voters feel somehow that we have not really tried the bourgeois alternative. And as long as there exists a notion that a bourgeois alternative remains untested, there is nothing much a Glistrup-type politician can do to the Swedish electorate.

The Swedish party structure seems to be very resistant to changes in size of the population groups that uphold the various parties. We have maintained the same fundamental party structure in spite of all the great demographic changes of the twentieth century. The primary sector has been drastically reduced, indeed is still shrinking, albeit more through natural depletion than through migration to cities and urban jobs. The proportion of self-employed has decreased and that of wage-earners has increased. Among the increasing numbers of wage-earners, the proportion of industrial workers has gone down while service workers have doubled several times over and immigrants have become a significant group. The median age of the electorate is shifting upwards in the long term despite the lowering of the voting age in the 1970s. But the party structure has remained the same and will presumably persist.

The Swedish party structure is relatively open to coalitions. Since the 1930s the Social Democrats have been so strong that coalitions have rarely been contemplated. In principle, however, our party system is open to coalitions even though they have been rare. If you look again at the party structure diagram in Figure 3.1, you will find that the Centre Party is a natural coalition partner in most feasible combinations. The Liberals also have such a position as to enter coalitions easily. The Conservatives and the Communists have such positions that their influence on policies is mostly that of a supporting party; their importance is clearly greater in the shaping of public opinion than in political decision-making. The propensity for coalition inherent in the party structure has good chances to make itself felt in the 1980s. Certainly, coalitions presuppose that strongly divisive issues are kept dormant while the coalition lasts. The lesson – a painful one as far as the Centre Party is concerned – from the Centrist-led coalition of Mr Fälldin is that a party cannot commit itself at the same time to a specific issue (nuclear power) and a coalition project.

Our task is not to investigate the probable size of the different parties in the 1980s. That is an impossible task, even though we can foresee quite some changes in size of the groups that constitute the nucleus of certain parties. Instead we shall try to indicate the social values that animate the men and women who occupy the party structure for the 1980s and constitute the most active and leading age groups in the country during that decade. These values will logically have their impact on policies, regardless of the size of individual parties and whichever party or parties are in government.

The Heritage of the 1970s

The 1970s brought a number of values into the limelight with the support of the environmentalists, feminists and several youth movements. An adequate expression of these values is found in the Shakertown Pledge. It is an oath (or perhaps one should say a collection of promises) that has engaged many college youths in the USA and is reflected, although partially and refractorily, in many of the typical opinion waves of the 1970s in Europe as well. It reads like this:

Knowing that the earth and its rich resources are a divine heritage and that we are called upon to use and enrich the resources of the world and give them our loving care, and knowing that life itself is a gift and an exhortation to responsibility, joy and festivity, I pronounce the following declaration:

1   I consider myself a citizen of the world.
2   I promise to lead a life that is sound and in accordance with the laws of ecology.
3   I promise to lead a creative and simple life and share my personal well-being with the poor of the world.
4   I promise to bring about changes, together with other people, to create a more just society on earth, a society where all men have

full access to resources necessary for their physical, emotional, intellectual and spiritual growth.

5   I promise that by being responsible in my work I shall avoid creating products which can hurt other people.

6   I consider my body as a gift and want to give it sound nutrition and enhance its well-being.

7   I promise always to be vigilant with regard to my relations with others and try to be honest, just, and caring to people around me.

8   I promise personal renovation through prayer, meditation and search for knowledge.

9   I accept being a responsible member of a society based on trust.

This declaration summarises beautifully the new values that appeared in the 1970s and are now being left in heritage to the 1980s.

The Shakertown Pledge also indicates a decisive weakness of the new values. By emphasising the individual components of a good social life they push the structural components into the background. Classes, institutions, markets, organisations, power centres surely wield a much stronger influence on development than the Shakertown values suppose. The personal interest pages of newspapers (those which used to be called family pages or women's pages) have given many more expressions of the values of Shakertown than the editorial pages. On the editorial pages and in the more qualified ideological debate of political issues, the 1970s have been a victory for the left and a defeat for the right. We have seen a renovation of leftist ideals and a gradual decline of the values of the right.

The renovation of the ideals of the left has been brought about by the amalgamation of two currents of thought. One is Marxism. It has come out of its ghetto and become academically and politically acceptable. The other is that of 1968, the new radicalism or the new left, which on the basis of suppositions of natural law has tried to challenge the existing social order. These two currents have a common denominator: both are anti-capitalist. The amalgamation, on the whole successful, of these two currents of thought within the left has given vitality to anti-capitalist values. You do not have to be an opinion pollster to notice that a vast section of public opinion – on the whole without regard to party affiliation – has begun to think of society in the terms of the left. Some people exploit other people, the needs of work are more important than those of capital, demands for justice from the weak have not been fulfilled, it is immoral to accumulate money and leave it as a family heritage; all this and much more of the common usage of political conversation in the 1970s shows how practically everybody muses about society in the terms of the left.

There has not been any corresponding revitalisation of rightist views. As to the ideals of 1968 non-socialists of the 1970s have been able to absorb but a few, for example to defend the integrity of the individual in a society where the authorities are armed with computers. Liberal thinkers in Sweden of the 1970s on the whole seem to have had a guilty conscience about the historical link between liberalism and capitalism. Against the more cohesive leftist views of society they have usually presented nothing more than a pragmatic argument, such as 'Yes, but the mixed economy has worked well and provided welfare'. Most of those who in this way have professed themselves believers in the survival of the market economy seem to have been rather ill at ease with people like Milton Friedman (they have not even discovered Gary Becker). Those of the left enter the 1980s with a revitalised general view of society, those of the right enter it without a general view and with their minds filled with the adversary's way of looking at the world.

Does this mean that the match is over and that the left is so sure of being the winner that we might as well hand them the trophy already? No, neither left nor right believes it to be so. Policies of the left and politicians directing the economy have not led to any greater enthusiasm for state intervention. Discontent with state interference is growing now that we enter the 1980s, just as scepticism about the capacity of the marketplace grew when we were entering the 1970s. So it seems we are gliding into the following kind of political dialogue:

The 1970s: all evil stems from the market forces.
The 1980s: all evil stems from state intervention.

It may prove possible to overcome this sterile contradiction. We need an economic policy which liberates creative forces but does not lead to an unjust distribution of resources and the marginalisation of certain groups (as the market forces do, according to the view of the 1970s) and at the same time remains liberal in the sense that it gradually makes itself obsolete and therefore does not lead to a thoroughly regulated, bureaucratised and unfree society (as state interventions do, according to the view of the 1980s). But where is the model for such a good solution? Well, this is something for the social thinkers and politicians of the 1980s to find out. There is very little in the political ideology of the 1970s that can cast light on a solution of this dilemma of the 1980s.

Homo 1980 or the Ugly Swede

The Swede of the 1980s is already living as a minority in our midst, and the values he has not yet incorporated have usually already developed abroad and are waiting for large-scale importation to Sweden.

The year is 1979. Mikael Karlsson, 31, sales engineer, wears a corduroy three-piece suit at work. He has let his hair grow a little, which he did not do before. He has borrowed money on his semi-detached house and fixed himself a respectable tax deduction. He does not smoke, but at a party the other day they offered him marijuana and he tried it. He has bought a new stereo, a new double-breasted leather coat and an old Pettersson motor yacht, which he is repairing. He has a friend who is trying to run his boat on methane. They sometimes ponder the possibility of using bacteria to extract gas from the marshland around his friend's summer cabin. But Mikael is reluctant to undertake so bold a project. Mikael has stopped buying the evening newspaper; instead, he has subscribed to *Boatowners*. He watches television less and less. He has started to question his well-paid but stressful job, and he has been talking to his wife about two kids being absolutely enough. His mother lives alone in an apartment half-an-hour from the semi-detached, but her son pays her a visit once a month at most. He does not take on salary savings plans or tax repayment savings plans which attract many of his colleagues at the office. He feels no strong party political commitment and speaks of politicians with some disdain and little interest. He considers his union fee as a kind of tax (it is also deducted at source, like income tax). A political issue that really interests him is the shortening of working hours; it is an issue that used to interest women rather than men in the 1970s.

Mikael Karlsson does not exist in the real world. He is a synthetic person, a literary construction compiled from opinion polls. We who have studied him have given him the nickname 'the Ugly Swede'. Mikael is up to his ears in a series of new sociocultural trends, such as 'live now pay later', 'self-realisation', 'autarchy', 'the simple life', 'small-scale technology', 'declining spirit of enterprise', 'diminishing faith in democratic institutions', 'lesser need for achievement'. He and many of his kind are thus of great interest to banks, newspaper publishers and radio dealers. He is a problem for companies selling baby articles and toys. But generally speaking he is not a danger to the retail trade of the 1980s. He consumes his income and thinks borrowing is a normal part of life. Mikael will be a good customer to a trade that can offer him goods and services that not only work well but also serve as individualised means of expression. For his employer Mikael Karlsson is a common problem, especially at those times when the job really demands overtime and acceptance of responsibility. Old tricks like pay rises and promotions work with Mikael only when it suits him. Mikael is also a problem to politicians – in particular those of the left – because he finds individual interests more important than collective ones.

To be sure, our apolitical Mikael will easily be drawn into the tax rebellions of the 1980s. But one cannot help worrying about his apathy with regard to the great issues of the 1980s: the content and discipline of working life, the care of old people, the overwhelming public sector, the temptations of protectionism and autarchy, the conflict between the demands of democracy and those of trade union democracy, the threat of fascism. If Mikael and his kind are allowed to decide then politicians will be left to a great extent to solve these questions on their own. That would give us a decade without strong political participation in spite of the fact that important problems require great political change. Mikael's political consciousness awoke a long time after 1968 and is not very developed. He is one of those who can fairly easily be dominated by the men of 1968.

Our Mikael of 1979 is consequently different from his counterpart of 1969. He is not attracted to the solidarity and community of the collective but to a small and rather selfish community. By contrast to the people of the 'green wave', he does not wish to revert to an earlier and well-known technology of the local community: he wants to develop a new technology. By contrast to the people of the 'red wave', he does not want to change society as a whole: at most, he wants to change himself or at least experiment with doing so. But in other ways he is similar to his counterpart of 1969. He is seeking to get away from the competitive drive, he accepts feelings and wants to use all his senses. No, Mikael will not be typical of the consumer of the 1980s, nor the working man, nor the voter. But the values he represents will in all probability make themselves more strongly and more shamelessly felt than hitherto.

A large number of Ugly Swedes can make a Beautiful Sweden with functioning markets, companies, authorities, taxation and political processes. But in order to accomplish that, a lot of adjustments are needed in traditional ways of doing things. Those politicians who do not understand which value changes are under way are not fit to lead such a development.

In conclusion, we might say that the values on the rise are individualist. People want to live a full and rich life; it means a disentanglement from established norms and conventions and a concentration on the inner life, the development and appearance of the self, the niceties of the small community. There is no ambition to participate in great accomplishments, no solidarity with larger communities, no identification with fixed ideologies. The new generation does not argue with the establishment and does not try to convert it as the flower children and the hippies tried to do around 1970. These days punk rock mostly screams at the establishment and dedicates itself to its own life of feelings and communion.

By the end of the 1980s we may have a reaction against privatisation, more or less as in the 1930s when people reacted against the individualism of the 1920s. At the time, the reaction was:

- anti-liberal, putting collective interests before individual ones, society before private life;
- anti-proletarian and anti-plutocratic, supporting the able workers and the able producers, an aristocracy of achievement;
- anti-democratic, acting politically by demonstrations and actions rather than secret balloting, thinking that a minority of strong-willed persons had a vocation to put things right, preferring corporate representatives to party representatives who were accused of following the whims of the decadent masses.

What we may fear, then, is a reaction in the form of values we usually describe as 'fascistoid'. However, we do not want to predict a fascism modelled on the 1930s for the late 1980s. Such a model combines fascist attitudes with a nationalism that does away with the conflicts between classes and regions and oppresses immigrants. Fascism as we know it from earlier decades also develops a para-military organisation of cells and a life style of uniforms, violence, belligerent songs and parades. There are no indications whatsoever that anything similar is under way in Sweden.

The New Phosphorism

How has that golden decade of leftist values, the 1970s, been able to produce a man such as Mikael Karlsson? The answer to that question is complex and partly unknown. But an important part has been played by a new wave of values which might be called the new Phosphorism. *Phosphorus* was a literary magazine published in 1810–13 with the participation of, among others, the poet Atterbom. The Phosphorists were romantics who broke with the superficiality of the Gustavians and the French academic conventions of preceding decades. Now the new Phosphorists are breaking with bourgeois superficiality and Marxist conventions. In the terminology of sociologists and psychologists the new wave is called 'intraception'. Intraception means that in relation to oneself one listens more to the signals of inner life than outer signals, and that in relation to others one tries to understand and empathise with their situation. Intraceptive activities do not result in indignation or condemnation or interest in the conventional but in understanding and humanity. The Shakertown Pledge has a latent streak of intraception.

Intraception is an ingredient of the cultural climate with great consequences. It can erode organisation and bureaucracy, dissolve ideologies and myths, undermine conventional ambition and motivation and weaken the will for national defence. Instead, it promises great compensations of another kind to its followers. Intraception concentrates on the self as it is here and now. It breaks with a conservatism that sees the self in a tradition from father to son. It also breaks with a socialism that sees the self as part of a larger fraternity. An intraceptive person normally dislikes nuclear power as a source of energy. His position is not really determined by calculations of risk or prognoses of energy or analyses of alternative sources of energy. Radioactivity, something invisible that can harm the self, is felt intuitively to be horrendous and is rejected without compromise.

Intraception dissolves myths. Here is a list of a few modern myths that are being eroded by the new wave:

- that the Gulag somehow is more excusable than Song My;
- that it is better to have many sexual partners than few;
- that factory workers have a historic mission to make a revolution;
- that money through work is different and better money than that obtained from public welfare;
- that work is the most important of all human activities;
- that it is better to die as a soldier in a war than as a civilian in your own bed;
- that it is more satisfying to work in public enterprises than in private ones;
- that public dental care is better than private dental care (or vice versa).

The intraceptive person meets these and other modern myths with the devastating answer: 'It doesn't feel that way to me. And if you ask yourself sincerely, I'm sure it doesn't feel that way to you either.' Intraception leads to a political life based on personal declarations of faith rather than doctrines and programmes. It will focus on Mr Glistrup's personal confrontation with the tax authorities, or Mr Fälldin's personal struggle with his conscience about nuclear power.

The Values of Working Life

The intraceptive elements of the cultural climate make themselves felt also in the lively discussion of working conditions. Demands are heard that work should not only provide bread but also develop the personality. Today some jobs have so little attraction that recruitment for them depends to a great extent on immigrant aliens. The pay structure does not stimulate hard and dedicated work (or stimulates it the wrong way). Leisure is normally felt to be more attractive than work. From this point of view, it is welcomed that work has become easier through the introduction of computers and robots.

Pay differentiation and job status are losing importance. People want interesting and self-developing jobs, not just jobs that pay well. On the job, recognition means more than a title. People want to work with products or services they believe are useful. They express fear that computerisation will make the jobs less interesting and leave less room for professional knowledge and pride. At the same time a certain kind of work with computers gives a new, creative dimension to the personality, much like the one an instrument gives a musician. Working is gradually being conceived as the key to a full and rich life. People want to do away with the isolation of work from society as a whole. Children must have the right to visit the workplace of their parents; politics, health-promoting activities, and so on, are being let into the workplace. Against such demands you have the need for security control of workplaces and extra protection awarded to expensive, complex machines such as computers, well-developed legislation for the protection of workers, as well as collective agreements on working hours. And, of course, the companies' drive for profit.

The most important changes in working conditions, however, have little to do with intraception as far as politics are concerned. The establishment of the welfare state has led to all jobs being secure (the Åman Laws) and to income being provided for those without a job. Instead, working for an income has become a symbol of full membership in society: 'work for everybody' means 'voting rights for everybody.' Work has become the new citizenship. A number of important benefits are attached to working: old age pensions, health benefits, participation in management, and so on. According to the plans of LO (the Confederation of Trade Unions) and SAP (the Social Democrat Party) for the 1980s, work will also entail the right to decide over capital by means of employees' funds.

However, society does not create job opportunities at the same rate as it expands the rights connected with having a job. This gives us a society with a large proportion of second-class citizens. A difficult question for the politics of the 1980s will be if work or citizenship should be the peg on which our rights should hang. The work peg may drop from the wall during the 1980s. If we want to continue hanging things on it society must be reconstructed in a feudal or corporatist direction and the labour market be abolished. Before, work had one dominant objective: to make a living. Now we have other objectives for work: rights, self-improvement, a full and rich life. At the same time the main trend of technological development has switched to some extent from large-scale mechanical systems to small-scale biological and microelectronic systems. This promises new possibilities for the 1980s to reach the new objectives – if the political problems can be solved.

Point of Explosion and Change of System in the 1980s?

When scrutinising the structure of large organisations in our world, one soon finds that they can be divided into two categories:

(1) those that get their resources from taxation and political promises of future tax support;
(2) those that get their resources from business profits and loans based on expectations of future profits.

This is an important dividing line in the human landscape. Future life on our planet is extremely dependent on the equilibrium between these two types of organisations. Roughly, they correspond to public and private activities. If present trends were to continue British, Dutch and Swedish taxes would be 100 per cent of GNP within thirty to forty years. This means that we have to put a brake on the development of the total framework for the public sector lest a point of explosion be reached and a change of system rendered inevitable.

If we look at how and on what basis decisions are made in the large structures, we find another important difference:

(1) decisions which are negotiated and based on the principle of contract;
(2) decisions which are taken by vote and based on the principle of majority.

In the first case a single person or a group can enter an agreement with several others and the agreement is valid even though there are few people on one side and many on the other. When a majority decision is taken the will of the many decides over that of the few.

Nowadays an ever increasing number of decisions are based on the majority principle, and the contract principle is losing ground. In large organisations employees are many and employers are few. There used to be and still is a contract of employment between employer and employee. However, ever-growing demands are being made that different varieties of majority decisions and co-determination should be applied also in situations previously determined by a contract. By invoking the majority principle, trade unions are acting as though they had a feudal leasehold on the factory floor. In many countries, and first among them Sweden, legal developments with regard to co-determination and union rights give their support to such demands.

Majority rule was a great step forward as far as tax-based activities are concerned. No taxation without representation in legislative bodies and no rules that run counter to the wish of the legislative majority. This is the centrepiece of political democracy and it has to be honoured and defended. But should majority rule apply also to profit-based organisations? Yes, say all those who support the slogan 'economic democracy'. At this point, however, we must ask ourselves whether we are not again getting close, though from another angle, to a point of explosion and a change of system. Entrepreneurs and innovators have thrived in a society of contracts and they will feel ill at ease if decisions concerning their lives and work are taken by a vote. Moreover business decisions taken by majority vote have a tendency to be slow, cautious and defensive, which is something quite different from the confident risk-taking of the entrepreneurial spirit. Substituting majority decisions for entrepreneurial judgement may well rob enterprise of its dynamic qualities. Experience shows that entrepreneurs are almost always a minority. Wherever you have majority rule there is thus a risk that entrepreneurs will lose to a majority of non-entrepreneurs. Entrepreneurship then ceases to be a catalyst between labour and capital.

This dilemma seems impossible to solve through 'fund socialism', that is, by employee organisations taking over capital. The union as a representative of wage-earners is liable to outweigh the union as a caretaker of capital in its internal votes. If we combine the two dimensions we have sketched, we get a table that defines more exactly how we are approaching a point of explosion and a change of system (see Table 3.1). The A sector is the traditional ground for entrepreneurship and the D sector is traditional political democracy. These sectors have constituted our system during the twentieth century. Sectors B and C represent other elements. In C we find a variety of things including public authorities (that is, the hybrids between state and private enterprise which administer toll turnpikes and bridges as well as many ports and airports in the USA), subsidised companies of all sorts and of course all forms of state capitalism. In B we find Maoist enterprises after the cultural

Table 3.1

	Decisions through negotiation: contracts	Decisions through a vote: majority rule
Profit-based resources	A	B
Tax-based resources	C	D

revolution, Yugoslav factories and other varieties of syndicalism, as well as different versions of enterprises run by co-determination. The A sector, the domain of entrepreneurs *par préférence*, is shrinking, whereas all other sectors are expanding. The same seems to be true in all industrialised countries. This is where we are coming closer to a point of explosion and a change of systems. As far as Sweden is concerned the crucial decisions will have to be taken as early as in the 1980s.

A Final Word: Be Considerate about Entrepreneurship

In the era of intraception allow me to end by pleading my own cause: a few more personal views stemming from my own slightly unusual background as a social scientist and an entrepreneur.

Industrial society arose in England around 1770 and is only 200 years old. It has developed with unprecedented speed. The result is so impressive that one is tempted to disregard any indication that industrial society is not built on unshakeable foundations. Very few people realise how little leeway there is in the balance of power – between private, public, political, technological, ideological and pedagogical forces – that has made industrial society grow and thrive. As long as that balance of power remains it will be highly profitable. If and when it is removed it will cause a deterioration of the comfortable and exciting social life we have grown used to in the rich countries. It brings immortal honour to the men who shaped the greater part of the nineteenth and twentieth centuries that they managed to save the delicate balance of power by letting dynamic entrepreneurship grow and by letting human compassion distribute the well-being that was created.

But by disregarding that frail balance of power, a few of the cornucopia of today, among them Sweden, have probably come dangerously close to stagnation and are actually faced with the threat of decline. They refuse to acknowledge that entrepreneurship and an innovative spirit are rare plants in the human garden, however stubborn they may be. They do not grow by themselves, but have to be conscientiously cultivated in order to grow and survive. Political, cultural, religious and other institutions can make or break them. Maybe it is because entrepreneurs and innovators have been so successful in their endeavours that politicians, journalists and teachers today tend to take them for granted. However, now entrepreneurs themselves complain that the entrepreneurial spirit and the drive for innovation are threatened by the complexity of government regulations, by the heavy tax burden and by the increasing application of the majority principle beyond the field of politics. Critics of private enterprise maintain that these are just the usual wails of grievance and greed to be expected of businessmen. And they are right in the sense that earlier generations of entrepreneurs have expressed similar concerns. But can we be sure that those critics know the difference between greed and the cry of distress of a drowning man?

So far entrepreneurs in Sweden have stood fast through the storms and managed to adapt to new political and economic conditions. But there are of course limits to that amazing capacity for recovery of entrepreneurs. The conditions of entrepreneurship should be thoroughly studied, clearly expressed, safeguarded and guaranteed in our society of the 1980s. After all we want a society that is not only just but also creative.

4

What Will Happen to Democracy in the 1980s?

JÖRGEN WESTERSTÅHL

A few predictions about the immediate future of Swedish democracy can be made with a fair degree of certainty. To these one can add estimates, secondary and tertiary, with a certainty diminishing in proportion to the introduction of new assumptions into the argument. Finally, one will arrive at a stage where it is difficult to decide whether one is judging probabilities or merely projecting one's own hopes and fears for the future. Then one had better stop. The difficulty consists in knowing *when* one reaches the critical limit.

The following reasoning rests on two assumptions. One is that peace will be maintained in our part of the world. The other is that Sweden's economy and industry will do sufficiently well in the next decade as to avoid any drastic decline in our standard of living.

Decreasing Political Stability

The political climate of Sweden in the 1980s will be different from the one we have been accustomed to. We cannot expect to recognise it, neither those who matured during the decades around the Second World War, nor the generation that raised the banner of rebellion in the late 1960s. The old Sweden is disappearing, the new will hardly be what its opponents hope for.

Among the things we can be fairly certain will occur in the 1980s is an increased mobility within the electorate. When in 1956 we began to poll public opinion in relation to Riksdag elections – this was in co-operation with the Central Bureau of Statistics – the proportion of people changing their party preference from the immediately preceding elections was 7 per cent. During the 1960s the figure rose from 10 to 16 per cent and in 1976 we reached the highest figure so far, 19 per cent switching from one party to another (Petersson, 1976, p. 168). There is reason to believe this tendency towards greater mobility within the electorate will continue.

Behind this development lies another and more fundamental change, namely, the decrease in importance of class voting. The social foundations for democratic party systems vary from country to country. In Holland and Austria religion plays the most important role in party preferences. In other countries regional differences are predominant and in the Nordic countries the class affiliation of voters has traditionally been the most significant factor explaining political preference. In Sweden we have been used to assuming that a third of total party preferences can be explained by class affiliation. This is a very high figure, internationally speaking, of explained difference in voting behaviour; only in Holland do they reach considerably higher figures – there, religion has sometimes explained about 50 per cent of party preferences.

What has happened since 1956, however, is that the importance of class voting has slowly diminished. The proportion of explained difference varies somewhat from one election to another but, roughly speaking, class voting in 1956 and 1960 was higher than in the two subsequent elections of the 1960s and the lowest figure for class voting ever registered was 1976 (Petersson, 1976, p. 22). The interesting thing is that this trend can be expected to continue. Class voting is still strong in older age groups but is weakened the younger the age group is.

The class vote index – which would be 100 if all workers voted for the Social Democrats and the Communists, and everybody else voted for bourgeois parties, and, conversely, zero if both groups divided their votes equally between those two blocs – is 54 for the age group 71–80 years and 24 for the age group 18–30 years (see Table 4.1). There is no reason to interpret the figures in such a way as to believe people vote more according to class the older they get, but rather that class voting was more important in the past.

Table 4.1 *Percentage of Social Democrat or Communist Votes according to Age and Profession in the 1976 Elections*

		18–30	31–40	41–50	51–60	61–70	71–80	Total
Total		54	46	52	48	52	47	50
A	Workers	64	65	71	67	74	73	68
B	Employees, entrepreneurs, farmers	41	33	35	29	29	19	32
Class vote index[a]		24	32	36	39	45	54	36

(a) Difference between percentages of lines A and B. Due to rounding, the more exact index value can differ from that difference.
Source: Petersson (1976).

Class voting is being replaced by more ideological voting. There has been a rather drastic change in this regard as well. A question that has turned out to be a rather good measure of position on the left–right scale has been included ever since the poll of 1960: those interviewed are asked to agree or disagree with the proposition that the managers of banks and industry get too much power unless the state has a chance to control private enterprise. Olof Petersson (1976, p. 128) has been able to show that up to the elections of 1964 class was more important to voting than ideology, measured in this way. Workers with a rightist view on that question tended to vote for Social Democrats or Communists to a larger extent than middle-class people with a leftist view. From the 1968 elections onwards the situation has been the reverse: midle-class people with a leftist view vote more for Social Democrats or Communists than workers with a rightist view.

In this case also, significant change appears between different age groups. Table 4.2 shows that in 1960 class meant more than 'ideology' – as measured by the question referred to – in all age groups. For the younger groups it was more of a balance, for the older the difference was very great between the influence of the two factors. In 1976 it is only in the oldest group that the class factor still weighs more heavily than ideology. What has happened is primarily a weakening of the class factor but also an increase in the importance of the ideology factor, and here the change is most evident in the older age groups. As Olof Petersson points out, the weakening of class voting can be explained to a great extent by the entry into the electorate of new voters who do not vote along class

Table 4.2   *Class, Ideology, Age and Vote in 1960 and 1976*

A 1960 Elections	Age 21–30	31–50	51–80
Effect on party preference of			
class	0·435	0·503	0·532
ideology	0·357	0·311	0·211
B 1976 Elections	Age 18–30	31–50	51–80
Effect on party preference of			
class	0·127	0·238	0·361
ideology	0·378	0·369	0·344

Note: The measures are beta coefficients, i.e., partial standardised regressive coefficients in a regression analysis with party blocs as the dependent variable and class and ideology as independent variables.

Source: Petersson (1976).

lines. However, voting along ideology lines cannot be explained by demographic change; behind it is an increase throughout the electorate of the importance of ideology or opinion.

Other results of the polls are also interesting in this context. Previously one could be reasonably certain that political interest and political engagement were voter qualities that accompanied one another. It was the people actively engaged in party politics who were also interested, and vice versa. This is still true for a large group of voters. But a new group of voters, whom Olof Petersson calls 'free-wheelers', has grown up. Members of this group are interested in political issues but only vaguely associated with a certain party.

Furthermore, confidence in politics and politicians has slowly diminished. From 1968 to 1976 the proportion of voters with low confidence has increased from 17 to 23 per cent (Petersson, 1976, p. 261). This has primarily taken place among those who vote for the bourgeois parties or for the Communists. In all previous polls of this kind Social Democrats have shown a significantly higher degree of confidence. In a renewed poll in the autumn of 1978 using the same question (Törnqvist, 1978) it turned out that the proportion of voters with a low degree of confidence had increased further by a few percentage points. However, this increase is due quite predominantly to the fact that the proportion of Social Democrats with a low degree of confidence had increased significantly. One may assume that Social Democratic confidence would be restored if a Social Democratic government were returned to power. Generally speaking, Olof Petersson has found (1976, p. 264) that confidence in politics and politicians is closely related to the judgement whether one's own preferred party is able to pursue good policies when it is in power. Distrust has increased among party activists and free-wheelers as well as passive voters who are neither interested in politics nor identify themselves with a party. Only among habitual voters, that is, those uninterested in politics but identifying themselves with a certain party, has confidence remained unchanged (op. cit. p. 276).

All these data point rather unequivocally in one direction. Swedish democracy, or, to use the terms of the constitution, popular government, will be characterised in the 1980s by less political stability and by less loyalty to the political actors. This is something we can predict with a fairly high degree of probability. It should be stressed, however, that Sweden has been used to an extraordinary degree of stability and loyalty in political life. Things were quiet and tranquil in the old conservative Sweden of the bureaucrats. Almost unnoticeably, without passing through much of a liberal period of individualism and the loosening of loyalties, we entered the new Sweden of social welfare. A new bureaucracy with

'Sweden, the people's home' for an ideal ruled for the common good of all. The popular movements that were the basis of this new Sweden had quickly transformed themselves from demolition balls to pillars of strength. Loyalty was strong once more, maybe stronger than ever. Now this Sweden, the people's home, will enter more troubled waters.

Swedish politics have been one-dimensional to a very large extent, maybe more so than those of any comparable country. One dimension of conflict, that of left and right, has dominated political life for a long time. Juxtaposed to it we have had other dimensions of conflict, particularly between agrarian and industrial interests, which have been important in some instances. In the last few years, the latter dimension has gained importance once more, through the issues of decentralisation, ward democracy and regional politics, through the environmentalist cause and, in particular, through the issue of nuclear energy. The remarkable feature of the nuclear issue is that it is probably the first time since the debate on prohibition that an issue outside the left–right dimension has dominated the political discussion.

Any forecast of Swedish politics will depend on the position of the left–right dimension. If it continues to dominate in the 1980s then certain basic conditions are already given. On the other hand if issues concerning other dimensions of conflict attract the main interest then our political development will become much more uncertain. If we assume that present industrial problems will continue to exist and therefore that economic issues will continue to play an important part then the left–right dimension will remain the central axis around which Swedish political life evolves. But we have reason to expect that issues related to other dimensions of conflict, particularly the industrial/agrarian, will appear and complicate the situation in a way we did not have to reckon with before.

New conditions for Sweden's political life were partly created by the introduction of the one-chamber system and the electoral method of nationwide proportional representation in 1970. The previous electoral method gave a measure of overrepresentation to larger parties which was further increased by the indirect elections to the upper house. That electoral method facilitated the establishment of a majority in a system where competition for votes according to the dominating political dimension tended to give a division in public opinion of about fifty-fifty. It provided an incentive for party mergers and discouraged the appearance of splinter parties by means of a considerable underrepresentation (however, without a cutoff at a given percentage level). The result, given the prevailing relations of strength, was a dominant position for the Social Democrats in spite of the electoral equilibrium between the two blocs that had existed since the 1952 elections. By contrast after the reforms of 1970 we can expect that recurrent shifts of majority rather than long-term stability will be the normal feature.

Another assumption for the 1980s and beyond, as far as one can see, is that minority governments must be the exception rather than the rule. Regardless of whether international trends lead to further integration or recurrent protectionism, the need for a strong and consistent economic policy will be strongly felt. At least the government must be able to carry out a consistent policy for the whole of the electoral term – and in this regard three years seems a rather short period.

The Decade of Coalition Governments

If you combine increased instability and the new difficulties in establishing a parliamentary majority with the need for majority governments, you have to conclude that coalition governments will be a normal feature. The Liberal minority government can be seen as exceptional, due to the special conditions prevailing at its inception. Of course, the Social Democratic Party still has a chance to obtain a majority of its own, for example, in 1982. But in that case there are several factors indicating that it will lose its majority again in 1985; by then some voters will have been disillusioned and other parties will have adapted themselves and enhanced their electoral competitiveness. We therefore have reason to believe that Sweden will be governed by coalition governments during most of the 1980s – and we have to analyse the implications of that situation.

Apart from the possibility of an all-party government, there are three possible majority coalitions on the left–right scale: a bloc of the left (Social Democrats and Communists), a bloc of the right (Conservatives, Liberals and Centrists), and a bloc of the centre (Social Democrats and Liberals and/or Centrists). We have recently experienced a bloc of the right, according to this terminology. It can be said to have worked as long as it was a matter of finding compromises along the left–right dimension. The coalition broke up when the issue of nuclear power, that is, a quite different political dimension, became acute. There was no longer a middle way in which one could seek compromises and there was no room for horse-trading, that is, an agreement in which everyone gets what he wants without caring too much about what the others get.

Generally speaking it is the extreme wing that is most enthusiastic about a coalition of the right or of the left. As long as there is no serious competition from a still more extreme party the extreme wing has nothing to lose, and a coalition of this kind is its only access to government (assuming the internal relations of strength between coalition parties are not drastically altered). Conversely a coalition bloc of the right is most dangerous to the party furthest to the left, in this case the Liberals, according to some recent policy indications. Otherwise it is well known that the positions of Centrists and Liberals, respectively, on the left–right scale, have not been constant but have fluctuated according to the times and the issues. This is the typical dilemma of a coalition of the right: enthusiasm on the right, hesitation on the left. Admittedly it does not prevent a coalition of this kind from being successful; however, it is hardly probable that all three parties will make electoral gains. Generally speaking three-party coalitions must be considerably more difficult to manage than two-party ones.

The left half of the Swedish party spectrum is completely dominated by the Social Democrats but there is also a small group of Communists. The relationship between the two has been significantly affected by the new electoral system. No party gained more through that system than the Communists – they had their seats in the Riksdag approximately doubled – though at the same time the minimum rule of 4 per cent represents a deadly threat to them. But this very threat leads to another consequence. The Social Democrats have to hold back criticism of the Communists in order to avoid weakening the total vote of the left. From the very beginning the Social Democrats have been the major party to compete most effectively for votes with the Communists.

The fact that the propaganda war is frequently most intensive between the two extremes of the party spectrum should not confuse anybody – the purpose is chiefly to stimulate one's own group and to influence the Centre groups, but hardly to win votes from the party one attacks. Social Democratic vigilance towards the left has thus been weakened by the new electoral system. If the Social Democrats get a large momentum in an electoral campaign, as in 1968, there is a risk that the Communists will be kicked out of the Riksdag. Presumably, therefore, the latter have gained slightly more votes from 1970 onwards than they would have if the Social Democrats had dared attack them across the board. Only in a situation where the Social Democrats were convinced that the Communists did not have a chance to pass the minimum anyway (or if they came to consider them a real threat, that is, if they were to grow) could one expect a wholehearted offensive on the left wing along previous lines.

There is no party less interested in coalitions than the Social Democrats. The rank-and-file Social Democrat hopes for a majority and is not inclined to think in terms of coalitions. The most recent coalition is twenty years away and it was not a very successful period for the party.

If the Social Democrats do not obtain a majority of their own the nearest option will be the kind of government we had in 1970–3, namely, a purely Social Democratic government which could rely on the Communists when necessary, without having to include them other than exceptionally in its political calculations: the Communists were there and they were normally unable to vote with the bourgeois parties, particularly not on central issues. We now have two changes in this respect. First of all, the character of the Communist Party has changed together with its base. Traditionally it has been a party mainly of workers. In the elections of 1979 the Communist Party had an electoral base mainly of the middle classes, with a strong element of students and higher civil servants. Secondly, the party has begun taking an interest in a great many issues other than those that can be included in the left/right dimension. This has made the party more active, less calculable and less suitable as silent support for the Social Democrats. There is a good likelihood that if the electoral results are similar to those of 1970–3 the Communists will want to negotiate a price for their support for a majority of the left in the Riksdag.

The Social Democrats, of course, do not want to negotiate with anybody. But if they do have to negotiate in order to form a cabinet, what will they do? If the left half of the party scale commands a majority they can choose between negotiating either to the left or to the right, but if the right half commands the majority a road to the cabinet is still open to Social Democrats through a possible agreement with the Liberals and/or the Centrists. What is then the most probable outcome? Judging from previous experience, there is reason to believe that the Social Democrats will consider being in government so important that they are willing to negotiate, and that an agreement with the Communists is not a realistic alternative. It should be kept in mind that a far greater proportion of Social Democratic voters have indicated a bourgeois party as their next best option rather than the Communist Party.

On the other hand there are currently certain factors that work against this prediction. The Social Democratic Party congress has strengthened its position; that is where the grass roots, or rather those who grow just above the mass of grass roots, carry the day, more often than not. Party activists can be assumed to be considerably to the left of the party leadership as well as its non-activist voters, and the policies they recommend are hardly suitable for a coalition with bourgeois parties. Such a coalition can also be expected to meet strong opposition from the trade unions.

There have also been new elements in Social Democratic propaganda during the last few years. Ever since the beginning of the century socialism has been like a big red balloon hovering above the workers' movement and offering space for each new generation to inscribe its objectives for the future. The common denominator of all these slogans, the red colour background, has been solidarity, primarily among the workers, later with all needy groups. Now there are voices saying that the march is approaching its end, that it is time to haul the balloon down to earth and take a third, decisive step into the society of the future. People dedicated to this kind of philosophical approach can hardly be interested in coalition with a bourgeois party.

Nevertheless if one assumes that the problems of economic adjustment will continue to make themselves felt through the 1980s and that the Social Democrats will not command a majority of their own for a longer period, a coalition between Social Democrats and Liberals and/or Centrists appears as a probable outcome. Admittedly if the three bourgeois parties once again win a majority they can also have another shot at a three-party coalition. One difficulty of all coalitions is that in order to continue to survive they presuppose that all participant parties obtain acceptable electoral results. This condition is particularly difficult to fill for a three-party coalition.

Is there any threat to Swedish democracy in the 1980s? A general and surreptitious threat has long been felt in the terminological field. Paradoxically it is the very popularity of the term democracy that constitutes a danger. Not only do almost all states, regardless of their political system, call themselves democracies but also all kinds of political endeavours are called democratic by their supporters, since democracy has become a general term of approval conferred on all that is good in society. This terminological confusion has been made possible by the use of a word borrowed from the Greek, the precise meaning of which is ignored. However, if instead of the Greek adjective you use its Swedish or English counterpart 'by popular government' – as the Constitution does – then such confusion of meanings is rendered impossible. Try 'administration by popular government', 'school management by popular government', 'smoking regulations by popular government', instead of 'democratic administration', 'democratic school management', 'democratic smoking regulations', and you will find the concept absurd or at least that the words point in a quite different direction. It is not the citizens but the employees and their organisations who are supposed to win influence through democratic administration, and so on.

In most cases this blowing up of the term 'democracy' is made without any sinister purpose, without any intention of hurting political democracy. But in the long run this situation will be increasingly embarrassing to political democracy. You cannot refer to or argue in favour of democracy without arousing a panoply of vague associations in your audience. Theoretically it would clear up things to switch to the terminology of the Constitutions and talk about 'popular government' rather than 'political democracy'.

Part of the popularity of the term 'democracy' is also to be found in the fact that there have been no important political movements in our country which refer to themselves as anti-democratic. If one is to look for real threats to popular government in Sweden in the 1980s one will have to disregard terminology. If one does this there are two fundamentally opposed trends in current political developments which may imply a threat. One of them can be defined as corporatist and collectivist, the other as extremely individualist.

Corporatism or Privatisation?

The new wave of corporatism, the intrusion of popular organisations into the state, the confusion of public and private functions, is a phenomenon of the 1970s. Here is an example to show how quickly this change came about. In 1969, at the proposal of Social Democrats and against opposition from, among others, a few bourgeois politicians connected with the teachers' unions, the Riksdag did away with the right of a union representative to attend the meetings of local school boards, with the explanation that there was no reason to maintain 'rules of a corporative nature'. Three years later the Riksdag adopted a law introducing union attendance, on an experimental basis, in all committees of local government.

It is the changed attitude of LO (the Swedish Confederation of Trade Unions) which primarily explains this extraordinarily rapid reorientation. The fundamental characteristic of the Swedish model of a trade union movement had originally been the strength of the trade unions. They were strong enough to obtain from their counterparts, through negotiations, not only annual pay increases but also a longer-term regulation of conditions in the labour market. They had condescendingly looked down on the continental trade union movements which strove to strengthen their position through legislation; it was a solution fit for the weak who could not solve their problems by their own strength. In the field of social policy it was acceptable to opt for legislation, but as far as power relations in the labour market were concerned the state was to stay out (cf. also the debate on profit-sharing arrangements).

Why then has LO substituted the continental model for the Swedish? A change of leadership, competition from TCO – the Swedish Confederation of Salaried Employees has been raised on legislative support – or direct influence of continental thinking through a university-trained secretariat? There is hardly any simple answer. The essential thing is to admit that we have got new corporatist tendencies, supported by the unions. Is it then not possible to see the activities of the unions as an extension, a deepening, of a popular government built on parties? So far, this is how the unions have to a great extent worked. But when they go into administering public tasks themselves, directly influencing the management of the public sector and taking sides on behalf of their members on strongly controversial political issues, then we are talking about competition with political democracy and a fundamentally different form of political decision-making.

The difference between a democratic and a corporative system can be illustrated at many levels. The simplest way is to point to the fundamental conflict between the individualistic way of shaping public opinion in a democracy and the collectivist methods of corporatism. In a corporatist system all members of an organisation are supposed to have identical interests and therefore want the same things. This may be applicable to the primary field of activity of the unions, for example, wages and working conditions, but it becomes problematic when it is concerned with other social issues; those who disagree with their organisation have no possibility of acting. The only thing they can do is leave the organisation. That is a meaningless option unless it is done massively, it can lead to personal harassment and it may run counter to the desire of the individual to support the organisation in its primary endeavours. Contrariwise, in a system of popular government operating through political parties it is up to everyone to vote for another party in case the party he used to support represents an opinion he dislikes on an important issue. The free forming of opinion in a democracy is directly related to the free choice between parties. In a corporatist society you do not choose your corporation or organisation: it is simply there.

Thus the minority lacks spokesmen and the opportunity for an adequate expression of its opinion. As a matter of fact even the majority can be in a bad spot. On issues which are not of primary importance to the organisation it is probably quite frequent for the leaders of the organisation to represent another opinion than that of the majority of the members. An example is the collective affiliation of unions to the Social Democratic Party. Here we have known for a long time that a majority of the LO membership is opposed to this kind of affiliation. Since the issue is secondary to the main motives for union membership the leaders have so far disregarded the opinion of the majority.

Corporatism, then, is something quite different from democracy and corporatist tendencies are a threat to democracy. How serious is this threat? Certain recent union proposals, for example, public subsidies for 4,000 regional union representatives, appear truly fantastic compared to previous experience with union activities. It seems as though they have lost their sense of proportion, as if they had been seized by a presumption similar to the *hubris* of Greek tragedy, which is doomed to be punished by the gods.

There are reasons for believing that the trend towards corporatism will continue for the time being. It is supported by a resurrected ideology, with terms such as 'participation' and 'self-realisation' as central concepts. The law on co-determination (MBL), the 'participatory bodies' in local government will roll on. But what happens some time from now when this has been established and tested? Will members of the organisations be happier, their job satisfaction greater, by virtue of the organisations having influence on companies and administration? Those who believe that like to think that power itself, the new position of power of the organisations, will give the members satisfaction. But modern wielding of power has nothing to do with the power of princes in a fairy tale. It is a time-consuming process, a careful balancing of different interests, an unwieldy anchoring of decisions in public opinion, and so on. Only a limited number of people are able and willing to participate in this kind of decision-making. For the vast majority of members, the promised power will be yellow mica rather than gold; it looks nice at a distance but loses its attraction as you get closer.

When you listen to the representatives of the unions and hear the reports of the mass media you usually get the impression that the trend towards corporatism is supported by a vast section of public opinion. But what is the real situation? There are many factors pointing in the opposite direction. The very basis of the unity of the collective, group solidarity seems to be on the wane all the time. Public interest and participation in the activities of the organisations seem to be weakening. The official emphasis on 'popular movements' you meet everywhere these days seems almost pathetic against the background of the withering of the very foundation of these movements. Trade union leaders put their faith in politicians at a time when the latter tend to be more unreliable than before from a union point of view. There is something that does not square in all this. Possibly the media are an important part of the explanation. They have a predilection for reports on action groups, protests and strikes. You get the impression of strong popular activities. Even at the local level, trade union initiatives have had a strong and positive reflection in the media. They have truly had the wind behind them. But mass media people are a fickle crew; you need only a slight shift in public opinion and local trade union leaders will be turned into a bunch of incompetent little dictators to be criticised and ridiculed.

To me modern Swedish corporatism appears as basically hollow, a movement of trade union officials with no real mandate from the members. It is therefore difficult for me to believe that it constitutes a danger to democracy in the long run. Nevertheless it is a palpable threat to a trade union movement of the Swedish kind. If the trade union movement does not reconsider, but limits itself to its traditional tasks, it will run the combined risk of decentralisation and bureaucratisation.

The opposite trend seems to me more dangerous to democracy. It goes in the direction of increased privatisation and diminishing solidarity with the public interest and with different groups. As far as invididuals are concerned a number of investigations indicate that increased well-being and leisure have been accompanied by an ever stronger concentration on the personal sphere, the family and private interests. In spite of all propaganda, solidarity, for example, with older generations, seems to be declining. The difficulty in recruiting competent people to public office is increasing and interest in voluntary work is declining. This change is making itself felt in the field of local government. It is not just a problem of recruitment. Those who do volunteer are increasingly demanding economic compensation and daytime meetings with pay to compensate for lost work income. It should be recalled that the older generations who were the backbone of local government by no means consisted only of well-to-do persons with abundant leisure but to a great extent of farmers and workers. It would appear, then, that precisely the public spirit that so many people hoped would be the fruit of democracy is on the decline.

This kind of development can go on for a long time without anything happening. Politics are taken over by entrepreneurs. But the great risk, as I see it, is that these privatised people may easily fall prey to extreme countermovements that want to unite everybody around some new common ideal that will explode the limits of privacy. At the end of the 1960s and in the early 1970s the extreme left had its heyday. Twenty years hence the time may come for movements with fascist elements. Swedish society with its uniform public debate, its lack of civil courage and its absence of a liberal tradition is presumably very vulnerable as traditional loyalties and old solidarity links lose their grip. Our democracy is not as solid as we like to believe.

References: Chapter 4

Petersson, Olof (1976), *Väljarna och valet 1976, Valundersökningar, Rapport 2* (Stockholm Statistiska Centralbyrån Liber).
Törnqvist, Kurt (1978), 'Opinion 1978', mimeographed report, Beredskapsnämnden för psykologiskt försvar.

5

Sweden and the International Economy

STAFFAN BURENSTAM-LINDER

Disturbances and alterations in the international economy have been considerable during the 1970s and it is likely that the 1980s will offer even more dramatic events. But it is difficult to discern any feature of current events that would undermine the principles of trade policy which have governed postwar developments so far. A free world trade will continue to be one of the most important pre-requisites for the safeguarding and further development of our standard of living. It is less than evident, however, that this pre-requisite will be at hand. There are two risks. One is that, for various reasons, growing protectionist pressure in the world takes the upper hand over efforts to liberalise trade further. The other is that we in Sweden on our own, and perhaps involuntarily, may gradually do away with the advantages offered by free trade and perhaps do so in such a way and to such an extent that we shall, additionally, be hit by measures taken by other countries against our exports.

The advantages of free trade have been taken for granted for so long that they have rarely been explained in recent years. The understanding of those advantages may waver in times of pressure. There may be some cause therefore to enumerate once more the advantages of free trade and particularly to underscore that they consist not only in other countries maintaining free trade but also in maintaining free trade oneself. Foreign trade makes it possible for countries to produce goods they are good at and import goods they are less good at. If a country tries, behind the shield of import duties or subsidies, to produce things it is less fit for, less productive employment results. A division of labour and specialisation produces a high standard of living. Foreign trade also makes it possible to lower costs by means of high volume of output. An additional advantage is that tough competition between companies in the world market increases their efficiency and gives the consumer more for his money. Prices will be lower. In principle so-called low-price imports are welcome, especially for low-income earners. The very point of foreign trade is to import at lower prices. Another important factor is that competition also enhances the search for improved methods and products which makes for economic growth. Foreign trade stimulates that search not least by making it possible to distribute the fixed costs of research and development over a higher volume of output.

These advantages are particularly palpable for small, highly industrialised countries such as Sweden. For these countries, possibilities of specialisation and high volume are more important than for the very large countries with vast home markets. To the small countries there are also additional advantages in the firm rules of world trade which have been negotiated during the postwar period. Large countries might by their very weight be able to bully their way through without such rules, but for the small countries uncertainty about the activities of their trading partners would create problems which would make risk-taking and investment more difficult. The fact that those rules are being respected is important to Sweden, especially at a time when we need to create a surplus in our trade balance to cover the deficit in our short-term balance of payments created by, among other things, tourism and foreign aid. In a world where free trade is not allowed to reign, countries will keep an eye on their bilateral trade balances and it will become more difficult to create a necessary export surplus.

Those are the advantages of free trade. Their strength has been emphasised in recent years by the progress achieved by a number of developing countries in the process of rapid industrialisation, precisely by focusing their development efforts on foreign trade. Nevertheless the situation with regard to trade policy is contradictory. On the one hand there has been a considerable and seemingly successful negotiating effort in the GATT for a number of years with a view to taking further steps in the direction of trade liberalisation. But on the other hand many governments have taken various measures which constitute barriers to trade.

There are several reasons why in the midst of current efforts to further liberalisation of trade one can see so many attempts in the opposite direction. One of them is the problem of economic instability, worsened by rising oil prices, which expresses itself through strong inflation and disturbances in the balance of payments. On top of that there is unemployment as a consequence of efforts to come to grips with price rises and balance of payments problems. Such an environment has always been fertile ground for protectionism, even though it has always been true and remains true that a beggar-my-neighbour policy harms everyone. Many factors indicate that the problems of stability will increase in the 1980s as a consequence of further oil price shocks, among other things. The industrialised countries will cope with such pressures with varying degrees of skill. That very fact will result in shaky currencies and a distorted balance of payments situation. It would be surprising if such difficulties were not also reflected in commercial tensions despite the fact that even the countries which do take to protectionism do not really facilitate their own stabilisation effort.

Structural stresses have also produced trade barriers and will probably continue to do so even more, although with a paucity of rational argument in this case as well. Economic growth means a need for restructuring. In a dynamic world economy the growth of competitors in one country warrants restructuring in other countries. But if the ability or propensity to restructure decreases – and this is what is happening in the industrialised countries – structural tensions will arise. Certain branches of industry become crisis-ridden. A country with a large sector of foreign trade is especially dependent on its adaptability. Inability to restructure will lead not only to stagnation but to regression when, as is often the case, it has export industries which are unable to keep up with competition.

In order to facilitate restructuring, measures of industrial policy have often been applied. The idea has been to increase competitiveness by aggressive means. However, it is easier to talk about restructuring than it is to bring it about. More often than not, measures taken under the pressure of political circumstances have degenerated into a more or less permanent policy of subsidies. Industrial policies, intended to be aggressive in practice, easily degenerate into preserving existing structures and distorting world trade. Once you grow used to having recourse to industrial subsidies the propensity to adapt and restructure declines even more. Subsidies lead to administrative pricing in many industries. Such interventionism has its risks for international trade. It means that you can no longer easily judge which production is economically sound. Prices no longer reflect real factor costs. Swedish exports of new ships are not good business for Sweden but an expensive aid programme which benefits foreign buyers. Interventionism entails risks for countermeasures, not only because other countries see their export market shrink, but also because they may be exposed, or feel they are exposed, to subsidised exports, which distort their own market. Subsidy programmes can distort competition within a country as well as between countries. In both cases there is cause for protest. Between countries such a protest can take the form of countermeasures in the field of trade.

There is reason to recall the foreign trade position of state trading countries in this context. Since in their case authorities administer the prices, market economy countries reserve the right to intervene with trade barriers in order to prevent arbitrary reversals of competitive conditions. It would be regrettable if we and other industrialised countries were to slip into a situation where it became increasingly frequent to have recourse to market distortion clauses and refer to the industrial subsidies of the others also in the trade relations between market economies. There is clearly a risk. Pricing methods and public planning have made it extremely difficult to have a lively trade conducive to growth even between Eastern European states.

Economic policy, including trade and industrial policy, must be shaped bearing in mind that in the long run you cannot save jobs with a support programme. Subsidies take resources from the industries which are better equipped to function and expand. Selective support threatens the jobs in competing companies. In addition, subsidies lead to increasing risks in private industry. Investment is hampered when one has to count on the risk that one's competitors will receive subsidies which distort competition.

One way or the other restructuring will force itself upon us. If you do not want to adapt the industrial structure gradually as conditions change, you will not be able to maintain the standard of living previously acquired, which was built on international specialisation. As the living standard rises it is tempting to use some of your wealth to try to avoid the stresses brought on by restructuring. But to cash in your wealth in such a way that adaptability is lost is to consume the very foundations of wealth. To modify a French saying: 'Il vaut mieux sauter pour ne pas reculer.' The existing structure or the existing standard – those are the alternatives when it comes to restructuring. Our living standard is not given and guaranteed by God. What we have is the opportunity to make an effort to safe-guard and develop our standard of living. This fact is worth repeating with the strongest possible emphasis, since there is a tendency to underestimate the challenges implied in the growth of other countries and to overestimate the chances offered by industrial policies.

There are thus a number of explanations – in the absence of rational motives – for the new protectionism. A remarkable phenomenon, however, is that countries continue to liberalise trade at the same time as they introduce new trade barriers. The explanation is that many policies which constitute obstacles to trade were probably not originally intended to be trade barriers but rather aggressive measures or short-term solutions. The contradiction has also been made possible by the fact that the new protectionism has manifested itself in a way that is different from traditional, contractual trade policies. Countries have resorted to non-tariff trade barriers, the most important of which have been industrial subsidies. There have been no rules for the latter, partly because they have not been so prominent before, but above all because rules are difficult to formulate and supervise. In the latest GATT negotiations, however, an effort has been made also to control and limit the long list of non-tariff trade barriers. Precisely because of the difficulties of doing this it is possible that the GATT negotiations, even if concluded, will end in disappointment. The necessity to come to grips with the non-tariff barriers to trade, the agreements to do so which have recently been concluded and the difficulty nevertheless of reaching concrete results pose a great and significant challenge to the GATT.

Special attention in the game of trade policies and new protectionism is attracted by a group of developing countries, the most rapidly growing of all countries and which are in the process of rapid industrialisation. These so-called newly industrialised countries confront the established industrialised countries with intense competition in a number of sectors. Structural tensions have led to the introduction of several trade barriers and demands for more of the same. Since protectionist arguments against those countries are voiced with particular emphasis, and since those countries will play an increasing role in the international economy, it is important to understand which threats or possibilities they offer us. Do we have any sustainable arguments for protectionist measures?

It is being said that one cannot compete with such extreme low-wage countries. This is true of certain industries, but not of all. As a matter of fact, Sweden has a large export surplus in its trade with those countries. That surplus has even been growing in the last few years. The same is true of the other OECD countries as a group. This means that it is possible to compete with the newly indus-trialised countries even in their own home markets. Nor can the fact that they are low-price countries be construed as an acceptable argument for protectionist measures. It is an advantage to be able to buy at a low price. In the case of certain industries, moreover, we are the low-price country, as is proved by our competitiveness, that is, we offer and sell a wide range of products at lower prices than other countries. Nor can we rationalise trade barriers with the argument that without them we lose jobs. Free trade means that you lose jobs in some industries and gain them in others. An export surplus indicates that we are on the winning side when we calculate the net result.

A new competitor is a new customer. He is a new customer because the export income he earns is used to pay for imports. Those developing countries, together with the oil-producing countries, will offer the most rapidly growing markets in the world. But a new competitor is a new customer only if you manage to restructure your own industry to produce the goods demanded by the new markets in newly competing countries.

A very special protectionist argument is that wages and work environments in the newly industrialised countries are supposed to be so bad that they justify a protest by means of trade barriers. That is the argument underlying demands for a so-called social clause. However, it rests on weak foundations. Working conditions in the newly industrialised countries are considerably better than those in developing countries which have been unable to get their industrial-isation off the ground. If one were to be consistent in such noble endeavours, trade barriers should first and foremost be applied against the poorest developing countries which have the worst conditions. Logic demands it, even though we are talking about imports which do not directly compete with domestic production. If noble feelings inspire intervention, countermeasures cannot be applied only when one's own production is threatened. For example, working conditions are bad from many points of view in a number of countries from which we import coffee. If it were really possible to improve those conditions by means of trade barriers, then the champions of the social clause should demand import restrictions on coffee. But they do not. This indicates that the rationale of the social clause, e.:cept perhaps in the case of a few misled idealists, is egotistic protectionism thinly disguised.

As a matter of fact, working conditions cannot be improved by means of trade barriers. Those conditions are bad in developing countries generally because the countries are poor. Poverty will be greater, not less, if we prevent the exports of those countries. The best form of development aid, which also helps us, is to give developing countries free access to our markets. As development progresses, working conditions will improve. This is already the case. To accelerate that process there are other methods than those which counteract their own purpose.

The protectionist arguments and the demand for social clauses have particularly focused on the so-called free zones, or export zones, established by several developing countries to stimulate their exports. It has been said that wages and working conditions in those zones have been worse than in the rest of the countries concerned which has enabled them to enforce acceptance of their exports there. But this is hardly the case. Instead the export zones have been made attractive by lessening the burden of taxes and other duties and bureaucratic interventions. Wages and working conditions are rather better in the export zones than outside.

The developing countries that have been the most successful in their development efforts have relied on the forces of a market economy, private enterprise and foreign trade. By contrast developing countries whose development strategies have relied on economic planning and import substitution have encountered great difficulties. This is worth noticing because *inter alia* it may mean that an increasing number of developing countries will adopt a more outward-looking development policy. An indication that this may be the case is that many developing countries have already taken partial steps in that direction by introducing export zones with greater economic freedom. To the extent that an increasing number of developing countries shift their strategies in that direction the share of developing countries in world trade will increase faster.

Conditions prevailing in the newly industrialised countries do not offer any new sustainable arguments for trade barriers. In many cases those countries pursue an aggressive industrial policy – which is easier at their level of development when they can copy previous patterns of development – and that means various subsidies which may distort competition. As those countries grow stronger we can demand that they should increasingly respect various international rules, in particular those of the GATT Agreement (so-called phasing-in). But we must not of course forgo those obligations ourselves. The forces and inertia I have discussed here give rise to processes which will shape a new pattern for the world economy. With all due respect for the awkwardness of prognostications, I can imagine the following scenario.

- The developing world, always heterogeneous in very many respects, will be increasingly so to an extent that will be crucial not only to it but also to the economic and political situation of industrialised countries.
- The newly industrialised countries will continue to grow rapidly and an increasing number of developing countries will try to copy their strategy for development; the problems of adaptation of the established industrial countries will grow; but their chances of fruitful trade relations with the newly industrialised countries will increase as well.
- Further scarcity of oil and rising oil prices will give oil-exporting countries a strongly increasing yield from their natural resources and cause trouble for the economic stability of importing countries (the political implications are another and perhaps even more serious matter).
- The great number of poor developing countries will pose a moral challenge to the rest of the world.
- The North–South dialogue, which lacks real content because of the lack of will on the part of industrialised countries to engage themselves and the difficulty of finding realistic methods of stimulating development by means of aid, will change its character with the transformations of the South as well as the North.
- The OECD countries as a group (and the Eastern countries) will see their strength decline in relative (but not necessarily absolute) terms because other countries grow faster.
- The OECD countries individually will be more or less skilful in meeting challenges to their economic stability and structure;

some of them will turn that challenge to their own advantage, others will fail; there may be great changes of relative positions within the OECD group and the gaps between countries may widen; as a consequence, the North will also become a more heterogeneous group.

- Certain countries will probably create further problems for themselves – and for their partners – by slipping into a more protectionist policy; the risk of a collapse of the system of trade rules cannot be excluded; in that event great efforts will be made to maintain respect for the European trade agreements; the agreements within the European Communities are more solid than those of free trade, which implies a great risk for Sweden.
- Working conditions of the GATT, OECD and UNCTAD will be strongly affected by those changes; as far as the OECD is concerned the problem arises that the organisation does not include several of the leading industrial and trading nations of tomorrow.

Where is Sweden in these general picture? – Well, our international dependence exposes us to a very high degree to changes in the world around us; it is important for us not to be one of the OECD countries which slip into a backwater because of their inability to respond to the challenge.

6

Can Sweden Remain a Leading Industrial Nation?

LARS NABSETH and JAN WALLANDER

This essay takes the form of a dialogue between the authors. They discuss three major questions. Does Sweden want to remain a leading industrial nation? How did Sweden become one? What will it take for Sweden to remain a leading industrial nation in the 1980s?

What Is a Leading Industrial Nation?

Lars Nabseth: I think we ought to start with a few words about what we mean by a leading industrial nation. There are many possible definitions but in my view the phrase refers to the five or perhaps ten nations whose relative wage scales are the highest. West Germany, the USA, Switzerland, Belgium, Holland, France and Sweden – probably Japan, too, in the near future – are leading industrial nations in this sense. The per hour compensation received by employees in the form of goods and services – private and public – is at approximately the same level in all these countries. One has to make the comparison on the basis of gross wages since countries often have different tax systems and different methods of financing health care, education, pensions, and so on. But the total wage and salary level still provides a good criterion for the living standard of a given country. Admittedly variations in working hours can't be taken into account when you measure in this way. If we have a shorter working year than another country our relative standard of living will be higher, even though our gross income stays the same. But since there is a clear correlation between increased relative gross wages and decreased hours, the countries with which we're comparing ourselves have working weeks of approximately the same length as ours. We do, however, have longer annual vacations.

Sweden is also a leading industrial nation in the sense that the material standard at which most people live compares favourably with the most advanced countries in the world.

Do We Want to Remain a Leading Industrial Nation?

Jan Wallander: The question, then, is whether we want to remain at or even raise this relative level in order to keep pace with the other leading industrial nations. This is a question many economists tend to brush aside. They take it for granted that we should pursue a higher living standard, scarcely even contemplating the possibility that Sweden might opt out of the general race for efficiency at some point in the future. Yet many people consider this conclusion far from obvious and wonder if we couldn't just stop where we are. Since we're having a damned good time already, why sweat and strain to go further? Can't we be content with what we've got?

Given this very natural reaction, let us try for a moment to imagine what would happen if in this country we chose not to climb higher on the ladder of development. What would it mean in concrete terms? Only a thorough consideration of that problem will put us in a position to decide whether we really find such an alternative attractive.

Lars Nabseth: A relative decline could have a number of different consequences. One of the most important is the risk of troublesome social tensions, which we have thus far been able to avoid. Our social reforms presuppose continuous growth. The best example is the ATP reform (the general wage-related pension scheme of 1959). Assuming a growing proportion of old age pensioners in Swedish society, it sets out to guarantee them a better standard of living, relative both to the past and to other groups in the population. The idea is that the elderly should receive some share of a rising national income and to most people that probably seems reasonable. But if national income should cease to grow these improvements for the elderly could only be paid for at the expense of the active population, that is, through a redistribution of income. That could create enormous social problems.

Jan Wallander: But if the overall living standard were stabilised wouldn't that include the maintenance of the elderly at the same standard they have today?

Lars Nabseth: The ATP system presupposes an improvement. Old age pensioners could be kept at the same standard of living only through an outright rejection of the provisions of the ATP system or an indirect attempt to cut into the increased income it guarantees – by charging higher fees for health care, say, or old people's homes.

Jan Wallander: But those who advocate zero growth surely must realise that such conditions require everybody to stay put. It isn't reasonable to stop growth and at the same time support demands to raise the living standards of certain major social groups. The notion of zero growth must apply to all essential groups in society, with only the most marginal exceptions.

Lars Nabseth: I'm not so sure the advocates of zero growth are aware of that. Think of the consequences in the public sector, too – the cost of health care for the elderly, for example. The forecasts indicate that without substantial growth local taxes will rise to undreamed-of levels. That raises the spectre of severe social tensions – another reason why I doubt the champions of zero growth have thought through the implications of such a development.

Jan Wallander: Our entire political and trade union system is built on the assumption that the parties and unions can deliver something to voters and members. Zero growth means there is nothing material to deliver. What will they do then? Of course they can channel popular interest into ideological areas – questions of religion or life style – that require no expenditure of material resources. But this would still involve an immense social reorientation that could easily arouse great tensions.

However, zero growth can also be interpreted not as a cessation of the drive for efficiency but as the utilisation of all gains in efficiency to increase and enhance one's leisure time. As a matter of fact I think that is what most people mean by zero growth.

Lars Nabseth: But that still wouldn't address the problem we have just discussed. The pension scheme is based on a desire to improve living standards and that means an increase not in leisure time, since that is irrelevant to the elderly, but strictly in material well-being.

One aspect of zero growth is the idea that we no longer need structural change. That is a serious mistake, for new international competitors are constantly emerging in fields where we led the way – the production of iron ore, for instance, or ships, or steel. We must not believe that restructuring would be rendered unnecessary by zero growth. Indeed it might very well put us in the highly disadvantageous position of producing goods that can be bought cheaper elsewhere. In terms of imported goods, a ship or a ton of iron ore might bring us far less in the future than it does now. Zero growth does not mean we can simply maintain the industrial structure we have today.

Jan Wallander: I think that people who desire zero growth often imagine that it would provide secure employment, a stable environment in which to live. Many people find that very attractive. But Sweden is heavily dependent on its foreign trade and we can continue to export and import only by adapting to the continuous restructuring of the world around us. Although we can attempt to become more self-sufficient there are many imports – oil, for instance – that we simply can't do without.

Lars Nabseth: What would Swedish forests be worth, for example, if we did not export them in the form of timber and wood products, pulp and paper, but turned them over entirely to domestic use? One possibility, of course, would be to burn them for fuel, but that would be of much smaller value than what we now get for our forest-based exports. This is only one example of our international dependence. We have a lot to gain from participating in the world division of labour.

What we have said so far does not mean that our future progress entails the same sort of restructuring and growth we experienced in the 1960s. Growth will probably be slower in the 1980s than in the 1960s. When we talk about growth we do not mean that everything must be exactly the way it was in the 1960s.

Jan Wallander: It is our belief, then, that most people would have second thoughts if they really reflected on the consequences of a conscious attempt to hold back the pace of development. In all likelihood, therefore, we in Sweden will continue our efforts to remain a leading industrial nation. So the next question is: What are our chances of achieving that goal? That is a difficult question. First, however, let us discuss how Sweden became a leading industrial nation – perhaps this will tell us something about our chances of success in the future.

How Did Sweden Become a Leading Industrial Nation?

Jan Wallander: Ever since the turn of the century Sweden's per capita gross national product has been growing faster than the GNP of the United Kingdom or West Germany, and at about the same rate as that of the United States. In the 1950s and especially in the 1960s an explosive burst in our growth rate brought us very close to the American level. At the same time the UK dropped further behind, while West Germany and still more dramatically, Japan, set a pace even faster than ours.

Lars Nabseth: Given such a long perspective, it is important to remember that Sweden did not take part in the two world wars. This has obviously affected the figures, particularly in the cases of West Germany, the United Kingdom and Japan. The United States is something of an exception since the American economy was not destroyed during the two world wars. In comparison with these countries Sweden may appear in too flattering a light – as if we had only our own cleverness to thank for our success. Thus it may be more instructive to discuss the post-Second World War period, when we prospered even in the absence of our earlier advantages.

Several important elements were involved in this postwar development. One was Sweden's traditionally liberal attitude – our espousal of low tariffs and sharp competition – in the area of international trade. This factor was further enhanced by the creation of EFTA (the European Free Trade Association), which has proved most advantageous to Sweden. Ample testimony to that fact is provided by all available figures concerning the development of Swedish market shares in EFTA countries during the 1960s. Already a leading industrial nation with a highly developed economy, Sweden is in a far better position than Norway, Finland, or Denmark to exploit a Nordic market that is now, for the first time, tariff-free. I also believe that positive conditions for growth have been created by our continued willingness to dismantle trade restrictions, to expose ourselves to stiff competition and to restructure our industry. Certain other countries may not have developed quite so much flexibility.

Jan Wallander: One significant factor in Sweden's rapid postwar development was that both internal and external conditions favoured a major transformation of our economy. We still had a lot of people employed in agriculture and forestry, where productivity was lower than in the industrial sector. Thus when many workers made the transition from agriculture and forestry to industry it brought about a very rapid increase in our standard of living. In 1950 over 20 per cent of the workforce was employed in agriculture and forestry; today we are down to 6 per cent. That is a considerable reduction. But it has been done once and for all. We cannot do it again. Many other industrial countries experienced such a change much earlier in their development.

Lars Nabseth: In 1950 over 700,000 people were employed in agriculture and forestry. Today the figure stands at about 200,000 – a difference of half a million people out of a total workforce of some 4 million. That is a very dramatic change. By way of comparison, look at the recent debate concerning the ordinary steel sector, which I happen to know particularly well. The Royal Commission on Ordinary Steel proposed a reduction in the industry's workforce from 20,000 in 1976 to perhaps 15,000 by the mid-1980s – a proposal that proved highly controversial. Yet each year in our agricultural sector we have laid off a workforce equivalent to the entire commercial steel industry. In retrospect one must say that it is remarkable that such a development was possible and that the farmers and their organisations accepted it with so little resistance.

Jan Wallander: We also experienced major structural changes *within* the industrial sector. If you compare our industrial structure of 1950 with that of 1977, you will find that at the beginning of the period the food industry provided 13 per cent of the total value added of the manufacturing industries. In the end that share had dwindled to 9 per cent. Textiles and clothing fell by two-thirds – from over 14 per cent to 4 per cent. At the same time the chemical industry almost doubled its share, while the engineering industries increased from 26 to 41 per cent. These were dramatic changes within the industrial sector, implying huge relocations of the population. Our improved living standard is in no small part due to the positive role played by the government and the unions in that development.

Lars Nabseth: A significant factor in Sweden's industrial development, and in the development of our society as a whole, has been the existence of a number of internationally oriented companies particularly within the engineering industries, that could capitalise on the level of world economic development. The presence of so many large international corporations is something unique, not shared by our Nordic neighbours. Swedish industry has found it a tremendous advantage to be able to allocate production tasks to foreign subsidiaries as well as to domestic concerns. As a result such corporations as Sandvik, L. M. Ericsson, Asea, Atlas Copco and Alfa Laval have been given a broader base for research and development. And in turn they create more jobs through their many subcontractors – Volvo is an outstanding example, but far from the only one. All this has contributed to our industrial expansion, not only making our corporations profitable – at least in the past – but also creating a markedly positive attitude toward their success.

Jan Wallander: And those corporations have been highly imaginative and innovative as well. Just think of the Swedish car industry. It was largely the product of artificial shortages created by the wartime blockade, a situation conducive to the large-scale domestic production of automobiles. Although these conditions gave the industry a flying start and a reasonable market volume, it still doesn't explain why since then it has been possible for us to produce cars that not only sell in Sweden but can also compete successfully on the world market. To me, this is a good example of how real possibilities cannot always be identified and accounted for through logical analysis.

I was heavily involved with the car industry in the mid 1950s, even making a detailed scientific study of the factors that would determine the development of automobile consumption. As a result I was invited by Volvo to give an expert analysis of its plans to export to America. I devoted a lot of energy to explaining the impossibility of success. There were many good reasons for considering it impossible. Volvo's main competitor would be the American used car, yet the alternative it offered was smaller, more expensive and less roomy. Admittedly, the Volvo consumed less petrol, but fuel prices were so low then that they did not really matter. Gunnar Engellau (the then president of Volvo) listened absentmindedly while I explained why his idea was hopeless. He had summoned me to solicit a positive opinion, to gather support for his vision. He felt intuitively that the idea *should* work so what the hell – why not give it a try? Against all scientific odds and rational arguments he got going – and he succeeded.

A major factor in our industrial success during that period was the creation of an environment favourable to innovation, in which those with ability and drive would be encouraged to overcome other people's reservations. Logical reasoning and established 'truths' are almost always ranged against the truly great innovations.

Lars Nabseth: Another excellent example of the same thing is the development of Sandvik. Their initial experiments with new materials that did not contain steel, for example, cemented carbide, met with enormous scepticism, particularly among metallurgical engineers. It just didn't seem reasonable for a long-established steel-producer like Sweden to devote itself to materials that no longer even included that metal. But here, too, there were a few innovative individuals who could see that the future of steel in Sweden would not necessarily be as glorious as its past. The important thing was that these people were able to continue their experiments despite the fact that many considered them odd and different.

Jan Wallander: Isn't it true that our natural resources helped us during this period? I am thinking of our forests, our ore, our hydroelectric power.

Lars Nabseth: In this regard I think we should go back somewhat further in time. From 1890 to 1914 technological developments favoured Sweden and the utilisation of our raw materials in three ways. As far as iron ore was concerned the phosphorous ores of Norrbotten and Grängesberg were made valuable through the new Thomas processing methods. With new techniques of chemical processing our forests could be used to produce pulp and paper; formerly they had yielded only timber and wood. And, finally, developments in the field of electricity made it possible to use Swedish hydropower in a new way. Previously it had been necessary to locate all factories by the rivers; now an industrial plant could be established anywhere in the country and still make use of hydropower. These three technical changes have had an impact on the Swedish industrial structure to this day, giving us comparative advantages in forest-based industry as well as in steel. Both these areas are energy-intensive – a positive factor for a very long time, although today it seems to be the other way around. As a result, these two sectors represent a larger proportion of industrial output in Sweden than in most other countries, while such industries as textiles, clothing, shoes and food are less important here than elsewhere. Once, our raw materials were an asset, but maybe they are now becoming a disadvantage.

Can Sweden Remain a Leading Industrial Nation?

Jan Wallander: So a number of rather special circumstances were involved in the accelerated development we have experienced since the 1870s and particularly since the Second World War. Since we cannot expect the process to repeat itself automatic- ally, it is quite natural for many people to have severe doubts about our chances of remaining a leading industrial nation. They ask themselves how we can possibly continue to produce the export goods vital to our standard of living in the face of competition from such places as Hong Kong, Singapore and South Korea, where wages are so much lower and the quality of production on a par with ours. After all they too have access to advanced technology and productive knowhow, and capital is available to them at about the same price as we pay in Sweden. Under these circumstances, say the pessimists, it will be quite impossible for us to go on producing all the goods on which our well-being is built. To many people the problem must seem almost insurmountable, and they are left with a feeling of hopelessness.

Lars Nabseth: The international division of labour and trade is based on the assumption that countries will concentrate on the goods they are best equipped to produce, then supply their needs through an exchange of products. So we need not expect developing countries to take over all production. As far as Sweden is concerned it is a matter of identifying those products that enable us to use our knowledge and ability better than other countries, thus inducing them to buy from us.

There are many, many goods the developing countries are

totally incapable of producing – things like heavy machinery, aeroplanes, or computer equipment. Just look at the comparative development of the world textile and steel industries. The textile industry has gradually shifted over to the developing countries, yet the machinery for textile production is still predominantly produced in the old industrial nations. West Germany is responsible for 40 per cent of world textile machinery exports but only an insignificant proportion of actual textile production. The same goes for steel: steel production is being shifted to other countries, but the production of blast furnaces, oxygen converters, foundries and rolling mills remains concentrated in a few advanced companies within the industrialised world.

Thus there are still many areas of production in which the old industrial countries are able to compete successfully. Can we in Sweden find a sufficient number of such products? I think so. My conclusion, therefore, is that it is overly pessimistic to assume that the developing countries are taking over the production of everything.

Jan Wallander: In addition, I think, people are really talking about two different things here. They point out that we face competition from countries where productivity is high and the workforce contented with a significantly lower standard of living; we, on the other hand, are less and less willing to work, although we demand higher wages. This just won't do, they say. No, it won't. No industry can survive in the long run if its employees try to get more than they are willing to produce. We simply cannot live above our means.

Yet it is something quite different to say that countries with widely divergent standards of living and wages can still trade with each other. In fact that is the whole basis for international trade. Economists have a glossy term for this sort of thing: they say it is the 'comparative advantages' that are decisive. Now, perhaps some people won't be particularly heartened by the term 'comparative advantage'. They might find it more comforting to hear that it is obviously quite impossible for all production ultimately to be taken over by Hong Kong, Singapore and Korea, *et al*. Why? Because unless those countries buy from as well as sell to other nations they will eventually have to give their products away. That would be nice for us, but not very desirable for them.

So we are misstating the problem when we draw conclusions from direct comparisons between the cost situation of various countries at a given moment. Although such comparisons and conclusions may be helpful to an individual company in a given situation, they tend to make one forget that in order to keep trade going adjustments are constantly being made through the medium of currency exchange rates. One of the most dramatic examples of this is Japan. A few years ago that country was widely regarded as an overwhelming competitor in most areas of production. But as a consequence of Japan's strong and successful expansion there has been a steep rise in the value of the yen, thus giving Swedish companies a fresh chance to compete effectively with the Japanese. Our capacity to compete, then, is dependent on continuing structural changes that enable us to exploit our comparative advantages. One serious obstacle to this is a strong contemporary trend toward the stabilisation of employment everywhere, filling the gaps left by production shutdowns through the creation of substitute activities. In doing this we only make vital structural changes more difficult.

Lars Nabseth: When it comes to finding and developing new products there is a great risk of error if you take an existing factory or form of machinery as your point of departure. The point is, you have to know which goods are in demand, for experience shows that the market is what spearheads the development of new products and ideas. I am quite sceptical about the notion that new products worth gambling on can be found through discussions in the Ministry of Industry, the Federation of Industry, the Board of Industry, or the trade unions, as the Boston Report[1] would have us believe. I do not think that is the way to find new products and ideas. It is out in the marketplace, within the companies themselves, that innovative ideas will be found. We must create an environment in which those ideas can be realised.

Jan Wallander: This is extremely important. When problems arise many people like to think that the solution lies in some sort of top-level meeting of the minds at which all possible data are collected and plans for the future are laid. That approach, in my view, is bound to fail. I can imagine that it might work in a country less developed than ours; in that case, its plans could simply reproduce what other countries have already done successfully at a similar stage of development.

That option is not available to those of us on the front lines. We have nobody to imitate. We have to find something new. We must bring about innovations, even though we cannot know in advance which of them will bear fruit. The central task, therefore, is to create an innovative environment. It is also important to remember that innovations and innovators are often seen in a negative light by the surrounding community. They break down habitual patterns. They are a pain in the neck to older companies, forcing them to change their line of production or else be forced out of the market. They are a pain in the neck to bureaucrats, planners and other people with a fondness for time-tested ways of doing things.

Thus it is essential to create a context in which new ideas can break through the opposition the way mushrooms break through an asphalt surface. It is worrisome that so many of our measures – the legislation on co-determination, the laws on the security of employment, and so forth – make it increasingly difficult to bring about innovations. In an effort to prevent social disruptions we keep on making the asphalt surface thicker and thicker. Eventually the mushrooms may be unable to break through.

Lars Nabseth: In our public debate there are some voices that advocate doing what the Japanese did in the 1960s. Let us sit down with the ministries and government agencies, they say, and decide where to put the money. The Japanese, taking advantage of their lower wage levels, made products for which there was already an established market. They have been successful in so far as they have been able to match the quality of existing producers while still charging lower prices. Today South Korea is doing the same thing. This, however, is not an option for any advanced industrial country. It is important to make this point, since many people believe we in Sweden can view industrial development from the same perspective as the Japanese or South Koreans.

Jan Wallander: You can illustrate the difficulty of planning for innovation by pointing to a few new developments that became obvious only in retrospect. If at the beginning of the 1960s you had said that the building trades would become an important Swedish export industry, scarcely anyone would have believed you. Today, however, we are a big successful competitor in that field. We have accomplished this by exporting products as well as knowhow. And if at the same time you had claimed that by the end of the 1970s Swedish commercial banks would have established banks in a number of other countries, many people would have found the proposition quite absurd. But the fact is that our banks can now be found all over the world – America, England, France, Switzerland, Germany, Luxemburg, Singapore and Hong Kong. I suppose many people assume that Swedish banks have a hard time in the domestic market, what with all the great international banking dragons in our midst. But the fact is that we are tough competition for those dragons – we manage our own international banking these days, and we do it very successfully.

Lars Nabseth: There is an area, however, which is well suited to centralised decision-making: public purchases of equipment.

On that point I agree with the Boston Group and others. Defence, energy and telecommunications are some of the fields to which this applies. It is reasonable not only for central and local governments to have competent buyers but also for the government to stimulate development projects likely to provide spinoffs. Through its purchasing policy the public sector can thus stimulate industrial development in the most advanced areas.

Jan Wallander: As far as the building trades are concerned one of the things we export is our expertise in planning systems. Similar possibilities exist in many areas of our large public sector. After all, every country needs hospitals, care of the elderly, and so forth. If we are good at those things we should be able to export our knowledge. But a regional government has neither the economic interest nor the capacity to offer to build and operate hospitals in other countries.[2] Perhaps the central government should take on the task of creating a suitable exporter in the area of health care as well as in other areas where the knowhow we have acquired in the public sector shows some commercial potential.

Lars Nabseth: As far as education is concerned such an attempt is being made in the form of a new corporation owned jointly by the state and private industry. The idea is to export various educational services which can often be related to the goods we export, especially in the case of developing countries.

Jan Wallander: In this context I should like to comment on the need for profitability in economic activities. 'Profit' has become a dirty word in public debate. It is almost as though people imagine that it would benefit mankind if companies were *not* managed in a profitable way. But all 'profit' means is that you should produce only those goods that are capable of covering their own costs. If you produce other goods you will stay out of the red only by subsidising their production with money borrowed from another area. In a few exceptional cases it may be reasonable to do so – the Swedish Royal Opera, for example – on a large scale it becomes devastating.

The demand for profitability, then, simply reflects the realisation that we should devote ourselves only to activities that yield a result interesting enough for consumers to find it worthy of production, unless we are consciously prepared to subsidise the price. From the companies' point of view, production is profitable in the latter case as well.

Lars Nabseth: It also means that if households, institutions and other investors are to be convinced that they should provide venture capital for private industry, their return on that money must be equivalent to that derived from other investments. But if profits dwindle to the point where these investments yield less than money put into private housing, summer houses, antiquities or stamps, then private industry will have a hard time finding venture capital and may turn instead to government subsidies and publicly financed investments.

Jan Wallander: A prerequisite for our continued development is the pursuit of efficiency, of maximum productivity.

Lars Nabseth: In that respect the last few years' development has been a dead loss. During the 1960s our productivity rose sharply – in industry an increase of over 7 per cent per working hour and working year. By international standards this was a very high figure. But during the last few years productivity has scarcely risen at all, which can only exacerbate our difficulties in maintaining a competitive position. One of the reasons we find ourselves in this situation is that it was broadly assumed – by politicians, the media, unions, even managers – that the positive trends of the 1960s would continue indefinitely. The main problem was thought to be one of distribution – apportionment of higher wages, more leisure time, improved public services, and so forth. Today it is clear to us that growth is far from axiomatic. Yet we have also introduced a number of laws and regulations whose effect is to restrict our productivity. One example is the Åman Laws, frequently reported to be holding back increases in productivity and employment, particularly in small and medium-sized enterprises. The purpose of the laws was to cut down on layoffs. But they have cut down on new jobs too: there are fewer now than at a comparable stage in the previous business cycle and it is difficult, particularly for young people, to find employment. Nor is the labour market flexible enough to provide people with the work for which they are best suited. It even takes longer than it used to for employers to fill a new job – they want to think it over first. Add up all these factors and what you have is a society-wide trend toward higher unemployment and a slower rise in productivity, since job openings remain vacant longer, on the average, than they did before. Finally there is what is known as the principle of seniority, which has reportedly created problems for many enterprises – for example, making workers reluctant to transfer from one company to another, even within the same town.

Jan Wallander: Clearly, the Åman Laws make an employer think twice, or perhaps even three or four times, before hiring someone. Once he's done it, he's stuck. If I try to visualise concretely what these laws have meant to my own field, the banking world, I suppose that we, too, have become increasingly meticulous in our hiring procedures, thus hoping to avoid errors. In addition the banks can sometimes, on the basis of a collective agreement, employ people on a trial basis.

Lars Nabseth: Young people who are just entering the labour market cannot always be expected to know which job suits them best. Since both employer and employee need a certain amount of time to adjust, wouldn't it make more sense to have a labour market in which some flexibility is possible, at least at the beginning of an individual's working life? In a system so restrictive of the employer the whole screening process is undermined. Indeed I think the arrangement is unfair to both parties since it prevents young people from getting a break. People should be given a chance to start working; then, if they fail, they must take the consequences and look for another job.

Jan Wallander: Absenteeism has been a major issue in the public arena over the last few years. Doesn't this development tend to disrupt the work process, with serious implications for our level of productivity?

Lars Nabseth: It is difficult for me to understand why some people regard absenteeism as a positive trend. Because one of its primary effects is to throw planning and production overboard – it leaves no one in the workplace untouched. It is far easier to adjust to a planned absence, such as a vacation. One recent study shows that young male workers are absent more often than older employees. Yet our health insurance system takes no account of this fact, with the result that older workers are financing the absence of the young. If the young people choose to shorten their working hours through absenteeism, then shouldn't they be the ones who take the economic consequences, rather than the older, steadier workers? Absenteeism is also considerably higher in large corporations than in smaller companies. This, too, indicates a need for some kind of differentiation in our system of insurance fees. All in all, changes in our health insurance system are clearly needed.

Jan Wallander: That is a proposition I support wholeheartedly. In the past it was a company's rate of absenteeism that determined what it paid. The banks have far less absence than industry, and we find it a bit strange that the present system requires us to pay for the high rate of absenteeism in industry. As for our own absentees, within the banks there are rather striking differences among the various departments, branches and regions – and between men and women as well. The general pattern is that women are absent more often than men and that big cities and large offices show a higher rate of absenteeism. One way of interpreting this might be to say that wherever working conditions are more demanding, absences are more frequent. In some instances that is probably the case.

But one can also argue that absenteeism is largely determined by social control. If you work in a modest-sized office in a small town and you're feeling a bit tired one day, you think twice before deciding to stay home. You are very conscious of the fact that you cannot go out shopping – everybody will notice in a small place – and you are aware, too, that your absence will create problems for your fellow workers. If you're not there someone else will have to do your job and there are only four of you in the office. But if you were one of 100 or 150 workers the effect of your absence would become more abstract. If the others were under extra pressure they would not feel so directly that it was because you, in particular, were missing.

We must realise that if we reduce social control and economic sanctions and if furthermore we maintain that people have a right to stay home if they don't feel like going to work, then we are bound to have a high rate of absenteeism. For a long time now we have been weakening the economic incentives for high productivity by such means as higher taxes and the elimination of piecework rates. It is all the more important, then, that we promote other methods of stimulating high productivity, of inspiring and encouraging workers to do a good job. We must constantly emphasise that one serves all of society by being efficient in one's work. Slacking off is not only socially unacceptable but also socially unjust, since low productivity restricts our ability to help the neediest sectors of the population. Today, however, an individual who works fast and efficiently may well be considered something of a social outcast. Under such circumstances it is no easy task to do a good job. Yet most people in my experience actually *want* to do a good job. It isn't difficult to steer them in that direction for it coincides with their deepest desires. You could say, as a matter of fact, that to deprive one another of that opportunity and gratification is a kind of mental cruelty. We all want to be useful to do good work and it is unjust to deny us job satisfaction.

This brings us quite naturally to the subject of productivity in the public sector. Increased efficiency in this rapidly growing aspect of economic life is a major prerequisite for an overall improvement in our standard of living. In 1950 some 8 per cent of our national product was devoted to public services; in 1960 the figure was 11 per cent. Since then we have expanded still more dramatically until by 1977 public services represented 27 per cent of the gross national product. It is unrealistic to imagine that we will be able to finance our rising standard of living solely by means of gains in productivity outside the public sector. Yet calculations of national income are made on the assumption that no improvement in efficiency is taking place within the public sector, and this assumption is believed to be an accurate depiction of reality. This is all quite absurd, of course, since there are plenty of ways in which the production of public services, too, can be rendered more efficient.

As far as I can see the central problem here is that there is really no incentive for workers in the public sector to strive for greater efficiency. To be sure, the government bodies that allocate appropriations to the various fields of public service do try to keep appropriations as low as they can and to maximise the efficiency of their subordinate agencies. There are even government agencies that specialise in efficiency, seeing to it that public activities are conducted as smoothly as possible. In my view, however, agencies at the top level of a large organisation will have little chance of bringing about increased efficiency unless all workers in the various units of production have a large stake in this goal. In fact they won't get anywhere. It is the same in both the private and public spheres. Those who work in the service agencies of the public sector must put in a yearly request for funds. It is nice to be able to expand your activities: it means you are entitled to a bigger staff and can hire more people. It is more prestigious to be head of a large agency than a small one: it means they make you a director general instead of a director, and so on and so forth. To be sure, civil servants are busy from dawn to dusk, always being pressured by their clients, that is, the public, to produce more and better services. Naturally you are more than willing to satisfy these public demands – provided you get more personnel.

The upshot of all this is a strong vested interest in larger staffs and a greater number of assigned tasks. The staff members and the union, not surprisingly, lend their enthusiastic support, as do those segments of the population that benefit from your activities. Many politicians join in too – after all, it wouldn't do to be accused of insensitivity to public demands for better service. The whole thrust is toward expansion. There is no real incentive for public employees to consider whether they are actually doing something worthwhile or whether they couldn't really get the job done with two people instead of three. The only way the public sector as a whole can be induced to strive for greater efficiency is to create a situation in which public agencies acquire a real stake in doing so. How, then, can this be achieved? One approach would be to stimulate competition among different public agencies that deliver similar services. Competition is a very effective method which might be applied, say, to education. That, however, would presuppose giving citizens some freedom to choose their own schools – a preposterous notion. Another method would be to get local governments to produce statistics showing clearly how much daycare centres cost in different parts of the country, how many welfare officers are assigned to a given number of recipients, and so forth. At Hande Isbanken we have such a system of comparative accounting for our regional banks. It is most effective.

It is also essential to mobilise the clients to exert pressure for increased efficiency – perhaps by establishing a scale of fees that reflects differences in performance among the various agencies. Thus Stockholmers who go to Hospital A may discover that they get good care there at a cost of X crowns a day; at Hospital B, however, the charge is X + 25 crowns and the care is not so good. As word begins to spread that there are differences between the hospitals, everyone at Hospital B will start wondering why this is so, and things which once seemed impossible to change will suddenly become quite amenable to improvement. This does not mean we should establish a system of fees that would prevent people from getting the health care they need. But even the introduction of minor differentiations might have a salutary effect.

It is very difficult to stimulate a desire for efficiency among workers in the public sector, and what I have said here merely indicates a few possible options. By contrast, I think it is quite hopeless to try and solve the problem by means of various supervisory agencies, budget systems, or whatever else we may come up with. Instead we must attempt to create a situation in which all the hundreds of thousands of employees in the public sector are concretely stimulated to make their work more efficient. A managing director, for example, can lecture employees endlessly on the need to economise, yet it is only when everyone working in the enterprise is given some incentive to do so that the preaching has any real effect.

Lars Nabseth: Yes, I quite agree with that view. But let me go back for a moment to your observations about fees for public services. I think there are a number of areas where a system of fees could be introduced without contradicting the fundamental principle that certain types of services should be accessible to everybody. In any case our economy has now reached a stage where the majority of the population has a high enough income to pay a few modest fees. Given our standard of living and wage level, it seems almost absurd to say that people cannot afford to pay anything for hospital care, to take one example, or in many other areas. Highway tolls are another case in which it is quite feasible for people to pay. And I don't think it will take much – just a little imagination and patience – to come up with a lot more suggestions. After all, local governments already have certain possibilities – fees for electricity, water, gas, and the like – that could easily be expanded. As far as shipping is concerned, here, too, fees are already being charged and the same is true of the civil aviation board. Of course it is possible.

Jan Wallander: A system of fees might also facilitate the allocation of resources within the public sector. This is currently done on the basis of guesswork – what the politicians' intuition tells them will be most popular in the next elections; what will be most likely to affect the mobile, marginal votes. Although this is what determines the priorities of the public sector it hardly seems a reliable method of discovering what voters generally want. Fees, on the other hand, would give us an accurate indication of the price people put on various types of public services.

Lars Nabseth: The possible drawbacks of a more generalised system of fees must be weighed against the huge drawbacks of our present tax system. After all, if the money isn't paid out in fees it will be siphoned off through taxation instead. Our current tax system has such a negative impact on productivity that it must in many respects be considered far worse than any system of fees, whatever the disadvantages some people claim it would impose. One important consequence of marginal income taxes is that a great many people find it more economical to do a job for themselves than to hire someone to do it for them and concentrate on what they really know something about. So the advantage of do-it-yourself jobs is that they are untaxed, while work in one's field of professional expertise is heavily taxed.

Jan Wallander: I can give an example of this from my own profession. A few years ago one of the vice-presidents of the bank gave notice that he could not attend a meeting we had organised since he was going on vacation. It wasn't all that important that he should be there; still, it seemed a pity, so I asked him to consider putting off his vacation to a later date. Well, he said, the thing was, he was moving to a new house and it would have been so expensive to hire carpenters to fix it up that he was taking time off to do it himself. Although relatively handy with tools, he certainly isn't as good a carpenter as he is a banker.

Lars Nabseth: Another crucial issue for the 1980s is Sweden's international dependence. We have already discussed Sweden's dependence on foreign trade and the advantages we derived from the creation of EFTA. As far as the European Economic Community (EEC) is concerned, we have a free trade agreement with its members but no other association with the community of nine (now ten). As long as these countries enjoy rapid growth and maximum utilisation of their capacity, it probably isn't too much of a disadvantage to stay outside. But when there is a great deal of underutilised capacity within the

EEC, the disadvantages tend to grow and we are repeatedly reminded that blood is thicker than water. When the EEC is suffering from a surplus of productive capacity in steel, ship-building, refineries, and so forth, its inclination is to solve its own problems first and only then enter into discussions with countries outside the community. Its industrial policies now tend to become rather introverted and we are forced to accept agreements we cannot influence. For instance, it has become difficult to export commercial steel to the common market. As far as shipbuilding is concerned, member countries tend to place orders with their own shipyards – a thorny problem for Sweden, with our large shipbuilding capacity and relatively small fleet. This is a strong argument for us to try and adapt ourselves as closely as possible to the policies of the European Economic Community.

The 1980s may bring even graver problems, especially with Greece, Spain, and Portugal as new members of the EEC. The temporary regulations for those countries will be significant to Sweden. My conclusion is that it's becoming more and more disadvantageous to stay out of the EEC; thus we should do our utmost to achieve the closest possible co-operation with the community within the framework of our present trade agree-ment. I believe that the EEC for its part is quite willing to co-operate with Sweden and with Swedish industry. In many areas our industry has more to offer than a number of the present and future members of the community.

Jan Wallander: When it comes to issues that have no immediate repercussions for the Swedish way of life and economy our attitude tends to be strongly internationalist. Indeed we are shocked by countries that do not show sufficient understanding of and concern towards nations we consider weak and oppressed. When our interests are directly affected, by contrast, we often become very isolationist and self-righteous. Neverthe-less we have done quite well in the past and EFTA proved a most propitious arrangement for us at one time. Now, however, that is over and we face a disquieting future. In order to export increasing quantities of paper, for instance, the Swedish forestry sector will have to eliminate a great many competitors within the EEC. And when we do increase our capacity in that sector we cannot expect EEC members to applaud our achieve-ments and aspirations. To them our pretty blue eyes won't look so pretty any more.

Summary

Jan Wallander: Let us now try to summarise our conclusions, our answer to the question: 'Does Sweden have a chance of remaining a leading industrial nation?'

We see a great many difficulties ahead, especially since Sweden no longer enjoys the same conditions it did after the Second World War when this country experienced such an exceptional rise in productivity. We also perceive a host of internal and external circumstances that could prevent Sweden from making use of whatever chances the future may bring. Maybe we simply won't be willing or able to exploit those opportunities. We certainly won't do it unless, among other things, we create a climate conducive to innovation and learn to accept change. Against that background it seems most unlikely that Sweden's efficiency will increase as rapidly in the future as it has over the last twenty years. It is likely to be a much slower process. What about the question of whether Sweden can match the pace of other Western European industrial countries? Here, too, there is no obvious answer. It is by no means certain that we can avoid slipping behind. If we revised some of our present attitudes, however, that would improve our chances of success. Though our prospects are no better than those of other countries, they aren't necessarily much worse, either.

Lars Nabseth: There is clearly a danger of dwelling so much on our own problems that we forget that other countries too, have problems – different from ours, perhaps, but just as troublesome. Look at Italy and England, to mention only two examples. There is a risk, then, that in exaggerating the relative importance of our own problems we will fall prey to an overly pessimistic perspective.

I do not think there is any shortage of ideas in Sweden. Those who claim that there is are too pessimistic. To be sure, many people – I am one of them – are very sceptical about the changes that have been made in the Swedish educational system, fearing that they may have grave effects in the long run. But to say that Sweden has *already* lost its creative capacity is to overstate the case. After all, we know of many companies in which there are still ideas, innovation, change. So my conclusion is that Sweden should be able to keep up with the other leading industrial nations but that certain changes will be required, both in our attitudes and in some of the laws and regulations passed in the 1970s when our economic situation seemed so promising. If such changes can be made, I think we will be able to keep up. But if conditions don't seem to favour change – if a political deadlock occurs, for example – then I would tend to be more pessimistic. Lacking the strength to keep up with the development of the others, we might, like

England, slip gradually behind. One crucial factor will be how Sweden deals with its energy problems. If we should opt for a phasing-out of nuclear energy I am afraid we would be far more likely to go the way of England.

Jan Wallander: So Sweden's capacity to remain a leading industrial nation really depends on our willingness to take the measures that will make it possible. And that willingness, in turn, depends to a great extent on how well the politicians understand the problem and communicate it to the voters. People will surely accept these measures if they're just given a clear picture of what it is all about. To the electorate Sweden's failure to keep up with the pace of development would be a far more unpleasant alternative. But the politicians certainly won't find it easy to make that clear to the voters and draw the necessary practical conclusions. It will demand great strength and involve considerable risk.

Lars Nabseth: If the Swedish people realised what the consequences will be if we *don't* make certain changes, I think they would be willing to accept them. But to make them understand that – through the politicians, the media, and so on – is a very difficult task. Indeed it is a task that has already defeated certain other countries. The British, for example, have wanted to break their vicious circle for some time, but the inertia of the political and social process has prevented them from doing so.

Jan Wallander: A democratic society has drawbacks as well as advantages. It is all too easy to give efficiency a low priority, and that can cause trouble in the economy. It is crucial to solve these problems.

Lars Nabseth: When the material standard of living is low the arguments for growth are so strong that it is relatively easy for politicians to convince people to accept the consequences – mobility, environmental changes, and so forth. But in countries like ours, where the living standard is already high, the consequences of growth may not be so readily accepted. Yet we cannot choose more leisure and a better environment and at the same time expect to make no material sacrifices. This may have been our big problem in the 1970s – wanting to have our cake and eat it. Perhaps, if it is resolved, we can expect a higher level of development in the 1980s.

Translator's Notes: Chapter 6

1   Report by the Boston Consulting Group on the present status of the Swedish economy.
2   In Sweden health care is the responsibility of regional government.

7

Knowledge – the Basis for Industrial Success

GÖRAN BORG and BENGT-ARNE VEDIN

The international success of Swedish industry has been built on concrete and solid ground: our basic commodities, mine and forestry products. But the same factors and the same technological development that once gave great market advantages to our commodity-based industries now benefit other countries and put us in a situation of keen competition.

However, other resources than the natural ones have proved at least as important to international competition. If anything characterises the development of international trade it is the fact that the production of goods as well as services requires increasingly advanced scientific methods and results. Corporations have built up a specific capital of knowledge. That kind of capital is now a resource of primary importance. It is in turn dependent on the scientific level of the country and the possibilities of scientific exchange with the world at large. As a consequence, the function and quality of the educational system have also become an important resource or – if you prefer – environmental factor for industry.

The industrial environment of a country is hard to define, but it is something that plays an important part for another indispensable resource, the entrepreneurial spirit. Our big corporations are based on the enterprising spirit of individuals. Many of them still retain that spirit, but it is being constantly threatened by organisational petrification within the companies and outside. We have many recent examples of that enterprising spirit: Anderstorp and Gnosjö, Almex and Lindén-Alimak, IKEA and Buketten, to pick but a few. We also have to take an external environment into consideration when a new enterprise is in the making: the conditions of our foreign markets. The more technically advanced the projected enterprise is, the more important it is that those external conditions should be positive as well. One commodity is indispensable and has gained in importance to our country: energy. To guarantee adequate provision of energy is a central problem for the policies of the 1980s. The complications constitute a problem in their own right.

An important asset is our developed infrastructure, communications, educational system, and so forth. Everybody knows that even those resources are subject to big question marks. What may be more serious than anything else is that the technological development itself and its basis, scientific research, are being questioned, not least by young people. After all, the potential knowledge available to an enterprise is held by people, and the enterprising environment is created by people through legislation, the media and public opinion. It is a question of fundamental values and it has been clearly demonstrated in the debate on energy. The industrial policies of the 1980s will be determined by the confrontation and the resulting synthesis of such values on the one hand and our national and international obligations on the other. Those obligations are, for instance, to guarantee education, health care, social welfare, pensions, interests on debt and international pledges through SIDA (the Swedish International Development Authority) and other organisations. Those obligations presuppose innovation and increased quality in our private industry. We assume that the policies of the 1980s will try to accomplish precisely that.

Education

Education is fundamental to the capital of knowledge available to enterprise and to some extent to the national environment for enterprise. Considerable criticism can be addressed, from that angle, to schools, universities and publicly supported research. It is said, for instance, that 'schools waste talent'. The practical meaning of that saying is that schools leave excessively narrow margins of choice for different interests and types of talent. If, as in this context, one has to be concerned with education for working life one may, for instance, point to the need for more alternatives of *intermittently vocational and theoretical education*. As far as the education of engineers is concerned one can demand changes on several points. Take, for instance, the subject of mathematics, the language of technology and natural science. The knowledge and ability of students in that subject has dropped to the point where applicants to technological universities must be offered preparation courses before starting their studies (this has been the case with the Royal School of Technology since 1973). M. Håstad (1978) has shown *inter alia* that the time available for the teaching of mathematics in compulsory schools (primary *and* secondary) has dropped by 30 per cent from the 1950s to the 1970s.

Another important deficiency is in the teaching of languages. For instance, in the late 1960s compulsory schools gave eighteen hours a week to French and German in grades 6–9, which were reduced to eleven hours a week (for either French or German. It has been suggested that the time should be further reduced to nine hours a week, but that proposal is likely to be turned down). At the same time the need of private enterprise for languages has become more extensive. Apart from the languages mentioned, there is a need for Spanish, Portuguese and Arabic.

An increased freedom of choice with regard to courses and the planning of individual studies needs to be part and parcel of the educational policies of the 1980s. There are many indications that they will have to be based much more than hitherto on the knowledge and enthusiasm of the teachers. This is also warranted by alarm signals concerning fundamental values of another kind. We refer to the values of high school students as reflected in their choice of available options. Table 7.1 shows that the number of students choosing the N line (natural science) has declined considerably. It is hard to determine whether this is due to a general negative attitude to natural science and technology on economic prospects or a tactical judgement of the chances of a good rating. In the short run it is reassuring to note that the number of students opting for the T line (leading to, *inter alia*, a high school engineering diploma) has remained fairly stable (but the loss of students is rather high on both lines: more than 20 per cent).

Table 7.1 *Number of Students Having Graduated from N and T Lines*

| High school option | Year | | | Change 1973/4–1979/80 | |
	1973/4	1976/7	1979/80	number	percentage
N line	7,321	6,000	5,500	−1,821	−24.9
T line	5,124	5,000	5,200	+76	+1.5
Total (N + T)	12,445	11,000	10,700	−1,745	−14.0

Source: Central Bureau of Statistics (1977).

However, there is a serious, long-term consequence hidden in those figures. If you consider existing data on school leavers' choice of further education courses you will find that of the 6,500 freshmen deemed necessary for the faculties of natural science and technology at the universities in 1980, fewer than half will be recruited from the N and T lines, the natural basis for recruitment. Since students seem to prefer the technological faculties, and since those faculties will require more than 3,000 of the 3,200 students available, the faculties of natural science and thus the education of teachers (including a possible improvement in the training of vocational consultants) will be jeopardised. As a matter of fact this has already occurred. The choices have been made and their effects will stretch into the 1980s. The lack of knowledgeable, interested and stimulating teachers means increasing difficulties, not only in terms of subjects taught but also with regard to other forms of objective and inspiring information for young people. This is how an ominous, downward spiralling trend may start for natural science and technology. Concomitantly, research and researcher training in those subjects will be hit by a lack of personnel (shortage of funds is the more usual difficulty). Materials development, microelectronics, biotechnology and other sectors of applied science will be of increasing significance in the technology of the future. They are among the subjects which are already having a rough time. It is remarkable that the educational policies of the 1980s will have to be focused on various methods of stimulating teachers, students and researchers in the field of natural science.

Lower marginal taxes are part of the necessary stimuli for most of the people concerned. Other more specific measures are needed. A systematic structure of contacts should be established between, on the one hand, schoolteachers and pupils and, on the other, scientists and prominent representatives of industry. Scholarships for teachers and opportunities for advanced studies at Swedish and foreign universities must be made a part of the normal pattern. Improved funding and structural changes are necessary to re-establish good working conditions for prominent scientists at the universities. The international exchange of scientists needs to be widened – we need to send a good number of our young people to foreign universities.

Scientific research in Sweden must be made more flexible. Universities and research institutes must be given improved scope for research, particularly basic research. It must become easier to hire competent scientists in new, important areas. Swedish research today shows clear signs of stagnation. An analysis made in part by foreign experts shows that in important fields of physics we face the threat of being left far behind. Those fields are connected to the dynamic sectors mentioned above – as well as to the machine and steel industries. The same tendency is found in other areas of a futuristic character. The situation is such that there is cause for a new organisation of experts to administer support for technical research (a technology research council, proposed by a governmental investigation committee in *Ways to Increased Prosperity* (Liber Forlag, 1979), p. 172 and appendix 1, p. 176).

A few important general areas have been neglected in Sweden. One is the field of innovations, where our foreign colleagues have made great efforts to explore the processes and to weigh the inputs at various stages against each other. This is also the case with advanced small-scale technology, which is rousing such great interest in countries such as Great Britain and the USA in connection with, for instance, local needs and foreign aid. Education at our technological universities is geared to the needs of industry for various kinds of specialists. Entrepreneurs and people with a talent for innovation are what Swedish business urgently needs today. It must become an important task for universities to create an educational environment for them as well.

The government's Bill 1978–79:180 concerning the curricula of primary and secondary schools contains constructive improvements. The urge for equality, which previously had destructive effects on young people with special talents for substantive subjects, is now given the interpretation 'a right to good knowledge and abilities' and is combined with an increased freedom of choice. However, it cannot be put into practice until 1982–3, and as far as industry is concerned its results will hardly be noticeable during the 1980s. Faster measures are required. A number of such measures have been proposed in, for example, *Ways to Increased Prosperity*.

The Enterprising Environment

Increased social security, full employment, economic stability and generous public services are social goals to which most people subscribe. Demands can be made without limits, but the costs are not connected with the benefits in a way that is visible to all. They still have to be paid by the individual and by the companies. In a number of interviews with corporate management in 1978 criticisms were voiced of the consequences for companies of legislation passed to further those social goals. The so-called Åman Laws and especially the tax system have been in the limelight. Dwindling profits combined with the system of subsidies for weak companies also have a negative effect. New enterprises and the will to take more responsibility and gamble on hazardous areas of innovation have declined. It is easy to demonstrate that the number of new enterprises has gone down.

We therefore face the 1980s with faltering basic resources, including those of knowledge and the enterprising spirit. But are we ready to take the necessary steps? Do we want to come to grips with the tax system, the growth of the public sector, the level of profits in private companies, the stimulation of talent and interest in enterprise and in education? Those are important pieces in the overall enterprise climate of our country. It has been good and it can be re-established, technically speaking. But do we have the political possibilities? It must be a central task of the policies of the 1980s to create them.

Markets and Competitiveness

A fourth of Sweden's gross national product, half of our industrial production, is exported. Many companies export more than 80 per cent of their production. Several larger companies have foreign subsidiaries. The production of Swedish subsidiaries abroad corresponds to about 40 per cent of our exports (*Ways to Increased Prosperity*, pt 2, p. 382). Sweden's standard of living and ability to comply with its obligations and commitments depend on its ability to export.

Sweden lost market shares in 1975–7 by an average of more than 6 per cent a year, partly as a consequence of the cost explosion of 1975–6. But that explosion also revealed deeper problems. The declining competitiveness of our natural resources has already been mentioned. Many industrial products have been exposed to keen quality-based competition from other industrial countries. In addition to the USA new countries appear as technological leaders with a great productive capacity. Western Germany and Japan together are already able to challenge the USA in the field of new technology. A number of Asian countries are following the Japanese example. Brazil and Mexico are also in the process of breaking into world markets. The penetration of those developing countries is admittedly rather limited so far but in certain sectors, including advanced ones, it is growing fast. The Swedish technique of breaking through trade barriers by establishing subsidiaries may run into difficulties as a consequence of a growing interest of the host country in nationalising foreign enterprises in various ways. France and Brazil are examples of this. One may be able to meet that trend by accepting the role of minority owner from the beginning, as KemaNobel has done in India (IDL Chemicals).

Growth Markets

All this makes increasing demands on knowledge, flexibility in production and market development. The study *Industriutvecklingen i Sverige* (SIND 1978, p. 52) predicts that a third of Swedish exports of goods will have to be changed to other products during the next five to ten years. At the same time the Royal Commission of 1978 on Long-Term Economic Trends (LU, 1978) calculates that Sweden needs to increase its exports faster than the growth of world trade as a whole (LU, 1978, p, 35). What are the chances of achieving this? We shall try to comment on the essential factors: competence and expanding markets. We have already touched on education, which is part of the competence factor. We shall revert to the problem of the competence of the companies. What remains, then, is the question of growth markets.

International markets with a good growth potential exist in the fields of information technology, biotechnology, and instruments and machine technology. Information technology comprises technological equipment and professional use of machines for the transmission and processing of information. In those fields Sweden has competence but also shortcomings. We shall revert to that. An ambitious attempt to evaluate market trends in relation to the Swedish industrial structure has recently been made ('Att utmönstra industrier med goda framtidsutsikter', in *Ways to Increased Prosperity*, pt 2, p. 277ff.). The analysis covers eighty branches exposed to competition. The growth rate of domestic consumption has been investigated for the three five-year periods of 1960–75. The branches are grouped into four categories with regard to their growth during the whole period and to changes during 1970–5 (marginal growth). Not surprisingly the computer industry (part of information technology) belongs to the highest-ranking group. So do agricultural machinery, electrical domestic appliances and wood-processing machines (parts of the sector of instrument and machine technology). Yacht building also, perhaps somewhat more surprisingly, belongs to that group. So do the pharmaceutical, instruments and plastics industries, although at a lower marginal growth rate. In the lowest group are rolling stock (but not electric locomotives), metal wires and cables, and headgear.

The machine and chemical industries are represented in the two highest-ranking groups to approximately the same degree as all industries exposed to competition. One would have expected that they should be overrepresented, bearing in mind the generally positive outlook for those groups. The machine industry has gradually geared its production towards products and branches with a slower growth rate during the 1960s. New market entries and diversification have not taken place sufficiently for a product-orientation change which would have been warranted by the growth of demand (op. cit., p. 297). The analysis also shows that the service sectors have grown in importance as consumers of industrial goods.

New Markets

New markets are also available in the newly industrialised countries, state trading countries, and commodity-rich, low-technology countries. Social infrastructure and plants organised to provide training and maintenance schemes are needed in those countries. Swedish companies are forced to change their business patterns and co-operate in groups including competitors (for instance LM Ericsson-Philips-Bell Canada in Saudi Arabia). Situations may arise where you have to help create competitors and cede markets to them. In trading with state trading countries, government participation is of growing importance. A country that has found an effective form of co-operation between government and industry in foreign trade is Japan, whose Ministry of Trade and Industry has the task of co-ordination based on common interests.

Developing countries with a weak infrastructure are important trade partners if they have raw materials (oil, ore). On that basis a differentiated economic structure can gradually be built up. This is what has happened in our own country. The starting position is more difficult if the country lacks important industrial raw materials or if they are difficult to exploit. It is nevertheless urgent to initiate a trade exchange with a view to future mutual interests. The international political situation (as presented in, for example, the United Nations, UNESCO, ILO) demands increased economic equalisation. Present industrialised countries have a long-term economic interest in a development in that direction. The problem is that initial investments are large and insecure in a new way. The Dutch company Philips has given an example of a new kind of initial investment through the Preufcentrum at Utrecht. New technology is developed there locally in a weak infrastructure and is then implanted into a realistic environment. Part of the knowledge acquired in this way has also proved useful to production in industrialised countries.

In England, a country with great knowledge and experience from colonial times, E. F. Schumacher has taken the initiative to create the ITDG, the Intermediate Technology Group. Its goals are similar to those of the Preufcentrum but the ITDG has focused mainly on basic needs. Better agriculture and forestry are crucial to a better economy. With SIDA as an intermediary, small Swedish industries have found new tasks in countries such as Tanzania and Botswana. It has proved possible to do that on the basis of mutual creative interests, probably in the long run a more solid ground than the aid donor–recipient relationship alone. Since Swedish industry may not be prepared to make the necessary investments on its own, and SIDA perhaps lacks the power and resources, it might be worth considering an effort in the form of a co-operative institution within the framework of the organisations of the machine industry, possibly with government support – maybe a centre for 'high technology in a weak infrastructure'.

Despite the difficulties presented by foreign competition, trade barriers, currency problems, state trading, and so on, it is necessary to maintain our efforts to keep and widen our share of the international division of labour. We must therefore assume that we shall choose the development option for our industry to which our initial discussion led us. The greatest possible degree of free trade and the fewest possible trade barriers, nationalisations, and so on, should thus be sought by the industrial policies of the 1980s. This does not, however, preclude the possibility that certain specific government measures may be necessary. We have mentioned the need for government participation in business with state trading countries. We have also indicated a need for government support in initiating production for and trade with developing countries.

Our scrutiny of growth markets has a specific purpose. Government tools for education, research and development should be directed towards strengthening Sweden's position in such markets. New posts for scientists should be created, for example, in the field of materials. Needs within the area of synthetics, solid state physics and electronics are very urgent. In the field of biotechnology new posts are needed in microbiology, preferably with a certain technological bias. Another method of spurring industrial and technical development in specific fields is to strengthen certain markets by means of public purchasing. Microelectronics and biotechnology are very interesting in that context.

Corporate Concentration and a Changing Employment Structure

Industrial production has been increasingly concentrated in the large corporations. Companies with more than 500 employees produced 63 per cent of industrial production in the early 1960s. At the beginning of the 1970s the proportion was 75 per cent and it has risen further since then. The reasons are many and they will remain in the 1980s. Economic and technological advantages of large-scale production, better resources for research and development and for marketing are obvious driving forces. More rational production processes have induced a decline of employment in the sectors of goods production and energy in Sweden. LU(1978) accounts for an annual decline of employment in those sectors by somewhat more than 1·4 per cent on average during the period 1965–77. There is a corresponding increase in employment in the service sector by 2·6 on average. A remarkable feature is the growth of employment in the public sector by an average of 5·7 per cent. This means that labour is shifting from sectors whose productivity grows faster to sectors where it grows less rapidly. Nevertheless production of goods and energy has retained its share, about 46 per cent in 1974, of the gross national product.

The transformation of the economy, with a growing share of labour employed in services and a slow growth in productivity in that sector, means a gradual worsening of our conditions for economic growth. Sweden's national and international commitments, however, presuppose the growth of our economy. Since growth is an objective, one can first consider devoting resources to new products and processes in the manufacturing industry. But new technological means can be expected to raise productivity further and possibly lead to a continued flow of labour into the service sector. An increase in the productivity of that sector is therefore desirable in any case. To the extent that this can be achieved by means of improved technology, it will increase the market for the manufacturing industry. An upward spiral can be created. This is one of the urgent tasks of the policies of the 1980s. The low productivity of the public sector must be attacked by organisational, technological and other means. The fact that private dental care, for instance, has proved more efficient than public dental care invites the conclusion that we should seek decentralisation, self-management and competition. That might lead to an upsurge of individual inventiveness to the benefit of the general public, the employees and technological development. The health care sector has proved to be a very good market for new technology.

Competence

When governments and scientists attempt to assess the future prospects of a country, a company or an industry, they also look at knowledge resources, relying on such measurements as their share of skilled workers, technicians, managers and salesmen, and the power output per employee of their machine equipment *(Ways to Increased Prosperity)*. If you categorise according to such criteria you will get other results than if you base your analysis on market growth. However, if you combine the two methods it is possible to assess which industries include not only expanding markets but also highly competent companies, that is, where general measures to improve the climate can be expected to yield the best results.

The computer industry ranks high in this case as well. It is also characterised by high labour intensity. Instruments, communications equipment, pharmaceuticals and various machine manufactures are also among the technical-labour-intensive industries. The plastics industry, by contrast, is technical-labour-extensive. Plastic is a versatile material – its qualities vary from porous and highly absorptive to elastic and almost as hard as steel – and its markets are growing, as we have already emphasised. These are pre-requisites for government research efforts to have a good effect. Paper and cardboard, packaging and parts of the rubber industry have similar qualities.

Technical labour intensity is obviously not a sufficient criterion for good future prospects. Market conditions are important. Ship-building and the aircraft industry are among the very technical-labour-intensive industries. Their situation needs no comment.

What is less visible, however, is the fact that very technical-labour-intensive industries such as communications equipment and other electronics, machinery and instruments must build on completely new technology in the future. Computer technology and micro-electronics are dominating parts of that technology. These areas are expanding explosively in the USA and Japan and great efforts to keep up are being made in England, France and Western Germany. In this field our country needs forceful contributions in the form of large public support for research, development and purchases. Such efforts will also be crucial to another important field, namely, office machines and entire office systems. There is an expanding market for modern office machines and they require an advanced technology based on electronics. In addition, it would enhance productivity in the service sector, that is, an evident contribution to the necessary increase in its efficiency.

Agriculture, forestry, food and pharmaceuticals have an area in common which is often called biotechnology. One might describe it as a kind of alternative technology, based on the living organisms themselves. To a growing extent, new knowledge in the field of microbiology, cellular and molecular biology has created processes which are economical with respect to energy and raw materials and may become of very great importance, not least to our co-operation with developing countries. This is another field where public support is desirable. Imported knowledge, here as in the field of micro-electronics, is another means. This leads us into a discussion on how to build up competence.

Industrial Research and Development

Swedish industry shows in comparison with other countries an exceptionally high degree of self-financing with regard to R and D, 85 per cent as compared to 50–60 per cent in the USA. The research effort of Swedish industry increased strongly up to 1975. The greatest inputs were made in steel and forestry. The mining sector has also made considerable development efforts. Even though R and D is not an obvious guarantee of success it is a necessary prerequisite. The previously rather good profit level has facilitated self-financing and that has led to R and D being market-oriented and goal-conscious. They have strengthened their competitiveness in their own markets, in sectors where no entirely new situations have appeared (as has been the case, for instance, in mining, steel, shipbuilding, and textiles and clothing). However, those research efforts have been of a short-term character. There are several explanations for this. The generally sinking level of corporate profits is the most important one. Public support for research and development in, for example, the aircraft industry and the Defence Research Institute (FOA) has declined, and the repercussions have already been felt. Research co-operation between industry and the universities is of limited scope, with the possible exception of pharmaceutical research.

Policies of the 1980s should primarily aim at providing business with incentives for wider and bolder development efforts and at creating once more an environment conducive to new market entries. Increased profitability and lower marginal income taxes are primary measures. Public purchasing in central areas of technology such as microelectronics, biotechnology and raw materials are similar kinds of measures. But increased stimulus to innovative talents in schools and companies, support for new market entries and support for research co-operation between industry and the universities should also be part of the policies for the 1980s.

Interest in future growth industries is a universal phenomenon. Government support for the furthering of competitiveness within them are legion, not only in France and Great Britain but also in Japan and West Germany. Joint action by state and industry directly aimed at new markets is replacing the indirect method of space and defence projects. These features of a new mercantilism in the world economy cause obvious problems to a small nation. The most ambitious Swedish attempts in the same direction can only be pale copies of what larger countries are doing.

The solution is to be found in direct support for market-oriented development projects and increased resources for basic competence. *If* one can predict needs in health care, the service sector in general, energy technology, central or local administration, then public purchasing should be used to speed up developments and stimulate the design of products which can later be exported. It is a historic fact that such action leads to success. It is only on the surface that technology seems to take violent leaps. The apparently quick, technologically determined social changes have had a long period of incubation. There is in fact ample time to predict the general trend – less, though, to decide on concrete, goal-oriented measures.

Thus the 1980s will be marked by a continued struggle with technological energy problems, in particular the utilisation of solar energy in various forms, for example, directly or by means of wave energy. Information technology, from microelectronics, computer technology and teletechnology, via computerised offices to the home video, home computer and education machine, is of rapidly growing importance. The information industry, a new concept, is in point of fact already the largest industrial sector both in the USA and in Sweden. Biological technology is another dynamic sector, materials technology a third.

New Market Entries

If its own R and D is insufficient for the necessary innovation, a large corporation can innovate by purchasing small idea-based companies and thereby at the same time giving the latter improved possibilities for expansion. Exxon Enterprises in the United States is a good example of systematic innovation of this kind. The method works well if there is a sustained supply of new idea-based companies with a good market potential. That is not the case in our country where on the contrary new market entries in industry are steadily going down. The proportion of newly established workplaces in relation to the total, during the period 1960–9, was merely 1·9 – 2·1 per cent a year (G. Du Rietz, 1977). It is of course a source of satisfaction that our large corporations do well internationally; this will be still more important in the future. Whereas Sweden has eighteen of the twenty biggest corporations in the Nordic area it only has a very small proportion of the small companies. Denmark has twice as many small companies as we have. New enterprises have been harder hit than other businesses by various social changes – changes with other aims, but which inadvertently have had such side-effects. It is a *sine qua non* of the future industrial health of Sweden that this trend should be reversed.

Expanding markets and a low density of technicians characterise many relatively new small and medium-sized goods-producing companies. The successful new businesses in the service sector, such as IKEA, Buketten, Kapp-Ahl, Uno-X, have similar characteristics. Companies using relatively large amounts of technical labour and knowledge face greater initial hardships. Sweden is a small market for their products, and a rapid expansion to foreign markets is necessary. It can be very difficult to create a market in cases where the product has been designed as a result of R and D outside industry, for example, at universities or research institutes. The costs of information and marketing are also swelled by consequential costs, when new technology does away with old techniques and structures. Nevertheless it is necessary to create new technology, less costly in terms of energy and raw materials and producing more durable goods. Everybody feels the need for new technology in the field of energy production and storage. Existing service organisations need innovation, including new technology (for example, mail distribution and waste disposal). The needs are unlimited.

Apart from the innovation that can take place in existing companies that enjoy good profitability, new companies are thus needed at a high level of knowledge. Larger companies should be able to harvest new technological enterprises in Sweden, as they do in the USA, if we provide a better environment for new market entries, more risk-taking capital and general incentives for the promoters of new ideas. Central and local administration should be organised in such a way as to leave scope for entrepreneurs and inventors. The institutions of higher education and the public or semi-public research institutes will be part of the process in two ways. First, they need to provide education for enterprising students (greater freedom of choice and more attention for the talented). Secondly, they must create an environment conducive to innovation and enterprise. The resources already exist. Scientists and teachers take initiatives on their own, which is the natural basis for the further construction of an attractive environment for innovative students and students with a talent for enterprise.

There is also the possibility of using so-called commissioned research in this context. This is a kind of research co-operation between universities and industry. Such co-operation has developed in several Western countries. For instance, Norway has special institutions for that purpose, Sintef at Trondheim and Sentralinstitutt at Oslo, both of which are growing fast in size and importance. Commissioned research in Sweden, by contrast, has very little significance at present. Perhaps the time is ripe for creating here as well a special institution in support of innovation, managerial education and commissioned research, with a link to the universities and the research institutes. In that case one objective should be to contribute to increase spinoffs of small, technologically advanced companies. There are inspiring models in Santa Clara County in California (Silicon Valley) and Route 128 in Massachusetts.

An important reason for the declining flexibility of the universities and their failure to keep up with the most advanced current research trends is the aforementioned tendency of Swedish research to stagnate. Another, which has to do with the innovation process, is the lack of contact between industry and the universities. In Sweden the economic division line between those two sectors is stronger than in any other OECD country. University research is almost entirely government-financed; industrial research is funded by industry. From the point of view of doctrine this may seem attractive. But such a division entails a weak flow of ideas and people between the two sectors. A small country with limited resources, in human as well as physical terms, cannot afford such high walls. We must increase the flow of people and ideas. A few methods are being tried, others can easily be developed on foreign models.

One method of enhancing the contacts with reality available to the research projects of universities and research institutes would be to channel funds through the industry that is expected to take care of the marketing. One way to get more spinoffs of university-based enterprises might be to create, on foreign models, some kind of development institutes which could – hopefully on a temporary basis – contribute risk capital, managerial knowhow and other support.

New ideas will also meet resistance in established systems of beliefs and moral notions. Technical innovation threatens existing systems and is resisted even though it leads to increased material well-being and opportunities for cultural progress. The media rarely have enough of a general view to be able to weigh pros and cons of a new technique and so they often get stuck in criticism: disadvantages are usually easier to identify. The great political task of the 1980s will be to create understanding, acceptance and a positive environment for innovation, the development of knowledge and technology in the schools, universities, research institutes and industry, and for the creation of new enterprises.

A strong manifestation of will in that direction is of great value in itself. But it is a politically controversial matter: to provide scope for individual action and creation all the way from schools to businesses. If and when we manage to establish an ecological balance between human society and nature at large, knowledge and technological development will still remain indispensable.

References: Chapter 7

Central Bureau of Statistics (1977), *Information i prognosfrågor*, no. 4.

Du Rietz, Gunnar (1977), '*Industrietableringen i Sverige efter 1918*', in *Hur skall vi kunna konkurrera* (Stockholm, Svenska Arbelogiva reföreningen).

Håstad, M. (1978), *Matematikutbildning från grundskola till teknisk högskola igår – idag – imorgon* (Stockholm, Royal Institute of Technology).

LU (1978), *Report of the Royal Commission of 1978 on Long-Term Economic Trends* (Stockholm, Liber Förlag).

National Industrial Board (SIND) (1978), *Industriutvecklingen i Sverige*, no. 9 (Stockholm, Liber Förlag).

Swedish National Commission for Industrial Policy, *Ways to Increased Prosperity* (Stockholm, Liber Förlag), nos 1 and 2, 1979.

8

Does the Mixed Economy Have a Future?

ERIK DAHMÉN

By a mixed economy we mean one that combines private capitalism and its market economy with state capitalism and its planned economy.

In a private-capitalist market economy, private ownership and private enterprise are supreme. The pricing of goods and services is free of government intervention. This means that consumption and savings, and hence the utilisation of productive resources, are determined by an interplay between individual consumers on the one hand and producers on the other, both of them guided by the profit motive. What happens in economic life, therefore, is the result of decisions made by a great many people. These decisions, by and large, are made independently of one another. Thus the system is often described as markedly 'pluralistic'. Although such interest organisations as trade unions may exist, even making some decisions of an economic nature, they have little influence. Apart from overseeing the monetary system and handling such chores as defence, law enforcement, and the like, the government has no major tasks to perform. It makes no attempt to determine the allocation of resources or influence the distribution of income. Only in an emergency will it intervene in economic life and individual affairs.

State-capitalist planned economies are characterised by state ownership and state enterprise as well as by the absence of free pricing of goods and services. Consumption and savings, and hence the utilisation of resources, are determined by political decisions in which profitability is not a factor. The same is generally true of the distribution of income. There are no interest organisations of any importance, and therefore such a system is commonly referred to as 'centralist'.

The Development of Mixed Economies

All industrial countries today represent some mixture of the two systems just described. There are no pure models of either a private-capitalist market economy or a state-capitalist planned economy. However, a comparison between the countries of the East and West shows such differences in the way the systems' elements are combined that it is not really a distortion of reality to distinguish between state-capitalist planned economies on the one hand and mixed economies on the other.

The following discussion will concern itself only with the Western industrial countries. The main characteristic of these mixed economies is that although the private-capitalist market plays a very large role, there are also considerable limits on its freedom. The government has a great deal of influence over the allocation of resources and the distribution of income, and there are many areas in which it intervenes – the determination of prices, for example – by means of economic policies and various laws and regulations. Admittedly, individuals still enjoy complete freedom of choice in large areas of consumption and production, yet this sector is by no means dominant. State ownership and state enterprise also exist, to some degree. There is a huge public sector comprising the activities of the central and local governments in which large income transfers are constantly taking place among various groups. Interest organisations are numerous and powerful, particularly in the labour market. In many respects one could say that society is organised into collectives, each using the political game to defend, often successfully, its own particular interests. This has given the system something of a corporatist flavour.

In assessing the future prospects of this kind of mixed economy, it is helpful to bear in mind that although the system has not been planned in any consistent manner, neither is it the product of more or less accidental conditions. Rather, it has been shaped by a gradual transformation of society, a change chiefly determined by technoeconomic forces. Admittedly there have been differences in the rate of change experienced by various industrial countries during one period or another. Yet we can also identify certain decisive characteristics and routes of development common to them all, regardless of shifting political patterns and government. Political ideologies can be said to have influenced development to some extent, but its main direction and content have not been affected.

How, then, have technoeconomic forces shaped the mixed economy? The answer lies in economic changes that occurred a century ago, when the private-capitalist market economy replaced earlier and quite different systems. Through industrialisation this new system liberated the majority of people from the misery, poverty and powerlessness to which they had formerly been subject and which, among other things, had prevented the creation of political democracy. Hence this new economic system had already begun digging its own grave. Its strong developmental forces provided the lower strata of the population with a rapidly rising economic standard and this in turn helped bring about a broadly based rise in the educational level. At the same time the working population was now more concentrated in the cities, which became hotbeds for the growth of trade union and political activities. Taken together, these factors led to an increasing emphasis on certain welfare goals that the private-capitalist market economy, left to itself, would not achieve. It was inevitable that such goals would gradually undermine the existing system, with its highly inequitable distribution of economic and political power. Thus the demise of the pure private-capitalist market economy was not caused primarily by a reaction against the stresses that had made up so large a part of each generation's experience: transformations of economic life; cyclical instabilities, with intermittent periods of severe unemployment; the often oppressive behaviour of the upper class. Rather, the system fell victim to the rise in economic standards it had generated. It is worth noting, for example, that the labour movement – unions and parties – took its initial impetus not from the most underprivileged groups but from those who had advanced furthest towards a relatively decent standard of living. It is also significant that in countries like Sweden, where the living standard of the broad strata of the population rose particularly rapidly and the gaps between rich and poor diminished considerably within a relatively short span of time, the struggle against the private-capitalist market economy of the period was less likely to become violent. Instead, that struggle was dominated by so-called revisionist tendencies in the labour movement with the support of liberal political parties.

Having provided a brief historical sketch of what has happened since the emergence of the private-capitalist market economy, namely, how that system was undermined and ultimately replaced by the mixed economy – I now propose to discuss how this mixed economy might develop in the future. In doing so, certain principles ought to be observed.

In the first place, such an analysis should demonstrate the working so far of the mixed economy in the postwar period. One would be ill-advised to depend primarily on an assessment of the present situation, in which pure chance must necessarily play a considerable part – the current status of the business cycle, say, or the political conditions of the day. Mere coincidence does not provide a solid basis for an evaluation of the future. Secondly, one should try to suppress one's own opinion of what is good or bad; one should assess rather than pass judgement. It would also be better to refrain from speculation on how economic policies might or should be designed. Experience shows that predictions can easily be distorted by wishful thinking – or its pessimistic opposite – unless personal values and policy recommendations are set aside. It is no accident that those who are more interested in the future than in the past are seldom the most successful in making forecasts. Thirdly, if one's assessments are to be taken seriously they should not be allowed to stretch over a longer period than five, or at the most ten, years. Futurologists may easily be misled by what Bo Gustafsson, in a penetrating and thought-provoking article, calls 'the tricks of history'.[1] One factor in particular tends to make the future full of surprises. If people do not clearly perceive the meaning of a given process then they won't think much about its consequences and for a long time they may simply permit the process to continue more or less as before – that is, without counteractions. Those who are aware of what is going on may manage to gain considerable insight into the character and implications of the process and it is quite conceivable that they will be able to predict its course of development for some years to come. But as the effects of the process are more widely felt its implications will become clearer to the general population and counteractions may well be forthcoming. We can only guess at what these counteractions and their consequences will be.

In most of what follows I shall try to be faithful to these three principles, although I do intend to end with a few speculations going beyond the period that can be encompassed today.

Systems with Inherent Conflicts

If we analyse how the mixed economy has worked over the last few decades we will see that while economic development was very rapid for a long time, during the 1970s the pace has been slowing down, and certain problems – ones that have been present all along – have begun to loom larger. These problems are inherent to the nature of the system. They cannot be explained by a series of unfortunate circumstances or a few 'mistakes' due, perhaps, to insufficient familiarity with the conventional tools of economic policy. The term 'nature of the system' refers to the fact that there are certain inevitable contradictions or conflicts that are built into the economy, and these are of two principal kinds. The most significant conflict is between a political way of making certain ambitious and far-reaching decisions – on matters affecting the allocation of productive resources, for example – and the way they would be determined by the multitude of individuals, companies and organisations that make up the market forces. After all, the whole idea behind political decisions is that they *should* be different. Furthermore, they are designed to provide certain groups with more money than they could have acquired via the normal route of income formation within the market economy. Here, too, we find the opposing modes of operation. The second major conflict is stirred up by the intervention not only of political decisions but of general wage agreements (which if not centralised, are at least collective) in the labour market. Their objective is usually to change the wage structure that characterises a completely free labour market – that is, to end the differences in income that result from individual wage agreements between employers and employees. Between these two modes of operation also collision courses are frequent.

The greatest problem created by these two conflicts consists in the fact that the same people who participate, through their represent-atives, in decisions at the central level can also act at the levels where the market forces have free play. Difficulties are bound to arise, since these free-acting individuals *will have no reason at all to behave in accordance with the decisions taken at the central level.* True, they may have participated indirectly in those decisions – they may even approve of them – but that is irrelevant here. Obviously, too, these difficulties will grow as central decisions become more ambitious and far-reaching.

These features of the mixed economy have several noteworthy consequences. One of the most interesting is to observe what happens when, in the midst of increasing efforts to exert political control over the allocation of resources and the distribution of income, there is an attempt at problem-solving by means of economic policy. Since the present format permits no closer scrutiny, I will have to be content merely to mention a few aspects of the process. For the rest, the reader is invited to study earlier publications.[2] So far, the most palpable consequence of conflicts between the two levels of decision-making and action has been almost continuous inflation.

There will always be more or less successful attempts on the part of wage-earners – with the crucial assistance of their powerful organisations – to compensate themselves for the higher taxes that logically result from political decisions to expand the public sector. These taxes, according to one well-established theory of fiscal policy, should make more productive resources available to the public sector. By limiting purchasing power, they are supposed to reduce the private consumption that might otherwise claim resources needed by the public sector. However, a certain amount of compensation for raised taxes is obtained in the form of wage increases, which the employees – largely due to their strong overall position *vis-à-vis* the employers – have little trouble pushing through. Many people, moreover, are quite successful at avoiding taxes altogether: there are thousands of tricks, many of them quite inventive. The net result of all this is a virtual obstruction of political decisions, inevitably leading to a deterioration in the value of money. Because of that deterioration, an increase in income never buys as much as one originally imagined it would. Inflation, then, takes over part of the job that taxes are supposed to do, according to the established fiscal theory mentioned above. As a by-product of inflation and tax evasion there is also an overall decline in efficiency throughout the economy. Reinforcing this more or less successful obstruction of the attempt, through tax increases, to prevent excess demand is a corresponding phenomenon in the labour market. Wage agreements aimed at certain goals – parity between those who work in less profitable enterprises and those employed in the more profitable ones, for example, or larger raises for low-income groups than for others – are met by opposition, even among those who, through their representatives, participated in those agreements and who generally agreed with their purpose. The aim of these opponents is to maintain the distance between themselves and those wage-earners the central agreements were intended to benefit most. High-income employees, partly because they are fewer and less well organised, are usually less successful in this endeavour than middle-income groups. The latter will always, sooner or later, win some concession – sometimes by means of strikes or the threat of strikes. Thus principles are one thing while concrete action – for which, by definition, there is always some scope in the mixed economy – is quite another. It would be very naive to believe that things could be otherwise.

It is, furthermore, typical of the mechanisms of a mixed economy that textbook attempts to block inflationary wage increases by means of monetary policy are bound to be less than successful. If well conceived and sustained, such attempts may manage to halt a spate of galloping, uncontrolled inflation, but they cannot establish monetary stability. They are capable of preventing the secondary self-generating inflation that is in excess of what is inevitably produced by a mixed economy. But when it comes to dealing with the primary cause of inflation, the central banks and their monetary policies are hopelessly outclassed. After a while, perhaps as a sort of compensation for their failure, they may try to hit the brakes too hard, causing a considerable decline in employment and production before monetary stability can be achieved. This is what is meant by 'stagflation'. Under these conditions, too, it becomes more difficult than anticipated for political bodies not only to fight inflation but to reach a number of other goals, including increased public services, social policies and general welfare measures. It is hardly surprising, then, that sooner or later the central banks, under high-level political pressure, are forced to abandon their monetary policies. It makes little sense to claim, as do some monetarist theories, that the inflationary problems of a mixed economy can be solved by steps to control the money supply, for the central bank that is taking those steps can never really be completely autonomous of the political powers-that-be. It is reminiscent of the proposition that you can stop someone from going out on the town by locking his door but putting the key in his own pocket.

In my view, the areas I have touched upon have not been sufficiently analysed and understood in economic literature or discussion. Therefore many people still cling to the belief that ambitious political goals can be achieved by means of economic policies whose theoretical underpinnings often date back to a period before the mixed economy, as we understand it today, had even been born. 'Politics is a matter of will' is a popular slogan, despite the fact that it is impossible to do everything one wants to, not only for the obvious reason that productive resources are limited but also because in a mixed economy, as I have already shown, the system itself constitutes an obstacle. Economists too frequently assume that policy can be made in a rational way – that if goals are set in accordance with the available productive resources, they can be attained, provided they are properly executed. Hence when any-thing goes wrong there is a tendency to explain it away by claiming that political or other special interests had an excessive influence on policy or that the policy's authors were simply incompetent. These economists miss the point when it comes to the problems of a mixed economy, and they are in grave danger of being caught short by its development.

Considering our experience with economic policy in a mixed economy, it is not difficult to understand why different forces were eventually unleashed – forces that have all tended to turn the development of the mixed economy and its 'mixture' in the same direction. Since efforts to use traditional methods of economic policy to reach established goals – but avoid upsetting the balance of the economy – have proved less successful than expected, those methods have gradually been supplemented by other, less conven-tional approaches. This has occurred in various countries from time to time, though not always to the same degree. Such supplementary approaches have placed increasing limitations on the private-capitalist economy and added many *dirigiste* elements to the economic system. Individual groups, companies, and the like, have thus seen their freedom of action impaired. Governments, mean-while, have taken to a panoply of subsidies for such purposes as limiting inflation and maintaining full employment. Furthermore, with those and other goals in mind, governments have repeatedly intervened in the determination of prices, while income policies of various levels and kinds, limiting the freedom of organisations within the labour market, have been introduced in many places. The common denominator of all these measures has presumably been an attempt to deal with the mechanisms of obstruction more effectively than conventional fiscal and monetary policies have done. It is clear that the mixed economy's move toward this sort of direct regulation has had little to do with political ideology or party politics. The fact that a given government has been socialist or conservative has not been decisive.

The aforementioned experience and its interpretation constitute a natural point of departure for the analysis that follows, in which I will chiefly concern myself with the not-too-distant future. However, since the whole area cannot be covered, even superficially, within the framework of a short essay, it is necessary to impose some reasonable limits on the discussion. Thus I shall not go into any detail on the subject of possible remedies, old and new, in the struggle against inflation. In this instance, moreover, it does not even require much discussion to make it clear that this struggle, as has already been the case for some time, will not be based exclusively on traditional fiscal and monetary policies but will include many measures of the kind indicated above, or new ones still to be invented. The result will still be far from a complete success. Admittedly the monetarist theory is currently enjoying renewed prestige as a guide to monetary policy, and this may prevent a violent and uncontrollable devaluation. But that does not mean the abandonment of a policy of direct intervention. If nothing else, the political clout of vested interests so characteristic of a mixed economy will undermine any attempt by the central bank to initiate a rigidly consistent monetarist policy. So in the not-too-distant future the struggle against inflation is hardly likely to bring anything essentially new to the 'mix' of the mixed economy. There are more interesting questions to discuss than the possibility of improving the economy through the use of monetary tools and other methods that are reasonably compatible with the present type of mixed economy. Other issues which have surfaced only in the last decade are not only more recent than inflation and the struggle against it but present more fateful problems for the mixed economy and its future existence.

The problem area I have in mind is broadly consistent with a social change that has long been implicit in technoeconomic development – that is, encompassing more or less the same forces as originally replaced a pure private-capitalist market economy with a mixed system. However, this phenomenon has now become more immediate, acquiring new elements as a result of the situation in which the Western industrial countries found themselves at the end of the 1960s or in the early 1970s. All this provides fairly clear indications of what will happen in the near future. In the interests of brevity and concreteness I shall limit my discussion to what has happened in Sweden and what it might tell us about the prospects for our own particular mixed economy.

The Long Downhill Slide of Swedish Industry

Since the mid-1960s, international economic conditions have deteriorated both for Swedish business in general and industry in particular. The nature of these external changes need not be explained here since it is irrelevant to the following analysis. I have described it many time in other contexts.[3] Let it suffice, then, to note that those changes required considerable adjustments and new directions if this country was to maintain its long-term chances for economic growth at anything like the previous rates. In this regard it is interesting to note that Sweden's capacity for adaptation and innovation proved insufficient. This had much to do with the appearance of new elements, or old ones that had been strengthened in the mixed economy, at a time when the war against inflation had already added a number of new regulations to its arsenal – with precious little success. Let us look a little more closely at these new or strengthened elements.

Some of them were related to the fact that central and local government was making greater claims than before on the resources of society. This was a natural development, quite in line with the technoeconomic forces that had originally shaped the economy and which continued to influence it. Neither in Japan nor in any Western country has the public sector staked out such a large share of total resources as in Sweden. These days almost two-thirds of national income passes through the budgets of the central government, local governments, or social insurance agencies. More than half that amount represents real resources, while the rest involves income transfers. Both necessitate an extremely high level of taxation. Other new elements had to do with the surge of demands, beginning in the mid-1960s, for improvements in the external and internal environment. Some aspects of this environment had been deteriorating for a number of years, in part because the nature of the private-capitalist market economy ruled out measures to prevent such a decline.[4] Environmental policies meant not only increasing utilisation of available resources but also regulatory interventions. Partly as a symptom of the same desire to define 'well-being' in a new way, demands for leisure increased, labour input declined and absenteeism rose, particularly in the 1970s.

There are many explanations for the fact that these elements of 'well-being' underwent a more significant increase in Sweden than in almost any other country. The most important reason is also the most obvious one: we felt we could well afford it given our highly advantageous point of departure after the Second World War and our subsequent attainment of a high national income and material standard of living. But the trouble was that when improvements were needed as a result of the new situation we encountered in the mid-1960s our industry proved incapable of sufficient adjustment and innovation. It is interesting to note that this reduced capacity for adjustment and innovation was also quite closely related to an influx of new values and demands, reflecting not so much any particular political strategy as a change of attitude in a society with a high material living standard and a mixed economy. Let us look at a few examples of what reduced that capacity.

Expanding enterprises found it more difficult to recruit labour as workers became increasingly reluctant to change their occupation and residential milieu. These demands for vocational and residential security were reinforced by the entry of more women into the labour market, and they were supported – contrary to earlier practice – by the unions. This can be viewed partly as a natural result of the high material standard and the new values it engendered and partly as a new expression of the recurrent demand, a longstanding feature of the course of economic development, for more influence over corporate decisions. Later on job security laws, demands for co-determination and several other factors further reduced the mobility of the labour force, with the result that expanding companies found it still more difficult to attract employees. This effect was reinforced by the principle, now fiercely defended by the unions, that in the case of layoffs those most recently hired should be the first to go. Since workers could no longer be certain that the company hiring them would not subsequently be obliged to reduce its labour force, they became even less willing to change jobs. The advantages of a higher income and change of residence promised by a new job had also been increasingly eroded by the fact that marginal taxes were soaring, even for those in normal income brackets. This in turn reflected an ever more ambitious level of political decision-making, bringing marked increases in total taxation, progressive tax scales and inflation.

While the development of expanding companies was thus hindered by both external and internal factors, the situation of the weaker companies grew still worse with the advent of changes in the principles of wage policy. The emphasis on special increases for the lowest-paid workers put too great a strain on their resources and many of them got into serious financial trouble. As a result they had neither the time nor the opportunity to plan and execute the restructuring that might have given them a new lease of life. Despite a heightened desire for 'well-being' and a reduced industrial capacity for adjustment and innovation, demands for higher per capita incomes did not cease. Money wages increased substantially under growing pressure from stronger unions, which now openly negotiated on the basis of after-tax income. Meanwhile the earlier resistance of employers had been considerably reduced by their belief that currency depreciations would soon wipe out the effects of increases in the cost of labour. They were also aware that widespread labour unrest would quickly drain their financial resources, while their adversaries could be confident that if employees were threatened by material hardship during a long strike a compulsory settlement would be imposed by political means in order to resume production. The pay increases were unrealistically high, given a situation in which resources had been mortgaged to the hilt for other social benefits, and conditions for growth had deteriorated. There was no rationale at all for what happened. The result of course was more inflation and further disruptions in the economy. The Swedish crown, which in the 1950s had been rather undervalued, gradually became overvalued, thus making the situation even worse and finally, after 1975, helping to create a serious crisis. This entire process, including all the major components we have just described, weakened the conditions for the kind of mixed economy – with predominating private-capitalist traits – that still prevailed in the mid-1960s.

This weakening is illustrated by what happened to the profit picture in the industrial sector. Owing to those new or strengthened elements of the mixed economy that affected conditions for industry, there was a tendency for corporate profitability to decline from one cyclical low to another. It is significant that shares registered in the stock exchange, that barometer of private capitalism, ceased to be a hedge against inflation. The annual average yield of such shares in terms of distributed profits plus value changes, which before the mid-1960s had consistently been about 8–10 per cent, now dropped to half that level. Until 1976 it hovered at a point barely above zero, then fell below that line. At the same time companies often got heavily into debt. If one looks beyond the averages the situation is revealed to be even worse than those statistical summaries would indicate. Since a large number of unprofitable companies are not even included the figures issued by the remaining ones provide a less than accurate picture of what happened. The statistical summaries further fail to reveal how fragmented things had become in comparison with the period before 1965. From the mid-1960s on, for example, many corporate owners lost on stock exchange values as well as inflation. Other interesting information is also obscured, such as the fact that in a remarkable number of cases profitability was sustained solely by foreign subsidiaries, or that for a growing number of companies the ratio between owned capital and loans dropped to a level where only small investments were possible.

In conclusion, then, we can say that since the mid-1960s the financial position of industry has been so weak that corporations have become more and more vulnerable to cyclical change, while their capacity to expand has in many cases been undermined. For a long time this went unnoticed, partly because many people failed to look beyond the surface of the situation, but also because they believed it was only a matter of deeper lows in the business cycle than before. In reality, however, the very foundations of private enterprise were beginning to sag under the pressure of new elements in the mixed economy. This long-term trend is far more significant than either the strong recovery in profits we experienced in 1973 and 1974 or the acute crisis that followed. Both the recovery and the backlash had to do with dramatic international developments and Swedish foreign exchange policy – with factors, in other words, that in the longer historical perspective appear as sheer coincidence.

The development I have described has significantly broadened the scope for government intervention in economic life. Not only have there been more interventions of the traditional sort, but new methods have been added as well. Their characteristics are so well known that I need not go into them here.[5] Many of the factors that have gradually undermined conditions for private industry may be explained by social developments similar to those that accompanied the original transition to a mixed economy. In a sense, then, this further shift in the 'mix' of the mixed economy may be considered a logical development. Admittedly the fact that a bourgeois cabinet happened to be responsible for an unprecedented increase in government intervention had a lot to do with the severity of the crisis that broke out in 1975. And that crisis in turn grew out of the international developments of the immediately preceding years, Sweden's economic policy at the time, and the general wage agreements of 1975. Nevertheless it would be wrong to view the shift in the mixed economy simply as a result of those events.

The Future of the Mixed Economy – Further Decline or Renaissance?

If on the basis of such an analysis of past events one now looks forward to what may be in store for the mixed economy, it is not very difficult to assess the main features of our immediate future. The best way to begin is with an assessment of international prospects over the next five to ten years and their implications for the Swedish economy. The only conclusion possible is that the external conditions for Swedish economic growth and an increased living standard will very probably remain less favourable than they were before the mid-1960s.[6] This assessment may turn out to be too pessimistic, of course, but it is extremely unlikely that it will prove entirely incorrect. The next question concerns our future response to continued demands for adjustment and innovation. We can assume that these demands will be similar to those which arose in the mid-1960s and proved so difficult to satisfy.

The first observation we can make is that our present system does not permit us to exploit the historically well-documented advantages of the private-capitalist market economy. At the same time strong elements of an opposite system – which may have advantages of its own, though so far they are less well-documented – are gaining ground. Thus today's 'mix' does not take full advantage of the best opportunities offered by either system. In the light of our analysis of past decades it is highly probable that the mixed economy we had during the first postwar decades, given its strong capacity for adjustment and innovation, would have been able to carry out the task of sustaining a satisfactory growth rate despite deteriorating external conditions. In any case this would have been possible if the Swedish crown had not become overvalued during the second half of the 1960s. But that mixed economy, as I have tried to demonstrate, was a far from stable system. It worked well, by and large, thanks to a number of more or less haphazard circumstances. Quite clearly, however, it represented a kind of artificial interlude. What came after that interlude was to a large extent a natural development whose effect, then and now, was to worsen conditions for growth.

But insights into the functioning of the present system obviously do not provide a sufficient basis for conclusions concerning the future. Today's economy is no closer to some kind of stable equilibrium than it was before. Everyone is entitled to make a few assumptions, according to his political or ideological lights, about what a future 'mix' should and might look like if everyone worked conscientiously for its realisation. This, however, is quite irrelevant to those in search of an accurate prognosis. There is ample historical evidence for the argument that future reality will bear little resemblance to such wishful thinking. Instead, let us attempt to evaluate that the 'mix' will *actually* look like – that is, how it is going to change. Such an evaluation may be based partly on an assessment of certain general political prospects, and partly on insights acquired through an analysis of past and present.

Given the current distribution of power and the fact that the political situation, with only the most marginal shifts in the electorate, is manifestly stable, it is difficult to imagine that there will be much scope for vast experiments with some completely different economic system. In any case, during the limited period I have chosen to comment on there will scarcely be any abrupt change of direction in relation to the long-term trends of the past. Instead, although changes in the mixed economy will continue under the pressure of prevailing circumstances they will probably be the same kind we have had before. The 'mix,' then, is likely to be more strongly marked by such elements as centralised decision-making, state enterprises, subsidies and other forms of support, and regulations for a number of different purposes. The direct influence of trade unions on management will also increase, although certain internal differences will doubtless appear in the unions in so far as the employers, whose power has already been considerably eroded, can no longer serve as the common enemy. Our entire analysis of the essential factors inevitably leads us to this conclusion. If any reader does not agree that this is probably the correct conclusion he has obviously failed to understand the underlying analysis. If a reader does not concur with the analysis that is of course a quite different matter. In conclusion, the mixed economy does have a future, since over the next few years – which is all one can seriously presume to assess today – it is scarcely going to be replaced by an entirely new system. But if one were to venture into speculations of what might happen in the long run, would the mixed economy still appear to have a future?

One such speculation might be that most of the forces that have influenced the 'mix' so far will continue to make themselves felt in the long run. By extension, then, one might hazard a guess that private capitalism and hence the market economy will lose so much ground that we shall eventually find ourselves with an essentially different economic system than the one we presently possess. Such a guess is supported by much of the recent debate over certain topical issues that has accompanied the phenomena we have discussed above. Part of this debate concerns what is currently called wage-earners' funds. This issue has been brought to the forefront by the fact that profitability, capital accumulation and corporate management to promote economic development are no longer considered acceptable within the present structure of private-capitalist ownership. These wage-earners' funds – or any similar arrangement that works against the principle of individual shares for employees – would give us an economic system best described by the term 'collective capitalism'. Collective capitalism would make even a high level of profit politically acceptable. The question, then, is whether such profits could be achieved by the kind of companies that would result if private-capitalist motives were circumscribed or abolished. Admittedly the market economy would not *necessarily* have to give way within fund-managed companies, but it is highly probable that this would be the case in practice. After all, such funds would create strong interest groups among wage-earners and it is hard to believe that they would simply accept the dictates of the market. They would call upon the government to intervene in many cases – for instance, if they were on the verge of being forced out of the market. Even today owners frequently side with their employees in seeking government support if layoffs are an alternative or made to seem so. It is probable, then, to put it mildly, that if employees come to dominate a company through their funds they will seek to

prevent or limit the impact of market forces by means of government intervention whenever the market is conceived as a threat.
A completely different speculation might be that state intervention and other collective elements in capitalism, including
alternatives to the market forces, will turn out to be such failures
that the political attitudes of the majority will turn against them. In
the current political debate, especially on the left, some concern has
been expressed that workable alternatives to the present mixed
economy might not be developed in time. Could it be that the step
from ideology and vision to the reality of a small country like
Sweden, highly dependent on the outside world, may prove too
difficult? Is it possible that the necessary political conditions will not
be present? There are those who think that the state-capitalist
planned economy can never ultimately be reconciled with political
democracy. If that turned out to be true even for countries with a
long tradition of political democracy, and people became aware of it
in time, then that realisation might trigger forces that are not very
active today. Is there, perhaps, something in all this that could help
us come to grips with the roots and origins of so many of our current
difficulties? Perhaps the discord and conflict will be modified
considerably if there is a moratorium on ambitious political attempts
to influence the allocation of resources and the distribution of
income. In that case the mixed economy might conceivably not only
be saved but even find its 'mix' changing in the opposite direction.
Perhaps having discovered that the problems of development cannot
be solved with the other methods that have been tried, Sweden will
even permit some reinforcement of the private-capitalist elements
which have been in retreat for so long. Today it is difficult, to say
the least, to believe any of the last few propositions. But 'the tricks
of history' have sometimes come up with greater surprises than that.

Notes: Chapter 8

1   Bo Gustafsson, 'Imperialismen, Tredje Världen och historiens list', *Ekonomisk
debatt*, no. 5, 1978.
2   See, for instance, E. Dahmén, *Kapitalbildningsproblemet* (Stockholm, Industriens
Utredningsinstitut, 1959); 'Hur användbar är den ekonomisk-politiska teorien i
dagens samhälle?', in *Samhälle i omvandling* (Stockholm, Bonniers, 1967); and
above all the concluding essay in Skandinaviska Enskilda Banken *Erfarenheter av
blandekonomin* (Uppsala, Almqvist and Wiksell, 1977; English translation
forthcoming).
3   See, for example, *Skandinaviska Enskilda Bankens Quarterly Review*, nos 1–2,
1977; the essay in *Erfarenheter av blandeconomin*, cited in note 2; and articles in
Svenska Sparbanksföreningen, *Vårt ekonomiska läge 1978*, and *Ekonomisk
debatt*, no. 1, 1979. Documentation may be found in *Teknik och industristruktur –
1970 – talets kris i historisk belysning*, produced by Industriens Utredningsinstitut
as part of the Kunskap och Konkurrenskraft Project sponsored by the Swedish
Royal Academy of Engineering Sciences, Stockholm, 1979.

4 For a description of the deficiencies of the market economy in this respect see E. Dahmén, *Sätt pris på miljön* (Uddevalla, Studieförbundet Näringsliv och Samhälle, 1968).

5 A good description of the genesis and characteristics of the more recent types of intervention is given in Erik Lundberg's concluding article in *Blandekonomi på villovägar?* (Uddevalla, SNS, 1972). Lundberg's extreme vision of the future has now become a reality in many respects, albeit more in the form of emergency actions than as active industrial policy.

6 In his essay, 'Fortsatt stagnation?', in the SNS booklet *Företag och samhälle*, no. 3, 1978, Ragnar Bentzel has summarised various assessments of international prospects and arrived at the same conclusion as far as Sweden is concerned.

9

The Historical Compromise and its Dissolution

WALTER KORPI

It is often maintained that the Swedish union movement has sharply changed direction during the 1970s. To begin with, they say, this was when the trade unions abandoned the traditional idea that the contracting parties of the labour market should regulate their relations by collective bargaining and without government interference. Instead they demanded and obtained legislation on job security, working environment, the position of union representatives, co-determination, and so on. Later, the trade unions also abandoned their own fear of doing away with the bargaining of the labour market and of sharing owner responsibility for production. Now they advanced the idea of wage-earners' funds, by which employees would get an important role as owners of companies.

These elements of trade union policy during the 1970s have confused many people who have been unable to see rational motives for such trade union demands. In the more superficial debate it has therefore been said that these elements are due to a lack of experience on the part of a new generation of trade union leaders or can be explained by the influence of a small group of university-trained functionaries working in the research departments of the unions. Many have also stated that trade unions in the 1970s have become dangerously hungry for power and even that they pose a threat to the democratic foundations of society.

Are these elements of trade union policy then something temporary to be overcome by the movement which will then resume its 'natural' role in society? Or do these apparently new elements simply constitute the latest stages in the old struggle of the labour movement for political, social, and economic democracy? Our answer to such questions will depend very much on our concepts of how society works and changes. Even those who see themselves as pragmatists guided by common sense look at society through glasses tinted by some kind of theory. They arrange their impressions and thoughts into categories and patterns which have been formulated by social scientists and philosophers. It is therefore of interest in this context to seek to clarify the points of departure and explanatory models behind various views on developments up to and including the 1970s. This should facilitate a fruitful exchange of ideas between people who have arrived at different interpretations and may be of some help as we try to speculate about how employees will act in the 1980s.

To begin with I shall briefly indicate the main traits of an explanatory model which has been dominant among social scientists in the postwar period and which easily leads to the conclusion that the kind of bargaining existing in the Swedish labour market in the 1950s and 1960s is the 'natural' final stage of the development of industrial societies. Secondly, I shall sketch an alternative concept which leads to somewhat different interpretations of what has happened and somewhat different expectations for the future. In my view the policy we came to see as natural to the trade union movement in the 1950s and 1960s was basically conditioned by a specific historical situation. That policy differed markedly from the trade union strategy prevalent up to the mid-1930s, a strategy shaped under different conditions. It is a change of conditions that has made it possible for the trade union strategy to change again.

A Pluralistic Industrial Society

The basic explanatory model of modern society used by leading Western social scientists of the postwar period can be called a model of pluralistic industrial society. This has been developed mainly by social scientists in the United States and Western Europe but has to varying degrees been adopted by a majority of Swedish social scientists.[1] According to the underlying argument the development of industrial technology is the most important force for social change. The argument goes as follows. The industrial revolution crushed the old agrarian society and its institutions. The development of technology demands an increasingly specialised and skilled labour force. This affects the composition of the labour force and consequently the class structure of society. The old social pyramid with its broad base of unskilled labour swells in the middle and becomes increasingly diamond-shaped. The middle classes will eventually dominate while the relative size of the working class decreases. In addition, growing occupational specialisation tends to fragment or disintegrate the working class.

In the pluralistic industrial society there are conflicts between management and employees as well as between different groups and classes of citizens. But industrial society has developed new institutions to deal with such conflicts. These institutions have replaced those which broke down in the early years of the industrial revolution, leading afterwards to dangerous social instability. The most important among the new institutions are, first, political democracy and, secondly, the institutions of the labour market created to regulate the relationship between unions and management, particularly the negotiation of agreements. The creation of these new institutions has also made it possible to separate the conflicts of the labour market from the conflicts of political life.

A central notion to the model of the pluralistic industrial society is that the power is fairly evenly distributed between a great number of interest groups which balance each other. That is how the industrial society is pluralistic. In the same way as the right to vote provides people with 'political citizenship', the right to negotiate gives employees 'industrial citizenship'. Agreements in the labour market are concluded by free and equal parties. Partly because of an ever increasing standard of living the various, equally powerful, groups of society are able to satisfy reasonable demands. The pluralistic industrial society will therefore both be capable of change and yet on the whole be stable, with no need for fundamental institutional change. The decisive factor in this model is that workers and other employees have been incorporated into society in a way acceptable to all.

Social scientists such as J. K. Galbraith (1967, chs 23 and 24) have stated that the gradual dissolution of the working class will also be reflected in a decline of the trade union movement. Class-based trade unions, according to him, are part of the infancy of industrialism. In modern society they lose importance and will increasingly become organisations for special interests based on profession. The working class would then gradually be dissolved and adopt bourgeois values in the welfare society. This stable character, founded on a reasonable distribution of power and well-being and on well-functioning institutions for the solution of conflicts, makes the pluralistic industrial society an ideal model, and close to being the final stage of the development of mankind. Since the driving force of industrial society is conceived as being the same in the East as well as in the West, industrialised countries of East and West are supposed to become increasingly alike, irrespective of political and other conditions. The most industrially advanced country, the USA, was assumed to show the way less advanced countries would also follow. Some social scientists have gone so far as to talk about the Western type of society, combining political democracy and private ownership of industry, as the 'end point of modernisation' and 'the good society at work' in which 'the fundamental problems of industrial revolution have been solved'.[2]

A person trying to understand the Sweden of the 1970s on the basis of the model of the pluralistic industrial society is likely to be confused. The trade union movement does not seem to remain willing to stick to its natural role in society. The subtle balance of the pluralistic society is being threatened by trade unions who want to appropriate more than their fair share. Generally speaking, it will be difficult from this point of view to understand why any groups would have rational grounds for wanting fundamental social change.

I shall now briefly outline one of the possible alternatives to the idea of the pluralistic industrial society, an alternative that in part offers different points of departure for the understanding of social development.

Social Change as a Solution to Problems

The model of the pluralistic industrial society had industrial technology as the driving force for social change. The alternative I want to outline starts instead with people and views social change as the result of their efforts to solve central problems they are confronted with. The most fundamental problem for mankind of all times is to organise in order to produce goods and services for its livelihood. The ways in which people relate to each other and co-operate in production are conditioned by certain factors of their environment. Some of these factors are given by nature (for example, the quality of the soil, and the climate) whereas others (for example, technology, tools and other means of production) are man-made. The way in which people co-operate in production is so fundamental that it puts a decisive stamp on the other institutions and conditions of society.

When the conditions of production are changed people are confronted with new problems. Efforts to solve those problems can lead to more or less thoroughgoing changes in society. But the social solutions to problems depend in various ways on the distribution of power between various groups and collectives in society. The distribution of power affects the demands of various groups as well as their notions of what is fair and reasonable. What they conceive and define as social problems will therefore also depend to a great extent on the distribution of power among them. Concomitantly the alternatives presented and chosen depend on this distribution of power. The distribution of power between groups, collectives, or classes will according to this concept be one of the most decisive factors in social change.

The Distribution of Power

The idea that the pluralistic industrial society is stable and definitive rests on the assumption that the distribution of power among the various groups and collectives in capitalist democracies is relatively even. As I see it this assumption is not valid. A way to shed light on the question of how power is distributed in a society is to analyse which means or resources of power are available to various groups and collectives. What, then, is a power resource? Power resources are characterised by their capacity to punish or reward other people. They can be of very different kinds. At the risk of entering areas which may seem unnecessary, I shall try to discuss a few.

Power resources may differ according to their area of operation, that is, how many people are receptive to a given kind of reward or punishment. They can also differ with regard to their applicability, that is, in which kinds of situations they can be used. Another important aspect is the degree of scarcity of power resources of a given kind. Furthermore power resources can be more or less necessary to other people in their daily lives. They also vary with regard to their ability to be transformed into other kinds of resources. Another important quality is the extent to which a power resource can be concentrated in a few individuals.

Let us now look at a few different types of power resources in society. Control of means of repression and violence has traditionally been a very important power resource in the history of mankind. Means of repression and violence can be said to have a wide area of operation. They can rather easily be converted into other resources. Even though they are not very scarce, they can be strongly concentrated. Their main disadvantage is that they cost a lot, since they provoke very negative attitudes against their users. Power based on violence and repression is therefore usually unstable. It has been said that you can do a lot of things with bayonets but you cannot sit on them. In modern Western societies, therefore, means of repression and violence are the extreme power resources, used comparatively seldom and subject to efforts to regulate their use.

A power resource of great importance in most societies is money. Money is a very effective power resource in many ways. It has a wide area of operation and great applicability. It is necessary, and it is easy to convert into other resources. It can also be concentrated to a very high degree. Control of means of production is another central power resource. It also has a wide area of operation and great applicability. Means of production are usually scarce resources. Of particular importance is the fact that they are a very necessary resource to most people, since it is a matter of their livelihood.

Labour, or as some economists call it, 'human capital', is also an important power resource in our society. The quality of labour may differ according to factors such as the degree of professional skill and education. But labour is rarely a very scarce resource. It also has a rather limited area of operation and a relatively limited applicability. Human capital, furthermore, is difficult to concentrate very strongly. As everybody knows, we live in an era of mass education, and education above a certain level can as a matter of fact give diminishing yields. Labour is also rather difficult to convert into other resources. The parallel some economists draw between physical capital and human capital is therefore not valid.

It is important to realise that power resources do not have to be used in order to have effects on the actions of other people. If you have the capacity to reward or punish you do not always have to use it in order to affect your environment. People learn from experience to expect the reactions of strong individuals, groups or other social actors in their environment and they can also be made to accept some of the values of such power-holders as their own. They also learn where the power resources are and where they are not, and thus they draw up a 'social map' of their sector of society which they use more or less consciously to orient themselves in their lives. In the capitalist democracies control of the means of production and of capital is one of the strategic power resources. Labour is another important power resource in those societies. Where the means of production are owned and controlled by individual groups the great majority of citizens must offer their labour on the market for their livelihood.

But let us reflect for a moment on what really takes place in the labour market. There are several more or less ideological terms to describe it. Economists chiefly discuss it as just another market where goods are bought and sold. But economists tend to forget that labour power is a very special kind of merchandise. It cannot be separated from its owner. It cannot be sold; that would amount to slavery. Labour can only be rented for a given time. The buyer obtains the right to dispose of the seller's labour power during working hours. Once the sales contract has been concluded in the labour market the person who has sold his labour power cannot take it off as an overcoat but has to deliver it in the workplace, where he personally must subordinate himself to the instructions of management. As the professor of labour law, Folke Schmidt (1968, p. 105), indicates, a basic principle of Swedish labour law has been that 'the employee must subject himself to management'. The labour contract therefore leads to a relationship of authority and subordination between human beings.

Seen as a power resource, labour power is fragmented and difficult to concentrate. However, its effectiveness can be increased through organisation which can co-ordinate the employees, weak individually, into united action. This provides a rational explanation for the creation of trade unions for the defence of the interests of employees against employers. It also explains why workers organise into political parties. The organisations that have the task of co-ordinating the action of workers, mainly trade unions and political parties, therefore constitute another of the strategically important power resources in the capitalist democracies.

Is either of these two types of strategic power resources, the control of capital and means of production or organised labour, dominant in the capitalist democracies? Let us recall what happens where these two types of power resources are most clearly confronted with one another, that is, in the workplace. There, control of the means of production is the basis for management's right of command over labour. This indicates that the workers in those societies are at a disadvantage in relation to capitalists in terms of power resources.

Nevertheless it is important to realise that the degree of disadvantage of the employees, that is, the difference in power resources between them and the owners of capital, can vary considerably over time as well as between countries. The difference is due in part to conditions affecting capital-owners, but maybe chiefly to the degree of organisation reached by workers for united action. Changing relations of power between employees and capital-owners can be assumed to be of fundamental importance to various elements of social development, such as the extent and character of labour conflicts, forms and methods of social institutions, the social distribution of benefits between various layers of the population and the consciousness and demands of the workers. The distribution of power resources can also affect the degree to which workers question the hierarchy of working life which is not legitimised by democratic elections but by the ownership of the means of production.

The Historical Compromise[3]

A person who considers the unions' policy of the 1970s to be a deviation from the natural role of unions in society, has a rather short time perspective for his judgement. What he sees as natural for trade unions has really been their line only for a few decades after the Second World War. But if you limit your horizon to 1945 you do not see the dramatic changes which had previously taken place within the workers' movement and Swedish society. Let us take an example. Many consider Sweden the promised land of labour peace. But that situation has really only prevailed during the postwar period. Up to the mid-1930s Sweden, together with Norway, was actually the country that led the world in strikes and lockouts.

How should we explain this dramatic change in a central area in which our country has gone from one extreme to the other in the course of a few decades? The assumptions built into the model of the pluralistic industrial societies are an obstacle rather than a help as we try to understand developments so far and speculate about the future. Instead of growing more and more similar to one another, as that model implies, Western countries have actually become increasingly different in the postwar period as far as labour conflicts are concerned.[4] Whereas labour conflicts have diminished considerably in Sweden, Norway and Austria they have increased very greatly in countries like France, Italy, Finland and Australia and they have remained at the previous levels in other countries. To understand this change we must abandon the assumption of a largely balanced and therefore stable distribution of power resources between various groups in the capitalist democracies. I suggest that we should rather study just how the distribution of power resources between workers on the one hand and capitalists and their allies on the other has shifted over time, and that we should then try to interpret developments and speculate about the future against the background of such changes in the relations of power.

In the early years of industrialism the differences in power resources were very large between the upper class, consisting of the then new bourgeoisie and other social élites of older origins, and a still fragmented working class. But as workers began to organise in trade unions and political parties those differences diminished. This led to an increase in labour conflicts. The conflicts brought limited but important gains to the workers' movement. The right to organise and negotiate collectively was accepted in the so-called December Compromise of 1906. The increasing force of the workers also led to an increase in their demands. In a few decades one of the most burning social issues was the fact that the right to vote depended on income and property. Strengthened by an alliance with middle-class groups represented by the Liberals, the propertyless workers were able to change social institutions considerably and, towards the end of the First World War, establish political democracy.

But in spite of the introduction of political democracy the Swedish labour movement remained largely excluded from political power and was therefore restricted to a labour market struggle for a more just distribution of what was produced. The strategy of the employers was tough. The struggle in the labour market intensified. Sometimes the struggle was also politically tinted, for example, the general strikes for the general vote in 1902 and against the Law on Collective Bargaining of 1928. The 1930s began with fierce labour battles, many of which continued to take the form of lockouts. The crisis of the 1930s and the election of 1932 led to a change in the front lines. For the first time the workers' parties got a trifle more than 50 per cent of the votes for parliament. The Social Democrats could form a government with the support of the farmers. In the elections of 1934, 1936 and 1938 that government received ever-increasing electoral support. By contrast to the earlier, weak Social Democrat minority governments, the Social Democrat governments of the 1930s could thus count on massive support from the electorate.

Such support was something new and remarkable in Swedish history. It meant that the workers' movement in the conflict between social classes, on a seemingly stable political basis, could open a successful offensive on a new frontline in the political field. This tangible shift in power resources within society made the two main antagonistic groups of Swedish society scrutinise and change their previous strategies for conflicts. For the workers' movement, government power meant great possibilities. They could avoid the costly labour market conflicts and instead use political means to redistribute the income and strengthen the position of workers. The level of employment could be raised and the spectre of unemployment be reduced. By means of social and tax measures they could in part influence the wealth-distributing processes of society. The workers' movement had much to gain from trying to pacify the labour market struggle and instead fight their battles over distribution in the political field. To employers, Social Democratic control of government signified a loss. The absence of a friendly government made it impossible for them to count on their extreme weapon, the general lockout. In addition political interference in private industry could be feared from the new government. While government interventions in the labour market had generally been to the advantage of employers before, they might now be tilted in favour of employees.

In the new situation a split occurred among employers as to the strategy to be used. As the historian of Lund University, Sven Anders Söderpalm (1976), has shown in his interesting book *Direktörsklubben* (The Club of Managers), the managers of our biggest multinational firms wanted to apply a very hard line against the new government. They wanted to co-operate with the bourgeois parties, chiefly the Liberals, to establish a bourgeois government as soon as possible. The majority of the Swedish Employers' Federation, however, led by Gustaf Söderlund, believed that the Social Democratic grip on government power would last a long time. They should therefore avoid open co-operation with the bourgeois parties and rather work as a pressure group with regard to the government and the Riksdag.

The palpable lessening of the disadvantage of the workers' movement in terms of power, brought about by the firm Social Democratic control of government power, thus led to a change of strategy on the part of the two main antagonists and made them reach, in the late 1930s, what might be called a historical compromise between capital and labour. The compromise came about gradually. Its symbol was the negotiation between LO (the Confederation of Trade Unions) and SAF (the Employers' Federation) that was initiated in 1936 for the first time since the great General Strike of 1909 and which two years later led to the Saltsjöbaden Agreement. The content of the agreement was less important than its symbolic significance. The spirit of Saltsjöbaden denoted the fact that the parties of the labour market and the main antagonists in society had adopted new strategies.

The historical compromise implied that the parties should work together to increase economic growth. They were to help each other to make the cake bigger so there would be more to share. Strikes and lockouts were no longer necessary. They declined towards the end of the 1930s and hit a very low level in the postwar period. A tacit understanding implicit in the agreement was that the labour movement would avoid using government power to interfere in the relationship between the parties in the labour market. Instead it was up to the two parties themselves to regulate that relationship. The new neutrality of the state *vis-à-vis* the parties of the labour market was part of a larger agreement based on a shift of power and not, as the model of the pluralistic industrial society implies, a logical consequence of industrial development. As far as the labour movement was concerned, however, the new strategy did not necessarily imply that they renounced their longer-term political objectives. Per Albin Hansson, Ernst Wigforss and Gustav Möller seem to have considered the strategy of growth as part of a longer-term strategy to increase electoral support for the Social Democratic Party and to expedite the 'maturation' of capitalist society.

The underlying conditions for the historical compromise between capital and labour in Sweden were, first, that the difference in power resources between the principal classes had decreased to a level where the working class had a fairly stable control of government power and, secondly, that the policy implied by the compromise appeared acceptable at least in the short term to both parties. The historical compromise was successful and lasted about thirty years, from the late 1930s to the end of the 1960s. Its dissolution was brought about by its own political consequences and another shift in the balance of power.

Since the compromise was made in a situation where the working class was still at a marked disadvantage in terms of power, the policy that ensued came to yield not only positive but also negative consequences to potential Social Democratic voters. During the 1960s, the bourgeois parties, in particular the Centre Party, were increasingly successful in mobilising electoral support for their criticism of certain negative aspects and consequences of the current policies, for instance, the geographical redistribution of labour, regional imbalances, environmental issues and energy questions.

However, at the turn of the decade, when the workers' movement was forced once more to review the old compromise line, it could do so on the basis of a position of power which in important respects was better than the one it had held thirty years earlier.

The Unification of Workers

The foremost asset for workers is their organisation. It combines their small individual resources into a strong unit. The development of trade unions in a country reflects much of the readiness for action and the general outlook of its workers. To understand the unique quality of trade union development in Sweden, we must look at it in an international and historical perspective.

Table 9.1 reflects the development of trade union organisation in sixteen Western countries during this century. It gives the number of union members in each country as a percentage of the total of gainfully employed outside the agricultural sector, according to the censuses. The figures are presented as averages for four periods: from the turn of the century to the First World War, the period between the two world wars and the periods 1946–60 and 1961–76. These averages may conceal large variations within the period, but they do make the presentation easier to interpret. The great strike

Table 9.1   *Degree of Unionisation in Sixteen Western Countries, 1900–76*

Country	Before the First World War	Period Between the wars	1946–60	1961–76
Australia	30	37	52	48
Austria	6	43	54	56
Belgium	5	28	42	52
Canada	8	12	25	27
Denmark	16	34	48	50
UK	15	29	43	44
Finland	5	8	30	47
France	7	12	28	(19)
Germany	16	46	36	34
Italy	11	19	27	(18)
Netherlands	16	27	31	33
New Zealand	17	25	44	39
Norway	6	19	47	44
Sweden	11	30	65	76
Switzerland	6	15	25	22
USA	8	10	27	26

of 1909 made LO membership drop by 50 per cent, which puts Sweden more or less at the middle of the organisation table for the period preceding the First World War. By contrast, a system of obligatory conciliation introduced in Australia made the Australian figure for the period very high. New Zealand, Germany, Denmark, the Netherlands and England also had relatively high figures, whereas Belgium, Finland, Austria, Switzerland and Norway ranked low. During the next period the degree of unionisation roughly doubled. The increase was particularly strong in Austria, Belgium, Germany and Sweden. Sweden had then reached the upper third of the table.

The degree of unionisation continued to increase markedly during the first part of the period between the two wars, on average by some 50 per cent in most of the countries concerned. However, the increase was uneven. Germany did not reach the degree of unionisation it had had before the fascist period. In the Netherlands, as well, the increase was weak. Several countries, including Finland, Norway and Sweden, more than doubled their degree of unionisation. Sweden reached the top position in the table. In the course of the 1960s and 1970s unionisation stagnated in several countries. Some decrease occurred in Germany, the USA and Switzerland and a significant slump was registered in France, Italy, New Zealand, Australia and Norway. By contrast, unionisation increased in Finland and Belgium and most strongly in Sweden. During the 1960s and 1970s the Swedish wage-earners were way ahead of their 'competitors' as far as the degree of unionisation is concerned.

When Per Albin Hansson formed his (Social Democrat) Cabinet in 1932 about a third of the male industrial workers were still unorganised. The women and the salaried employees were almost entirely unorganised. During the first postwar years the male workers became almost entirely organised. The women followed suit. The organisations of salaried employees made a considerable step forward during the first years of the postwar period, but the great increase in organising them occurred only in the latter half of the 1960s. What distinguishes Sweden from the other countries is that not only industrial workers but also women and salaried employees have organised to a very high degree. This has not been the case in Norway, for instance. The swelling proportion of salaried employees and women in the labour force has therefore meant a lower degree of total unionisation in several countries. In the United States, Canada, Germany, Switzerland, the Netherlands, Italy and France a large part of the workers also remain outside the trade unions.

What then does the degree of organisation have to tell us about the attitudes of wage-earners and their readiness for action? We can observe that, contrary to what the model of the pluralistic industrial society assumes, it is not professional but class-based organisations which have become dominant among our trade unions, namely, the industrial unions within LO and the 'vertical' unions within TCO (the Swedish Confederation of Salaried Employees). This means the wage-earners do not want to use the trade unions to defend their separate professional interests but rather their collective interests as wage-earners. Within LO the unified wage policy of solidarity became truly effective only in the 1970s. Also TCO applies principles of solidarity to the pay structure. In addition, co-operation between LO and the unions of TCO improved considerably in the 1970s.

It seems therefore that the increasing degree of unionisation in Sweden reflects an increasing readiness of the great majority of Swedish wage-earners, salaried employees as well as workers, to think and act collectively in relation to the employers. An example is the wage policy adopted by the Swedish Federation of Industrial Salaried Employees (SIF) at its congress of 1978. That programme stresses that the type of work rather than the quality of the individual should be the decisive factor for salaries. This means that not even the higher employees of private industry want to retain the old individual relationship to the employer as far as salaries are concerned. Instead they seem to want to advance collectively. In conclusion, the strong increase in unionisation has thus led to an increase in the power of wage-earners and reduced their disadvantage with regard to the adversary.

Politics Shifting towards the Left

Now then, if the readiness of wage-earners to think and act collectively has increased, why is it that the socialist parties have not increased their share of the electorate at the same pace? As everybody knows, their share has floated around the 50 per cent level and in the elections of 1976 it fell clearly below that level. This difference between unionisation and political action can be explained by the fact that the trade unions are shaped according to the class structure, whereas the political parties operate along the lines of social stratification among the citizens.

The trade unions are based on the conflict of interest between employers and wage-earners. This is a stable contradiction. Few people change camps and switch from being wage-earners to being employers or vice versa. In principle the trade unions can grow until they include all wage-earners. By contrast the political parties base themselves primarily on conflicts of interest related to the social stratification of citizens. The position of the various parties on the political scale from left to right roughly corresponds to their having the bulk of their electoral backing in different parts of the social hierarchy. But the political parties can modify their programmes and their actions in such a way as to attract the greatest possible number of voters. It is logical for the two blocs to seek to obtain at least 50 per cent of the votes lest their action be limited to politics of demonstration. To accomplish this the parties may have to shift the content of their policies in one way or another. The result of these adaptations is that we keep having a roughly even distribution of voters between the two blocs.

Even though increased unionisation, which reflects the increased power of wage-earners, has not led to an overwhelming majority for the socialist bloc in the electorate it has had other palpable political effects. It has made it possible for the Social Democrats during the postwar period to shift the front lines of Swedish politics towards the left from time to time. This shift is palpable in the fields of social policy and taxation, but maybe most dramatic in the field of labour market policy. For example, during the years immediately after the Second World War the Liberals under the leadership of Bertil Ohlin could still say that Sweden should not aim at full employment since this was inflationary and could make private industry less efficient. According to bourgeois spokesmen, therefore, the desired degree of employment should be put somewhere below full employment, the defence of which was left to the Social Democrats. However, the ever-stronger Social Democratic support for full employment has driven the bourgeois parties to accept that policy. Therefore during the 'stagflation' years of the 1970s the Swedish bourgeois government pursued a much more ambitious employment policy than, for instance, the Social Democratic governments of Germany and England were able to do. In the United States, where wage-earners have a very weak position, President Carter could at the same period write off unemployment as a serious social problem once the unemployment figures had come down to 5 per cent, a staggeringly high figure by Swedish standards. By contrast the bourgeois Swedish government had to devote large resources to keeping unemployment below 2 per cent since it realised that the judgement of the electorate would otherwise be severe.

The Dissolution of the Compromise

The dissolution of the historical compromise in the 1970s, symbolised by the withdrawal of LO from the Saltsjöbaden Agreement in connection with the adoption of the law on co-determination in 1976, was a consequence of the fact that the conditions for the previous strategy of compromise had been removed or at least weakened. Part of the background was the international economic crisis, which drastically reduced economic growth and made old-style welfare policies more difficult. Another important factor was that the previous strategy had had a few consequences which had provoked political resistance. As indicated previously, the Centrists since the late 1960s have been able to mobilise voters against a number of drawbacks in the strategy of growth. Even in the workplaces resistance was felt to some of the consequences of that strategy, such as stress, layoffs, piecework wages, unsatisfactory jobs, and risks of the working environment. The big mining strike of 1969–70 and the forestry workers' strike of 1974 were two clear instances of protest where such issues were central.

But the increasing power of wage-earners also turned conditions which previously had been accepted as natural into important problems. Wage-earners began more and more to look at their subordinate position in the workplace with consciously critical eyes. Furthermore, the demands of wage-earners were extended to bear on the distribution of wealth and economic power in society. The demands for greater influence of wage-earners in the workplace could not be satisfied by the usual method of negotiation. This being so, LO abandoned its previous line that the state should stay neutral and avoid interfering with the relationship between the contracting parties of the labour market. Instead LO now wished to use the political power controlled by the Social Democrats in government and the Riksdag in order to obtain by legislation what could not be obtained by negotiation. As a response to these demands from the wage-earners and LO, the Social Democratic Party in the early 1970s initiated a series of laws which strengthened the position of wage-earners in the workplace. Now that the factors underlying the earlier compromise were no longer present, those laws broke up something which in the model of the pluralistic industrial society is considered an important criterion of social maturity, namely, the distinction between political and economic conflicts.

But perhaps the most farreaching initiatives towards social change in the 1970s stemmed from the urge to solve the fundamental problems of organising and securing the livelihood of the citizens. The historical compromise had meant, among other things, that living standards were to be improved and employment secured by providing private industry with broad opportunities for expansion. This was done, for example, by various tax breaks for companies as well as subsidies financed by taxation. The solidaristic wage policy also helped provide the most profitable enterprises with scope for expansion. These policies contributed to accelerate the concentration of capital in private industry. During the 1960s there was a wave of mergers which further concentrated the already strongly centralised economic power.

Wage-earners for a long time accepted this as a necessary

prerequisite for economic growth and secure employment. But as the strategy of compromise was being scrutinised during the 1970s the strengthened power of wage-earners led to a change in their views of what was right and equitable. They began to see the ever-stronger concentration of economic power in private industry as a central problem. The proposal for wage-earners' funds must be seen against that background. As a condition for their support for a policy which would create economic conditions for industrial expansion so as to secure employment, the wage-earners demanded that they share in the wealth created by them and have a share of the economic power that goes with it. A proportion of company profits to be reserved in the form of shares, and constituting wage-earners' controlled funds, is what they proposed as a method for obtaining a long-term shift in the distribution of industrial power.

Where Are the Wage-Earners Heading?

The future is determined by an elusive interaction between many factors and is therefore notoriously difficult to predict. We can nevertheless speculate a little about future changes in what we have assumed to be a central factor of social development, namely, the distribution of power resources between wage-earners on the one hand and employers and their allies on the other. This is of great importance to our way of dealing with the central problem which has once more become so difficult to solve, namely, that of maintaining our standard of living and full employment. We shall limit ourselves here even further and only discuss the question of how wage-earners' co-operation can be expected to develop within the not-too-distant future.

For wage-earners as a whole co-operation is rational since it increases their power against the employers. For individuals and groups, however, it may – at least in the short run – be rational to go it alone and seek a privileged position as compared to other wage-earners. There is therefore always a tension among wage-earners between tendencies to collective and individual action. The relation of strength between these opposed tendencies depends partly on which issues are in the focus of the political struggle, that is, in which field the political battle will take place. Some fields are conducive to cohesion among wage-earners while others tend to split them up. Wage-earners can be united on issues of primary concern to them. Full employment is one such issue. Almost all wage-earners stand to gain, directly or indirectly, from full employment. Issues such as the influence of wage-earners in the workplace and in society are other examples where they can unite against the employers. By contrast the issues of distribution of income, such as marginal taxes, have a splintering effect since it is much more difficult to find a solution to them which will satisfy all wage-earners. The political strategists' manoeuvres to decide where the political battle is to be fought can therefore partly affect its outcome.

We have assumed that the demands of wage-earners for influence on the workplaces and a less inequitable distribution of power and influence in private industry reflect the relative strengthening of their power during the postwar period. This has led to what some economists call too low a tolerance with regard to corporate profits sufficiently high to secure industrial expansion. A logical way to increase the tolerance of wage-earners with regard to high corporate profits is therefore to split and weaken them as a group. Thereby wage-earners' demands would gradually be lowered and their view on what is just and equitable be modified. Perhaps the easiest way to weaken the wage-earners' cohesion is to attack the still rather new and vulnerable co-operation between LO and TCO. The parties in government have considerable opportunities for doing this, as was demonstrated by the tax proposals of the Liberal government in the spring of 1979.

But unless the cohesion and striking power of wage-earners are weakened their view of what is just and equitable will be such that their tolerance of high corporate profits will be too low. Propaganda and moralism may for a while hold back their demands but cannot be expected to do so in the long run. If the strength of wage-earners can be maintained we must therefore expect that they will seek solutions which combine the preservation of living standards and full employment with a lessening of the present concentration of power in private industry. It must be considered probable that such a solution can be brought about in ways which do not weaken or threaten democracy but rather strengthen and expand it. The notion that changes in present ownership patterns of private industry would threaten social pluralism is based on arguments according to which history has all but concluded its course and the best of capitalist democracies have come close to the final goal of social development. This may, after all, be too presumptuous a supposition.

If the cohesion of wage-earners and thus their relative power are maintained and strengthened we must expect that the endeavours to solve the old problems of a secure standard of living and full employment will lead to proposals which will question important tenets of our present society. We can therefore assume that the wage-earners remain a force for social change. The methods of making decisions for social change, however, are likely to be similar to those we have been used to, debates within organisations and between political parties, elections, systematic preparation of legislation with active contributions from competent authorities and concerned pressure groups, and parliamentary decisions by the Riksdag.

Notes: Chapter 9

1 Researchers of various disciplines have contributed to the model of the pluralistic industrial society. Among the main contributors are Dahrendorf (1959), Kerr *et al.* (1973), Moore (1951), Galbraith (1967), Lipset (1960), and Dahl (1961). Even though there are considerable differences of opinion between the authors thus classified as champions of the model, they nevertheless agree on several of the basic notions of the model.
2 The quotes are from Lerner (1958, p. 64) and Lipset (1960, pp. 403 and 406).
3 A more extensive discussion of Swedish developments can be found in Korpi (1978).
4 The development of labour conflicts in Western countries during the present century is more extensively discussed in Korpi and Shalev (1979).

References: Chapter 9

Dahl, R. A. (1961) *Who Governs? Democracy and Power in an American City* (New Haven, Conn., Yale University Press).
Dahrendorf, R. (1959), *Class and Class Conflict in Industrial Society* (Stanford, Calif., Stanford University Press).
Galbraith, J. K. (1967), *The New Industrial State* (New York, Signet Books).
Kerr, C., *et al.* (1973), *Industrialism and Industrial Man* (Harmondsworth, Penguin).
Korpi, W. (1978), *The Working Class in Welfare Capitalism: Work Unions and Politics in Sweden* (London, Routledge & Kegan Paul).
Korpi, W. and Shalev, M. (1979), 'Strikes, power and politics in the Western nations, 1900–1976', *Political Power and Social Theory*, vol. 1, no. 1.
Lerner, D. (1958), *The Passing of Traditional Society* (New York, Free Press).
Lipset, S. M. (1960), *Political Man* (London, Mercury Books).
Moore, W. E. (1951), *Industrialization and Labor* (Ithaca, Cornell University Press).
Schmidt, F. (1968), *Tjänsteavtalet* (Stockholm, Norstedt).
Söderpalm, S. A. (1976), *Direktörsklubben – Storindustrin i svensk politik under 1930- och 1940-talen* (Stockholm, Prisma).

10

Towards a Labour-Managed Sweden?

BO SÖDERSTEN

The Swedish economy has been subjected to considerable stress during the 1970s. Some of the difficulties have been caused by international factors. The oil crisis led to a redistribution of income and an increase in global savings. This in turn had a strongly depressing effect on the international economy. Internal factors have also contributed to the deviation of the Swedish economy. The development of wages has been very uneven in the 1970s. During the first years of the decade wages rose slightly. Then followed a very steep rise during 1975 and 1976. Since then nominal wages have risen only by a few per cent while real wages have gone down. Moreover industrial investments during a period of fifteen years (starting in 1963) have had a slow pace of growth and in later years they have fallen considerably. At the same time housing investment has decreased and the total savings ratio of the economy has diminished by 25 per cent. In spite of this our country has borrowed more than 40 billion crowns abroad over the last few years in order to finance investments. These are all well-known facts. I am sure one can find an explanation and a cure for each one of them. The real question is whether there are not deeper explanations for the *malaise* that bedevils the Swedish economy. Maybe the solutions are not to be found in the kind of measures economists normally discuss. Maybe we have to look at certain institutional and structural obstacles to expansion that may be embedded in the Swedish economy? In this essay I shall try to do that by describing an alternative to our present economic system.

Every economic system works according to a kind of inner logic. In our present economic system profit plays a central role. Production is organised by a company. Capital is offered in a market and cleared at a price, interest. In order to survive companies must allocate the resources they use in such a way as to be able to pay wages and interest on capital according to the norms established by the market. The existence of a profit guarantees that this will be the case. The role of the profit is primarily to guarantee that resources are allocated efficiently.

An alternative economic system must also be organised in such a way as to work according to some kind of inner logic. An alternative presented in international literature is that of a labour-managed market economy. From certain points of view the difference between a capitalist-managed market economy and a labour-managed market economy may seem small. While in the former companies will maximise their profits, in the latter they are presumed to maximise their income per employee. But this distinction alone causes important differences in the way companies act even in the short term. When you go into other aspects, such as the role of capital and the form and importance of incentives in the two systems, the differences become more evident.

The way in which production is organised is also important to other aspects of society. It influences the orientation and tasks of the public sector. The tax structure will depend to a great extent on how economic life is organised. There is a tendency in public debate to disregard the fact that an economic system must be considered as a consistent whole. People imagine that it is possible to combine at will elements of different systems, to 'pick the best' of every system. This is not a very realistic view; it is not possible to have an efficient capitalist market economy without profit as a carrot or without the inequalities it creates. Against this background I shall discuss a few essential qualities of a labour-managed economy as an alternative to our present economic system.

The discussion of labour-managed companies and a labour-managed economy does present a theoretical interest but it also offers insights of practical relevance. Someone who is favourable to the idea of wage-earners' funds can hardly avoid taking a strong interest in their logical conclusion: the labour-managed economy. During the 1970s the Swedish labour market has undergone important changes. Security of employment has been improved by the Åman Laws; it has become more difficult and more expensive for companies to fire people. Board representation for employees and the introduction of the law on co-determination have also strengthened the position of wage-earners. Many academic economists and enterprise representatives have criticised the new laws, emphasising that they make the economy function less well; that the mobility of the workforce and the adaptability of companies are diminishing. But these reforms give all employees greater security and influence and contribute to the view of the workforce of a company as something cohesive and permanent. Precisely such qualities are typical of the labour-managed enterprise. We are thus already moving towards a new system with many of the characteristics of labour-management. Therefore we have practical reasons to discuss the qualities of a labour-managed economy. Against this background it is remarkable that so little interest has so far been shown in these questions.

In the present essay I shall first examine some fundamental characteristics of the labour-managed economy. Secondly, I intend to examine alternatives such as companies managed jointly by capital, labour and the state. I also mean to show how the principles of labour management can be generalised into comprising the public sector and, finally, I shall add a few remarks on the alternatives we are facing.

Some Fundamental Characteristics of Labour Management

The fundamental decision unit in a capitalist company consists of capital-owners and managers. They are the monitors who lead and distribute work; in a capitalist economy it is capital which hires labour. Laws and regulations can limit the traditional rights of management. Nevertheless it is true that the right to decide rests ultimately with corporate management which is responsible to the shareholders. In a labour-managed company it is labour that hires capital. The ultimate responsibility rests with the 'employees'. Everybody has the same degree of influence. The fundamental principle is one man, one vote. In this sense, labour-management represents economic democracy. It is then natural to imagine that the 'employees' will form a collective, looking at themselves as a cohesive unit. The collective that shapes the enterprise is the strength of a labour-managed company but at the same time its weakness.

A community is always defined in relation to something outside it. This is what gives community its meaning. Labour management rests on the fundamental idea that work is essential to human life. Those who form a team, a company, to work and produce, must all have the same degree of influence on the team/company. This is why only those who are members of the team can exert influence on it. Outsiders, be they capital-owners, consumers, or representatives of the state or the local community, cannot be given the same degree of influence. A company can have potential sources of conflict with society. A company may also need supervision in order to protect the interests of consumers and other legitimate interests. This does not change the fact that, ultimately, only work can qualify for influence.

In the last few years we have seen the labour force take the shape of a fixed or constant factor in the companies. The latter hesitate to fire employees even during a recession. Efforts of the public sector reinforce this. The laws on security of employment make companies less likely to fire their personnel. The state offers subsidies (such as the twenty-five-crown subsidy and stock support) to make companies retain their employees even though sales and production are down. This kind of measure and the labour viewpoint it represents do not fit into a capitalist pattern of organisation. On the contrary they must be considered obstacles to rational company activity. However, they do point in the direction of labour-management. In the labour-managed economy we can expect the number of employees to become more of a constant unit. There are several reasons for this. One of them has to do with the rule of optimisation that it is reasonable to apply to a labour-managed company. It is natural to assume that employees will try to maximise income per employee (see Vanek, 1970, Meade, 1972, and Södersten, 1973). They try to get as big a surplus to share as possible after paying the cost of raw materials and interest on rented capital, and after correct depreciations. The residual is then shared between the employees as their income. How this distribution is to be made is their own business. It is thus not at all necessary to share it equally. It is more probable that the residual will be shared according to some rule that more demanding, responsible or heavy jobs, or jobs that need special education or special skills, should be better paid than easy and comfortable tasks.

To maximise profits is not the same thing as maximising income per employee. The easiest way to illustrate this is to show how a company reacts to a price increase on the goods it produces. A profit-maximising company will employ more workers and increase production. In a labour-managed company employees normally have an interest in having as many people as possible working in the factory, since they have to outweigh the fixed costs of the machines. But the fewer people are employed in the company, the higher will be the value of production per employee with a given machine equipment. If the price rises, then, the latter tendency will dominate. It will be profitable to cut down the number of employees as the price goes up, for then the average income will be higher than otherwise. Therefore the supply of a labour-managed company will be rather insensitive to price changes. This may lead to short-term inertia in a labour-managed economy and a lack of adaptation to changing conditions of production, as compared to a profit-maximising economy.

This mechanism is important. However, there may be other reasons why a labour-managed economy may be preferable to a capitalist profit-maximising economy. In order to shed some more light on the differences between the two systems, I shall now undertake a discussion of the role of capital.

The Role of Capital under Labour Management

As we looked at the role of labour and the different optimisation norms that prevail under capital management and labour management, respectively, the difference between the two systems may not have seemed very important. However, it is absolute as far as the role of capital is concerned. Private ownership of productive capital cannot exist in a purely labour-managed economy. The only thing that qualifies for influence is work. It is therefore logical that capital should be owned collectively. However, ultimate ownership of capital must be the privilege of society as a whole, for example, by means of a social fund or a number of regional funds. But the right to dispose of capital being used in the individual company is the privilege of the single labour collective. This is an important distinction.

Capital will remain an important factor of production in a labour-managed economy. It has to be allocated according to criteria of economic efficiency. The method that comes to mind most easily is that labour-managed companies that need capital will rent it from the social fund. In exchange they will have to pay a certain annual rent (interest). The interest rate will be decided by supply and demand. The right to dispose of that rented capital, however, will pertain exclusively to the company. It decides how the capital is to be used. It will also receive the direct dividend of that capital. If the capital is invested in a competent manner, so that it yields a higher dividend than the rent exacted by the market, then this extra dividend will go to the employees of that company.

The problem of capital accumulation is elegantly solved in a labour-managed economy. The bulk of capital income will go to the public owners of capital (the social fund). Suppose the ratio of total capital stock and national income is 3:1. If national income is 400 billion crowns then the total capital stock is worth 1,200 billion. Suppose, further, that the rent for capital is 8 per cent. Then 24 per cent of national income, or 96 billion crowns, will go to public purposes in the form of capital income. This income can be used in many different ways. The natural way is for capital income to go back to production by financing new investment. We can assume that the optimal savings ratio of the Swedish economy of the 1980s will be around 25 per cent of national income. Public ownership of productive capital, in combination with a reasonable pricing of the resource that capital use represents, could thus solve the problems of savings and capital accumulation in a labour-managed Sweden of the future.

Several factors indicate that labour-managed companies may wish to self-finance part of their investment. Modern factories and machines are often the best guarantee for innovation and hence the best guarantee against unemployment. It is probable, therefore, that labour-managed companies would put part of their surplus into new investment. From the point of view of innovation this may be desirable. However, it may be doubtful from the point of view of distribution of income, since company employees who own part of the capital will receive part of the income from that capital. Since that income comes on top of their income from work, this may easily lead to employees of self-financed companies receiving a higher salary than those of other companies.

Capital supply may also come from sources other than public ones. Household bank savings will also exist in a labour-managed economy. There is no reason to try to influence the buying pattern of households over time.

Incentives and Technological Progress

The fundamental driving forces behind demands for labour-management have to do with the position of employees. In traditional, monitored, capitalist companies employees are considered as separate from management, whose main task it is to supervise the employees, judge their performance and see to it that they receive a salary according to their performance. Employees themselves are regarded as mere factors of input whose main motivation is some kind of performance-related salary.

In a labour-managed company, however, employees are given another role. Here they are considered in principle as equal, regardless of the function they fulfil; here the manager and the errand boy have the same degree of influence, since the only thing that qualifies for influence is work and the principle of one man, one vote. In real life, however, one may have to admit that experts – and the management mandated by employees – will presumably have a greater influence than that of the average member of the labour collective. But no particular education is necessary to be part of the labour council that ultimately has the governing function of the company. These different principles must give rise to different structures of incentive.

In a capitalist, profit-maximising company there is usually little reason for an employee to make an extra effort. Of course he may be proud of his good performance. And he must probably comply with certain minimum requirements in order to keep his job. But every extra effort on his part will primarily benefit the company in the form of increased profit. This can be partly counterbalanced by piecework pay. However, experience shows that piecework is not a very attractive form of wages, not least because it is often difficult to apply in a just and effective manner. This is why there is a trend towards other forms of wages. In any case the problem of incentives includes other elements than wages. In a labour-managed company it is the employees who are collectively responsible for the development of the company. If someone makes an extra effort he will also benefit from part of the increased residual thereby produced. This is most evident in the case of the small company, or the one-man company (for example, the landowning farmer). The one-man enterprise decides alone on working speed and effort. He is free to weigh leisure against income. Every improvement or useful innovation he can make will benefit him.

The one-man enterprise is of course an extreme case. Large-scale economies will require that labour-managed companies are of a certain size. We shall then encounter something economists call the $1/n$ problem. Suppose n persons are employed in a labour-managed company. If one of them makes an extra effort he will still receive a certain proportion of the result of that effort, that is, $1/n$ of the total increase. The larger the number of employees (n), the smaller his share. Therefore there will be a limit to personal incentives in the labour-managed company as well.

Still, there is a considerable difference in the structure of incentives between a capitalist profit-maximising company and a labour-managed company. In the latter, employees will know they alone are responsible for the result. This is a strong incentive to make an effort. Social control will be a positive factor. If someone goes slow under labour management he takes a piece from the common cake. If someone goes slow under capitalism, he primarily takes from the residual that goes to the owners. It is probable that employees will control and stimulate each other in a labour-managed company. True enough, the $1/n$ problem can make itself felt if the company is large, but it is always possible to present the accounts of the company in smaller parts, every one of which will be responsible for its performance.

Co-determination and self-management have an intrinsic value. It is probable that a degree of co-determination can have a direct positive influence on production. In addition, co-determination itself is rewarding. It is therefore probable that co-determination will be carried further than strictly production-oriented arguments would justify. Technical innovation is closely tied to the issue of co-determination. Technical progress and education, together with capital accumulation, are the strongest driving forces of economic development. Also the quality of technical progress is of great importance to the distribution of income. In the capitalist, profit-maximising company it is natural to invest primarily in technology of a low labour intensity, that is, innovations which raise the yield of capital and facilitate substitution of machines for labour. By contrast employees under labour management will seek innovations that raise the productivity of labour *and* capital. We can expect them to invest primarily in technology of low capital intensity, that is, innovations that raise the marginal productivity of labour in absolute terms. The reason is that such innovations will facilitate the employment of more people while at the same time raising the salaries of those already employed. In conclusion, this structure of incentives can be expected to be different under labour management than under capitalism. This advantage inherent in labour management can be important in the long run.

The efficiency of the educational system of Western industrialised countries has been subject to criticism in the last few years. It has been pointed out that their educational systems are used as instruments of categorisation rather than vehicles for the teaching of positive and useful knowledge (Arrow, 1973, and Stiglitz, 1975). In a labour-managed economy schools would presumably be less inclined to apply categorisation and income distribution criteria to the education they provide. At present it is quite possible that the social yield of categorisation may be negative, while the private yield for certain individuals may be positive. In a labour-managed economy, where the majority principle rules, it is difficult to imagine that a minority could impose on the majority an educational system which would be disadvantageous to the latter. It is more probable that schools in a labour-managed economy will focus on giving students knowledge relevant to their future contributions to production, while the aspect of categorisation will play a less prominent part (Södersten, 1976). Another weakness of capitalist education is that education within the company threatens to be less than adequate. Companies hesitate to invest in education since their employees frequently move somewhere else after completing their education. In fact that specific, company-related education is inadequate is well known from economic literature (Becker, 1964).

As pointed out previously, we can expect employee loyalty to the company to be strengthened under labour management while average employment time will increase and mobility of labour decrease. It will then be more profitable to invest in company-related education. The difference between the social and private economic yield of education tends to diminish; the labour force will be better educated and the companies more efficient.

Plan and Market under Labour Management

Fundamentally, the labour-managed economy is a market economy. The individual companies will act on a market and compete with one another. The key word of labour-management is self-determination. Let us imagine a number of companies of different size and character managed by those who work in them. In a labour-managed economy power is decentralised. Democracy in the economic context means a possibility to influence one's own conditions of work and production. Therefore individual collectives of employees must have a high degree of autonomy. They can have that only if they act as individual decision-making units in a market. Decisions on the organisation of production, wages and work conditions must therefore be the privilege of the individual collective of wage-earners. They will have the sovereign right to make decisions in the economic sphere.

In addition to the economic sphere there is the political one. It comprises problems of importance to society as a whole. This is where the laws and regulations are adopted that establish the framework for the economic sphere. The power to decide over the political sphere belongs to the parliament and the government. There is an area where the economic and political spheres inter-relate in a decisive manner. It comprises the investments of a company and other decisions that have implications for its future size, orientation, location, and so on. This is where the two spheres unite. Figure 10.1 illustrates what we can call a sphere of planning. The signals of the market will orient the day-to-day decisions of the companies. As far as the future is concerned, however, market information is insufficient. At the same time investment decisions affect the functioning of the economy as a whole.

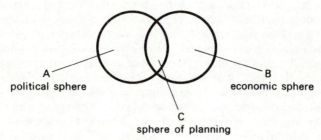

Figure 10.1   *The sphere of planning*

This problem is particularly important in a small country such as Sweden. Investment decisions by a small number of large Swedish companies have a decisive effect on the functioning of the Swedish economy. At the same time the propensity to invest depends on the economic policies pursued by the state. This is an interesting and important problem of general balance for which the structure of economic organisation is highly relevant.

During a number of years investment trends in the Swedish economy have been unsatisfactory. In many sectors innovation has been slow or non-existent. The overall savings rate has decreased significantly, from 26 per cent of GNP in the mid-1960s to less than 20 per cent in the last few years. In my opinion this trend must be explained to a considerable extent by the tension between attitudes and political objectives on the one hand and the structure of economic organisation on the other. Traditionally, Swedish industry has to a large degree been able to finance its own investments. A precondition has been a relatively high level of profits. The desire for a high level of profits has run counter to the concept of the desirability of economic equality that has prevailed in broad layers of the population. This has constituted a contradiction which has been detrimental to investment as well as expansion. At times it has expressed itself in conflicts of fateful consequence to efficiency. A good example is the wage explosion of 1975–6 following the good profits of 1974.

This problem is still making itself felt. The Royal Commission of 1978 on Long-Term Economic Trends is very optimistic as regards the potential for industrial expansion and increased exports. On the other hand it depicts the margins for a rise in private consumption as rather limited. The assets created by industrial expansion should primarily benefit our industrial companies. Their profits in 1983, according to the calculations of the commission, should be 18 billion crowns higher than in 1977. We have every reason to question the political feasibility of such a development. In principle one can imagine four different ways to raise the rate of savings and thus create the conditions for increased investment. One possibility is to pursue a strict financial policy and thus create public savings, another is to increase the profits of industry in order for companies to finance their own expansion. A third option is some kind of wage-earners' fund arrangement, by which employees hand over part of the wage total for the purpose of capital accumulation. The fourth alternative is borrowing abroad.

It will probably be necessary to opt for a combination of the alternatives mentioned. Simply to raise the level of profits would not be politically acceptable. The existing economic structure makes that alternative unattractive to large groups. It is after all a matter of large wage-earning groups having to restrain their consumption. The balance between consumption and savings must presumably be different in the next few years from what it has been in recent years. It is hardly reasonable to demand that the large wage-earning groups should accept such restraint in consumption without receiving something in exchange. Against this background the alternative of wage-earners' funds will grow more relevant in the years to come.

Increased co-operation between state and industry for investment and industrial innovation seems inevitable. Such co-operation is difficult to bring about; we have heard disquieting noises from the co-operation mechanism throughout the postwar period. An alliance between the state and labour-managed companies must appear as much more natural. An important reason is that the objectives of a privately owned company are defined by specific, private interests; capital-owners and managers have too much power and their interests do not always coincide with those of employees. Let me mention a few present conflicts which would be overcome by a change to labour management. Every sector has an 'optimal technology' comprising the most advanced methods of production. But the diffusion of new methods is often slow. It can be decades before the most retarded companies of a sector even know about the availability of new technology.[1]

Labour-managed companies are based on the principle of solidarity between all the people who work in a company. It should be possible to stretch out that principle to include even those who work in other companies. This principle of solidarity is after all already a cornerstone of the unified wage policy today. It should be possible to make labour-managed companies share their knowledge with others. In the short term even such a company might have an interest in keeping certain information secret. In the longer run, however, labour-managed companies will have so much of a common interest that knowledge of new processes and methods can be diffused more quickly and effectively than now.

A change to labour-managed companies should facilitate much new information which could lay the foundation for a high and even rate of growth in industrial investment and production as well as for a planned structural adaptation. But the important problem of how to create new market entries, introduce new sectors of production or promote large-scale innovative investment is not automatically solved by a change to labour-management. The environment, however, for co-operation between the state and the enterprises will be transformed. State support will be more natural and effective when it is granted within the framework of a labour-managed economy; it no longer leads primarily to profit for a limited group of owners. Instead it aims at creating employment and strengthening or establishing strong companies in regions that need support in order to survive.

There are several reasons why the application of exclusively microeconomic criteria in a market economy such as Sweden's does not necessarily lead to a macroeconomic optimum. I have already mentioned the problem of information; research and development are normally inadequate in a private capitalist economy, and the diffusion of information between companies is ineffective. This has to do with the fact that scientific findings are essentially a collective utility. The use of particular knowledge by a company does not prevent other companies from using the same knowledge. Therefore knowledge must be put at the disposal of everybody. We know this is not the case under present conditions. On the contrary, individual companies have a great interest in preventing the diffusion of exclusive knowledge of production and marketing methods. An additional reason for the prevailing lack of macroeconomic optimum has to do with private and public economic functions being separate. The state has to consider certain external effects a private company need not take into account. A good example is dependence on the international sector. We cannot channel our foreign trade too one-sidedly lest we run too great a risk of wartime isolation, trade blockades and economic warfare. We saw some examples of this during the oil crisis of 1973.

The use of domestic raw materials should also be planned so as to reach optimum investment in industries depending on them. Certain resources, such as forests, are limited. The expansion of an industry with the forests as their commodity base must therefore take place in an organised manner and the resource be used in a systematic way. This has not been the case in the postwar period. It is also natural that we should strive to process our own raw materials to the greatest possible degree. It is a fundamental principle of state industrial policy that we should choose investment projects that correspond to domestic relative factor prices. Wages are high in Sweden. This reflects primarily the fact that Swedish labour is highly productive and well educated. We must therefore choose investments which are skill- and labour-intensive. We must concentrate on projects which use advanced technology but are not necessarily capital-intensive.

Generally speaking it should be easier to solve the problem of investment under labour management than under capital-owner management. Wage-earners can be assumed to be much more willing to accept a higher level of public savings if it is used to finance the expansion of labour-managed companies. Increased co-operation between state and industry will also be warranted in order to solve the problems of industrial innovation in the future. On the other hand co-operation between the state and private capitalist companies is problematic. Co-operation with labour-managed companies can be more effective and create fewer conflicts, especially as far as the equalisation of income and wealth is concerned.

Participatory Companies – an Alternative?

An economic system constitutes a logical entity which has to be governed by reasonable economic criteria. This view, however, is not accepted by everyone. Especially people with a sociology or political science orientation tend to look at the economic system –

and, for that matter, at the individual company – as part of a power structure. From that point of view it is tempting to consider our system 'constitutionally' incorrect or ineffective. It does not concede influence to all the groups that should be entitled to it. According to this view, the influence of groups now marginal to the system should be amplified. It is frequently advanced that two elements which are marginal at present, the wage-earners and government, must be given a larger measure of influence. What we should have, they say, is tripartite co-operation. In such a model a company should be led by representatives of the owners, the employees and the government.

Such proposals may seem practical, reasonable and just. Capital-owners should not lose all their power, only move over. Further-more management is conceived of as an entity opposed to the employees. This, after all, is something we are used to in the present system. From this perspective the proposal appears truly reformist; you just take a relatively short step away from the present organisation structure, even though this step – as it must appear to all progressive persons – is in the right direction.

It is evident that companies are dependent on the government and vice versa. Why then should not the government have its representatives within the companies? The project of participatory management runs counter to the principle that an economic structure constitutes a logical entity and must perform according to clear-cut economic criteria. This is fairly evident if you examine the criteria according to which the participatory company should work. Which optimum should it seek? It is impossible to maximise profit, income per employee and some vaguely defined public interest at the same time. The company needs an unequivocal guiding principle and we must choose *one* that we find suitable. On a more practical level we might ask ourselves: who should represent the public interest in the direction of the company? Presumably it would have to be some kind of bureaucrat. How can a company work efficiently if it has to have bureaucrats exercising some kind of controlling function within it?

The idea that economic systems are entities composed of inter-related variables and that every economic system has to be guided by simple criteria of efficiency is fundamental in economic thinking. A great number of the misunderstandings caused by economic analysis have to do with the fact that people in general find it hard to accept these propositions as fundamental to any economic argument. Desiderata of how the economic system 'should' be are therefore often irrelevant, precisely because they disregard the fact that an economic system has to be shaped in such a way as to correspond to its own fundamental conditions. The idea that the public interest should be directly represented in the individual company is caused by ideological myopia. It is enough that politics and economy are interconnected. But the relationship is not such that they should be connected on the company level. On the contrary it is very important to distinguish between an economic and a political sphere. Their activities should in principle be separated. Only in one respect do they necessarily interrelate: with regard to investment and company expansion.

The idea of a participatory enterprise is thus not a fruitful one. One cannot judge economic activities in a constitutional perspective shaped by political science or sociology. An economic system has to be constructed in such a way as to meet reasonable criteria of efficiency.

Wage-Earners' Funds and Labour Management

The most politically relevant proposal for a change in our economic system presented so far is that of LO (the Confederation of Trade Unions) and the Social Democratic Party for wage-earners' funds. How does that proposal relate to the idea of a labour-managed economy? The project adopted by the LO congress of 1976 had an evident element of hesitation. One reason was that it feared that labour management might not be consistent with a wage policy of solidarity. Part of the doubts also stemmed from fear that individual labour-managed companies would be 'company egotistic', that is, the individual wage-earners' collective would not show solidarity with the larger wage-earners' collective.

On the other hand the individual wage-earners' collective would have a fairly strong position according to the LO project as well. This is because the project would give the first 20 per cent of the wage-earner vote in the company to the local union representatives. It would then be the trade union representatives of the local wage-earners' collective that would be the first to have their power increased, according to the project. In addition the person to exercise the next 20 per cent of the voting right could be appointed only after having been accepted by the local wage-earners' collective. In the proposal put forward by the working group of LO and the Social Democratic Party in February 1978, that project was slightly modified. Influence was to be shared equally between local wage-earners and regional representatives up to 40 per cent of the voting rights; beyond that the increase would go to a so-called regional parliament.

It follows that the project for wage-earners' funds has been rather ambiguous as far as labour management is concerned. It is true that the tasks of the trade unions would be different in a labour-managed economy. It is also understandable that it would put the unified wage policy under strain. But we must not make the good the enemy of the best. Wage-earners' chances of influence would of course be much greater under labour management than under capitalism. The possibilities of equalising income would also be quite different from what they are today. All significant capital income under labour management would go to the public owners of capital (or households having bank accounts). This income is easy to control. Other income would be predominantly income of work in labour-managed companies. These would also be easy to control. One could therefore conceive a tax system much more effective than under capitalism. This is yet another reason why the potential for equalisation would be different. In addition the structure of incentives would be different. One would not have to take the interests of any capital-owners into account.

The projects for wage-earners' funds so far presented all give a strong position to the local wage-earners' collective. This is undeniably a step towards labour management. It is only natural; it would hardly be possible to outline a system for wage-earners' funds which did not strengthen the role of employees in the individual company. Nevertheless there are a number of ambiguities and dubious elements in the projects presented so far. As far as I can see they have to do with the authors' doubts of the capacity of the individual wage-earners' collective to manage its own company. This is why the projects have become complex and difficult to explain. For example, the introduction of regional representative bodies has given the impression of opacity and artificiality.

The projects have had two aspects, one of influence or power, another of capital accumulation. According to the proponents' political view, one aspect or the other can be emphasised more. It seems inevitable that wage-earner capital will be needed in the future to finance economic development. And it is natural that influence should accompany that investment. However, the projects for wage-earners' funds have been floating in the air since they have not been based on a thorough analysis of economic systems. A truly logical argument for wage-earners' funds must, as I see it, be advanced against the background of a general desire for a decentralised, labour-managed economy. It is all reasonable as soon as you see the proposal as a solution to the problem of capital accumulation and at the same time as a move towards growing influence for wage-earners, which would dissolve the knots and contradictions that are the hallmark of our present system. Only when short-term reforms are presented in a perspective of long-term social change in the direction of labour management can we build up an effective argument for wage-earners' funds.

Labour Management and the Public Sector

We have so far assumed that labour-managed companies will operate in a market in the same way as capital-managed companies. However, the public sector has grown strongly in the postwar period. Does a system of labour management have any relevance for the organisation of the public sector?

The key concept of labour management is self-determination. That principle is of course not limited to companies operating in the market. Admittedly the principles of labour management have been elaborated with such companies in mind, but the fundamental principles of self-determination are applicable to the public sector as well. In order to apply them we must first define the public sector correctly. Several public companies act in the market or under conditions strongly reminiscent of those valid for the market. In this category are most public utilities including local ones such as energy and waste disposal; in short, those which provide well defined products or services. There is no difficulty in organising such companies as labour-managed companies. In some instances they appear so clearly under market conditions that the analogy to the labour-managed market-oriented company is complete. In other cases conditions may be different without prejudice to fundamental principles. The point is to define as clearly as possible the products and services expected of them. In most cases this should not cause any serious problem.

A hospital, for instance, has to provide a certain number of health care services of a certain quality. The buyer, in this case the regional assembly *(landsting)*, will then define the demands for these services and calculate the cost they would entail during a given period. It is then for the labour-managed hospital to decide on its own organisation, on how the daily production of services is to be organised, on the wage scale for employees, and so on. The hospital should obviously be organised along the principles of a labour-managed company and we must assume that employees will seek to maximise income (or more generally the well-being and the wages that their work provides) in the usual way. To the extent that no market pricing is possible, it is up to the controlling authority (the regional assembly) to try to buy the services as cheaply as possible, with due consideration to reasonable demands for quality.

In a similar way the tax administration can be converted into a labour-managed company. The government, and possibly the local authorities, will then buy the tax-controlling services from the labour-managed tax administration. The latter has to 'deliver' a tax scrutiny of a certain quality and the government pays for it, while looking after reasonable citizen demands for legal guarantees. The tax administration will collect a lump sum fee from the government.

The organisation of its activities will be the privilege of its employees, applying the principles governing labour-managed companies.

The expansion of the public sector seems to have taken place in a partly uncontrolled manner. It is unclear whether important parts of the public sector really meet reasonable demands for efficiency. Public administration seems to devote an irrational proportion of its time to producing information for internal use; in the absence of reasonable criteria for the efficiency of the public sector, it tends to maximise size; the growth of the number of employees in various sectors of the administration turns into a goal *per se* (Ståhl, 1977). The ideas of labour management or self-determination are based on decentralisation and on the fundamental distinction between the political and the economic sphere. With regard to the expansion of the public sector the latter distinction has not been maintained. Bureaucracies have been allowed to grow as *ad hoc* solutions to political problems (cf. the unfettered expansion of university administrations during the 1970s in connection with a stagnating or rather decreasing amount of education and research) while criteria of efficiency and alternative solutions are put aside. If the principles of labour management were applied to the public sector the productive tasks would be clearly separated from the controlling or political function. Then the authorities would also be forced to present clear criteria for each public activity. The most efficient way of organising these activities would then be left to those who should know best, that is, those who are to do the job. The controlling or political function would thus be delimited from the executive function – a clear division of responsibility between those who are responsible for establishing political objectives and those who are to perform the activity necessary to reach them. At the same time a great proportion of the bureaucracies that have grown strong for the last fifteen to twenty years, shielded by the concept of 'a strong society', can be thrown away as unnecessary and inefficient.

Towards a Labour-Managed Sweden?

The ideas behind labour management are hardly known to the public at large. They also tend to get lost in the current political debate which is oriented towards short-term and topical issues. Consequently the discussion of fundamental political issues such as that of wage-earners' funds tends to be muted and largely incomprehensible. It seems to me that wage-earners' funds are well worth considering as an option in the discussion of the future organisation of the Swedish economy and the public sector. Before entering into the question of its practical relevance for Sweden, it might be useful to mention briefly some international experience.

There are wage-earners' funds in several countries. Admittedly their degree of success varies, but it is not difficult to find examples of stable and successful projects of this kind in various countries. Of particular interest is the so-called Mondragón co-operation in northern Spain. This comprises a bank, a number of co-operating companies and vocational schools, all managed by labour. The Mondragón experiment has proved its feasibility. It has expanded steadily and it currently includes fifty-eight producing co-operative companies with a total of 14,000 employees, including among others, the largest Spanish producer of refrigerators, stoves and washing machines, as well as the leading producer of machine tools.

The single most interesting country in this respect is Yugoslavia. The Yugoslav system of self-management is marked by several of the fundamental principles of labour management, such as one person, one vote, and the effort to maximise the income of employees. However, there are certain deviations or contradictions as well. Yugoslavia is a communist country and purports to apply Marxist economic principles. There is an inherent tension between the political dictatorship and economic democracy as expressed in the system of self-management. Furthermore the development of Yugoslavia has hitherto been marked by many of the problems we encounter in underdeveloped countries. The general economic development of the country has been very successful. From 1960 to 1976 national income grew by more than 160 per cent in real terms, or roughly 10 per cent a year. Per capita income grew at a rate of 7–8 per cent a year. This is why Yugoslavia is nowadays referred to as one of the newly industrialised countries which increasingly make themselves felt as efficient competitors in international markets.

Yugoslavia's problems of unemployment and underemployment are due primarily to its ongoing development from a primitive agricultural economy with huge labour reserves in agriculture to a modern industrial economy. A certain inequality of income and inefficiency in the allocation of resources must primarily be due to certain Marxist characteristics of current doctrines having been less than useful as guidelines for the shaping of economic policy. On the whole, however, self-management in Yugoslavia has worked remarkably well and has proved itself to be a system that permits a strong economic development. The lessons we can learn from foreign experience as regards a transition to labour management in Sweden must nevertheless be limited. Sweden has already come a long way, both in terms of economic development and social progress. This is why there is hardly any existing system for us to copy. Whether we want to or not, we shall have to develop our own model.

I see labour management as an alternative to our existing capital-managed economy. Labour management is directed against privately owned monopolies – it is anti-capitalist. In this respect labour management seems to be a fairly realistic proposition. The contributions to capital accumulation made by private capital-owners, for example, in the form of new issues of shares at the stock exchange, have been insignificant in the postwar period. Privately owned companies will in the future hardly be necessary for the supply of capital. That can be solved collectively, regardless of whether savings are made by the public sector by means of a budget surplus or created through some kind of wage-earners' funds.

Precisely in this field proposals for labour management have good prospects. The possibilities of increasing the rate of savings without too strong inflationary disruptions depend on restraint with regard to consumption and wages. This demands some kind of social contract. A contract always needs two contracting parties. If wage-earners are to refrain from an increase in consumption they must get something in return; influence through wage-earners' funds and labour management offers a solution. Labour management could solve some of the other problems which have impaired the functioning of the Swedish economy. The disparity in wage trends is one of the problems which have to be solved. A policy of planned investment is another necessity. In both fields labour management offers an alternative superior to what exists today.

In popular debate the proposals for wage-earners' funds and the drive towards labour management have been depicted as a threat against a pluralistic economy. Admittedly productive capital under labour management will largely be owned collectively; but it can easily be channelled to labour-managed companies in a decentralised manner, for example, through labour-managed banks. Otherwise, labour management is a decentralised system by definition. In a labour-managed Sweden we shall most probably have much less concentration of economic power than today. One can hardly imagine a more decentralised economic system than that of labour management. To talk of labour management as a threat to a pluralistic society is therefore nothing more than political propaganda. Those primarily threatened by a transition to labour management are the big capital-owners. Their power and influence would disappear. Managers would not be affected in the same way. Their services will be needed in the future as well. But they would no longer be responsible to capital-owners and a shareholders' meeting but merely to the collective of wage-earners they serve.

A comparison, then, between our present capitalist-controlled companies and labour management will provide strong arguments in favour of the latter. But capitalist management and labour management are not the only conceivable alternatives. There may be other forms of organisation which have even better prospects for the future. We touched upon this possibility when discussing companies managed jointly by capital, employees and representatives of the state.

Labour management may include features that are less attractive to many people. It may seem to give too much scope for competition. Just as a profit-maximising economy, labour management offers an alternative which follows its own economic laws. The need for rational behaviour, consistency and discipline is evident in the labour-managed company. In a way there will also be scope for competition. The companies most able to satisfy demands registered by the market will be the most successful.

At the same time it is clear that a labour-managed company leaves scope for the principle of solidarity. We would have a strong sense of solidarity between those working in it. It is solidarity at the level of society as a whole that would be more problematic. But it is doubtful whether such solidarity emerges by itself in any system. It must surely be cultivated through education and social pressure, regardless of the system. There is no evidence that a labour-managed system would not work as well as any other. The employees of a labour-managed company have the advantage of a natural feeling of closeness among themselves. That solidarity can then be extended to larger groups. Furthermore, even a single labour-managed company will be dependent on society as a whole, for example, in relation to the problems of technical and structural innovation. This provides a natural point of departure for co-operation towards a greater sense of social solidarity.

However, in labour management the connection between effort and result will be evident to everyone within the single company. This may be something certain groups will feel disheartened by. There is in our society a widespread reluctance to think in terms of efficiency. Such phenomena are to be found in many areas. For example, many people are reluctant to admit that the fundamental task of the school is to provide children with knowledge. Instead they demand social training, adaptation to the group, indoctrination into desirable social ideas. Labour management presupposes a rational behaviour. It needs knowledge and rationality and adaptability. It is therefore hardly probable that people who stress the inferior role of knowledge and advocate a school which demands nothing from its pupils will be very interested in a system such as labour management.

The ideals of a society which demands nothing, which gives all people the right to the same standard of living, utilities, leisure, and so on, regardless of their input, do not lead to a system of labour management. If they want to get away from the present system it is more likely that such people go for more public influence. One way of reaching that goal is the establishment of participatory companies. Another is to increase the role of bureaucracy. The weakness of this approach is that it is hard to combine with demands for economic consistency and rationality. It is difficult to see which principles of optimisation would govern the activities of participatory companies or bureaucracies. This is an obstacle to the efficiency of such enterprises. They may, however, be attractive from other points of view. They can balance conflicting demands. They can provide job security in the short run. The likelihood of *ad hoc* solutions and bureaucratic measures in order to remedy economic ills is thus considerable. It is easier to try and maintain employment through subsidies and create new posts at the unemployment agencies than to go for increased investment and new ideas, products and markets. That kind of activity might gradually transform our economy into a bureaucracy. If so, we can expect a system devised to maintain existing patterns and guarantee traditional employment, while the capacity for adaptation, development and innovation will be scarce.

It is not easy to prophesy concerning the options of Swedish society. An abstract discussion such as the one presented in this essay may be misleading since it seems to exclude intermediate shades of grey. It is not necessarily true that capitalist management or labour management are the only or even the principal systems available. On the contrary it may be said that the demands for consistency and rationality presented by the systems in their pure form are too repugnant to many people to appear as real candidates in the fight for an economic system of the future. It may well be that hybrids of different systems are equally probable.

Still, it should be clear that labour management has many attractive qualities. It demands something from the individual but gives him a chance to solve problems with other people and produce collectively what is needed to survive. It offers autonomy and self-determination and rich possibilities for initiatives of the group or the team. It points clearly to the need for co-operation between the company and the government in order to solve common problems. It gives value, independence and dignity to individuals. The remaining question is whether Sweden of the 1980s will be ready to take the decisive steps necessary to bring about economic democracy in the form of self-determination. The temptation to let ourselves be manipulated by politicians and leave responsibility to bureaucrats, managers and other traditional authorities will be great – it may prove insurmountable to the majority of our people.

Note: Chapter 10

1 For an interesting study of experience from the diffusion of eight new industrial production methods in six different countries during the postwar period, see Nabseth and Ray (1974).

References: Chapter 10

Arrow, K. (1973), 'Higher education as filter', *Journal of Public Economics*, vol. 2, no. 3.

Becker, G. (1964), *Human Capital* (New York, National Bureau of Economic Research, Columbia University Press).

Meade, J. E. (1972), 'The theory of the labor-managed firm and of profit-sharing', *Economic Journal*, vol. 82.

Nabseth, L., and Ray, G. F. (1974), *The Diffusion of New Industrial Processes* (Cambridge, Cambridge University Press).

Stiglitz, J. E. (1975), 'The theory of screening, education and the distribution of income', *American Economic Review*, vol. 65, no. 3.

Ståhl, I. (1977), 'En ekonomisk teori för blandekonomin', Skandinaviska Enskilda Banken, *Erfarenheter av blandekonomin* (Uppsala, Almqvist & Wiksell).

Södersten, B. (1973), 'Arbetarstyrd ekonomi', *Ekonomisk debatt*, vol. 1, no. 8.

Södersten, B. (1976), 'Mikroaspekter av löntagarstyre', *Ekonomisk debatt*, vol. 3, no. 1.

Vanek, J. (1970), *The General Theory of the Labor-Managed Market Economy* (Ithaca, NY, Cornell University Press).

11
Energy Policy and Economic Vulnerability

LARS BERGMAN and KARL-GÖRAN MÄLER

In the course of only a few years public opinion on the problem of energy supplies has changed radically. Considered a technical problem at the end of the 1960s, it is now, a decade later, closer to being a question of human destiny. At the same time there have been major political struggles over the ends and means of energy policy. Behind the gunsmoke of the nuclear debate, however, there is a striking unity of opinion on the central elements of a future energy policy. Primarily, perhaps, this unity applies to the role of the state in the field of energy. There are not many people who question the notion that the state should have a role in governing the production and use of energy in Sweden. Few people believe that energy problems can find an adequate solution within the framework of a market economy that is uncontrolled in certain important respects. Another opinion, supported by most people, is that energy conservation should be a fundamental element of our energy policy. This idea, as well as the notion that the state should have a role in the field of energy, is something new in Swedish politics as far as energy is concerned.

Before 1973, the year of the large increase in the price of oil, energy policies in Sweden were geared largely towards facilitating the use of the kinds of energy and energy-production methods that imposed the lowest costs on consumers. In addition the need for strategic reserves was considered very important. However, the development of total energy use was not a subject of much interest to the government and Riksdag. Admittedly there had long been a system of energy taxes, but its rationale was primarily fiscal. The taxes were not intended to have any significant effect on the use of energy; they were simply a secure source of income for the state. The government's 1975 Bill on Energy Policy, however, included quantitative objectives for the long-term development of energy use. Gradually energy taxes have come to be considered a means of achieving those objectives, even though loans, subsidies and consumer education have been the principal methods used so far. The resources appropriated by the Riksdag for these purposes are very large, which indicates that energy conservation has a high priority in Swedish energy policy.

This essay has two purposes. The first is to discuss the motives and orientation behind governmental guidance of energy production and energy use. One conclusion will be that there were equally strong reasons for a government policy on energy before the oil-price rise of 1973 as there was afterwards. Our second purpose is to scrutinise and attempt to define the vague concepts of vulnerability and freedom of action. We shall also try to give those concepts some content by examining various scenarios for the 1980s and their consequences during the 1990s. Our main conclusion will be that the debate on energy policy has been too preoccupied with energy conservation and haggling over the number of nuclear reactors. We believe that factors essential to our future freedom of action, such as flexibility of energy use and production, have received too little attention. Our analysis will indicate that discussions of energy policy should be focusing much more on how the Swedish economy is affected by changes in the price and availability of various kinds of energy; compared to that issue, one or two percentage points in the growth of energy consumption is of secondary importance.

Our primary instrument of analysis is a specially designed computer model which describes certain strategic relationships between economic growth, production in various sectors of the economy, investment, foreign trade and energy use. The calculations presented in this essay have been taken from a recently initiated research project. Our results should therefore be considered preliminary.

Why Do We Need a Government Energy Policy?

In a functional market economy Adam Smith's 'invisible hand' is working, and there is no need for a government energy policy.[1] This statement, however, rests on a number of assumptions regarding the market for energy products, energy technology and the side-effects of energy production and consumption. In the following discussion we will take a critical look at the operation of energy markets. However, it must first be pointed out that a market economy does not automatically lead to a desirable distribution of income. Intervention in the market system could therefore be justified on the grounds of income distribution. Furthermore, it is quite clear that energy policies have effects on the distribution of income. The extent of those effects, and their impact on different social groups, is not very well established.[2] Often, however, those effects are distributed completely at random between high- and low-income groups; thus energy policy seems unsuitable as a tool for modifying the distribution of income. We shall therefore entirely disregard the income distribution argument. If one should want to eliminate certain less desirable effects this can usually be done by means of such general policies as taxation. For similar reasons we intend to disregard the regional effects of energy policy.

The world market for energy products is far from what economists would call perfect. Oil production is dominated by a cartel with wide powers to establish monopoly prices. It has also been suggested that because the production and pricing of oil is such an integral part of the foreign policy of the oil-exporting Arab states, the actions of the oil cartel cannot be analysed on the basis of economic theory. However, various studies have shown that economic factors remain a powerful analytical tool in that field. By contrast we think another kind of imperfection is more important. In principle, decisions concerning the price and production of non-renewable resources during a given period are linked to corresponding decisions in all other periods. Under certain conditions a market system can generate a process that ensures an optimal balance of production from one period to the next. That, however, assumes a perfect knowledge of future prices. And such knowledge in turn requires a whole system of so-called futures markets in which producers today can contract for deliveries at a determined price during all future periods of time. Needless to say, there is no complete system of futures markets for energy or any other product. This means that producers of the raw materials for energy will try to limit their dependence on an insecure future by keeping current production at a higher level than would normally be desirable. The result is a too-high consumption of non-renewable energy resources, though this is modified, in a way that is difficult to quantify, by monopoly pricing.

It is important to point out that these probable excesses in the consumption of oil are a global problem; a small country like Sweden can affect the situation only marginally. On the other hand our argument does suggest that world market prices of raw materials for energy are likely to rise more sharply than they would in the case of a 'perfect' market. There is reason, therefore, to consider whether it would be possible to facilitate the adaptation of the Swedish economy to future increases in energy prices by means of energy policy measures today. We shall revert to that question in the next section.

The energy market shows imperfections in areas other than the supply of raw materials for energy. Demand is also characterised by imperfections. The most significant are probably the following three: patterns associated with insecurity about future prices and supplies, the fact that energy consumers are not always the ones who pay for the energy they use, and various deficiencies of the capital markets. Since these imperfections concern domestic markets they are accessible to government intervention.

Expectations about future energy prices and supplies can vary strongly among different groups in society. One reason is that information collection is a costly business requiring large-scale systems. Public authorities should therefore strive to disseminate information on factors relevant to supplies and prices in the field of energy, and they should provide price forecasts as well. As a result various decision-makers will be more inclined to take such factors into account when designing structures for housing and production. However, since the assimilation of such data is costly too there may be a need for special measures giving people a stronger incentive to act on the information. To cite an example: the builder of a one-family house might design its insulation in accordance with current energy prices, even though a higher degree of insulation might be advisable on the basis of informed estimates regarding future price trends and the durability of the house. In such a case some kind of political intervention is obviously necessary if the builder is going to take anticipated future increases in energy prices into account.

Another element tending to lessen the effectiveness of the market system is the fact that energy consumers do not always cover the costs of their consumption. A good example is provided by cases in which consumption of heat and electricity is measured collectively. In such situations the individual has little or no incentive to take price changes into account, since the energy price transmits inadequate information on the marginal cost of supplying energy. Thus to the individual consumer the cost of a small increase in consumption is practically nil, while the expenses of production and distribution to satisfy increasing demand are frequently higher than the average cost – that is, the basis on which collective charges are being calculated. This obviously leads to an unnecessarily high consumption of energy. In such cases an institutional change may be an effective way of improving the use of energy resources.

Yet another important element is the fact that various kinds of credit restrictions make investing households and companies less inclined to consider their initial outlay in relation to future operating costs. Hence the use of capital-intensive techniques with a low energy consumption is being held back.

Credit restrictions and other imperfections of the capital market also discourage long-term R and D projects – developing new energy sources, perhaps, or devising new technologies for energy conversion. This could be an argument for government to improve the functioning of the capital market or, failing that, to offer subsidies for investments in certain types of construction.

Government can also take responsibility for financing risky research projects. This may also offer the important advantage of avoiding monopolisation of the results of research and making them available to all who want to use them.

There are additional reasons why a free market economy can be expected to fall short in certain ways. Some reasons are purely technological. Certain production technologies are so dependent on large-scale structures that the market economy either cannot use them or lets them result in monopolies. The distribution of heat through pipelines falls into this category, as do certain kinds of power plants. The environmental effects of energy production and consumption provide another rationale for government intervention in this field. In general, however, energy policies are blunt instruments when it comes to protecting the environment.

Thus there are a number of reasons for initiating a government energy policy, all of them based on certain deficiencies of the market in this particular field. Such a policy should aim at correcting those imperfections, which in some instances are due to policies pursued in other areas, particularly that of credit market regulations. When designing a policy for energy, it is important to be aware of factors other than direct energy consumption. Equally important is the energy we import in the form of industrial products. Changes in our energy policy might lead to the use of imported goods, the production of which has consumed energy, as a substitute for direct energy use at home. For instance, if Sweden raises energy prices in relation to those of other products this will lead to a decline in our direct energy consumption and a concomitant decline in our imports of energy products. At the same time, energy-intensive activities will be encouraged to relocate in other countries, and we can expect a corresponding increase in our imports of energy in the form of other products.[3] We pointed out earlier that future energy prices can be expected to rise. Thus it is tempting to suggest that we begin to 'prepare' the Swedish economy right now, raising the domestic level of energy prices in relation to the outside world. The idea would be to accept higher energy costs in order to facilitate a future adjustment of the Swedish economy. This argument, however, is incorrect, since it disregards the fact that the relative prices of goods on the international market will be affected by future increases in energy prices. An isolated rise in our domestic energy prices might lead to the premature elimination of certain activities that *would* be profitable if there were an international rise in the price of energy.

Our arguments for an active energy policy are valid also for the period preceding the large rise in oil prices and the debate over nuclear safety. These phenomena simply revealed that a number of uncertainties attend a system of energy supply like ours with its heavy dependence on imports and its need for a technology which, in the longer run, can take on the role of hydropower in our system. For instance, it is difficult to predict the amounts and prices of future oil deliveries. It is equally difficult to anticipate the problems that may be associated with the introduction of a new, advanced technology.

The strongest arguments for an active government policy on energy are related to those uncertainties. Against this background government measures in the field of energy should aim at reducing the uncertainties that plague decisions on the production and consumption of energy; they should also attempt to reduce the vulnerability of our economy to large, unexpected changes in the system of energy supply. Mistaken predictions about the oil market and the problems of nuclear power are but a reminder of the uncertainties to be taken into account when shaping energy policy. One way of reducing our vulnerability would be to reduce our consumption of energy although this, as we have already pointed out, could lead to an unfortunate restructuring of the economy. An alternative strategy is to make use of cheap energy but also commit resources to increasing the flexibility of our economy. We shall study that alternative more closely in the next section.

Vulnerability versus Freedom of Action

The concepts of vulnerability and freedom of action are frequently used in public debate on energy. 'Freedom of action' has become a catchword. It is commonly thought that energy policies should be designed to preserve maximum freedom of action. It is rather unclear, however, what is really meant by that. The discussion goes on but there is no attempt at clear definition or quantification of the terms being used.

In this section, we will try to arrive at a working definition of the concepts of vulnerability and freedom of action. In the next section we will present an attempt at quantifying the problem. Obviously the two concepts can be defined in many different ways and there is no certainty that our definitions are the best for all purposes. We believe, however, that they represent a marked improvement over current vague uses of the concepts. In addition, our definitions can be related to economic theory and thus to various kinds of economic models of prognosis and simulation.

One feels intuitively that the concept of vulnerability should denote the sensitivity of the economic system to disruptions – in its energy supply, for example. Freedom of action should be a measure of the real freedom of choice afforded by energy policies – that is, to what degree government regulations on energy interfere with other social goals. The less the realisation of a given energy objective interferes with other goals, the greater our freedom of action can be said to be in the field of energy policy. Generally that freedom of action should increase as we become less vulnerable to disruptions in the energy supply. We shall now define these concepts, using a highly simplified example as our point of departure.

Let us imagine two different scenarios. The first assumes continued economic growth – the kind that has prevailed since the Second World War – in combination with unchanged energy prices in real terms. The second scenario involves a steep increase in the relative price of crude oil in 1990. Let us also assume that we have two possible strategies at our disposal, A and B. Strategy A means sticking to the status quo: no measures will be taken either to modify the growth in energy demand generated by the market economy or to increase the capacity of the economic system to substitute one kind of energy for another. Strategy B means that part of the annual volume of investment will be devoted to increasing the system's capacity for energy substitution. It is uncertain which scenario will prevail in 1990, so we must choose our strategy without prior knowledge of the ultimate consequences of that choice. However, the consequences of each combination of strategy and scenario are known. It seems reasonable to measure the consequences in terms of private and public consumption of goods and services. To complete the picture we should measure annual consumption before and after 1990. According to our simplified assumptions, then, the consequences of each strategy/ scenario combination can be determined by means of two figures: the first indicates consumption before 1990; the second consumption after 1990.[4] The decision-making problem facing our society can thus be described in terms of the matrix in Table 11.1.

Table 11.1

Strategy	Scenario 1	Scenario 2
A	200,200	200,100
B	175,175	175,150

Obviously all figures are mere examples for the purposes of illustrating the point we want to make. In the next section we shall try to develop more realistic examples. The basic idea is simple. If we choose strategy A and scenario 1 occurs, then consumption will be high – 200 both before and after 1990. But if oil prices rise sharply, the chosen strategy will reduce consumption to 100 after 1990. If the probability of scenario 2 is high, then strategy A implies considerable risk. If we choose strategy B instead, the same high consumption cannot be achieved in scenario 1 since resources have to be reserved for increasing the flexibility of energy use and decreasing total energy consumption. However, if scenario 2 does occur, then strategy B will pay off in the form of higher consumption after 1990 than would have been the case with strategy A.

The choice of strategy obviously depends on how you assess the probability of the two scenarios and your willingness to take risks. At this point it is unnecessary to discuss the decision-making problem in further detail; our purpose is simply to use this example as a means of defining vulnerability. Obviously vulnerability has to be defined in relation to the scenarios. It seems natural to express the vulnerability of strategy A with the figures (0,100). These two figures illustrate that for the period up to 1990 there is no difference between the two scenarios, whereas for the following years there is a difference of 100 to the disadvantage of scenario 2. For strategy B the vulnerability is lower (0,25). By increasing the capacity to substitute one kind of energy for another, vulnerability has been reduced in our numerical example. We can now define the vulnerability of a given strategy as the maximum difference between the consequences of different scenarios. In our example we have expressed those consequences in terms of consumption but it is clearly possible to measure other things as well. With this definition of vulnerability it is possible, at least in principle, to measure the vulnerability of various energy strategies on the basis of a quantitative economic model.

The cost of reaching the lower degree of vulnerability in 1990 is the consumption one has to give up before that time (200 − 175 = 25 in our example). In order to choose between the strategies, however, one must also consider the outcome after 1990. If scenario 1 turns out to be correct then strategy B means that the scope for consumption will be smaller (by 25 units) than would be the case with strategy A. If on the other hand scenario 2 is the correct one then the scope for consumption in strategy B will be larger (by 50 units) than in strategy A. The choice will thus depend on the probability of scenario 2 becoming a reality.

In order to define the concept of freedom of action we shall develop our numerical example a bit further. Suppose there are two different grades of crude oil. They are equivalent in terms of energy but the cheaper one has a higher sulphur content. Let us now introduce a third scenario involving the discovery, in 1990, that sulphuric emissions cause intolerable pollution of the environment. In order to avoid them a switch must be made from the cheaper to the more expensive oil. Let us call the two options now facing society in 1990 α and β − α being the option of continuing the use of high-sulphur oil and β that of changing to the higher-priced low-sulphur variety. We will sum up the alternatives in the matrix in

Table 11.2 (although for the purposes of simplification we have disregarded the pre-1990 scope for consumption).

Table 11.2

Strategy	Option	Scenario 1	Scenario 2	Scenario 3
A	α	200	100	$200-m$
A	β	140	80	140
B	α	175	150	$175-m$
B	β	135	125	135

Note: The symbol m indicates the option scenario combinations that result in intolerable environmental pollution.

If either scenario 1 or 2 becomes a reality there will be no reason in 1990 to choose option β, regardless of the strategy chosen today. However, option β will be chosen if scenario 3 occurs, thus avoiding damage to the environment. Now, if we had chosen strategy A, this would lead to a contraction of consumption by 60 units after 1990. If strategy B had been selected, the corresponding cost for eliminating the environmental danger would be only 40 units and the freedom of action, in our opinion, would be greater. The freedom of action provided by a given strategy is defined by the maximum negative effect exerted on the economy as a whole by various potential adjustments in energy policy as quantified in our example by the effects on the margin for consumption.

This definition of the concept of freedom of action is not generally accepted. As a matter of fact most people are likely to have some other meaning in mind. To us, however, it seems reasonable that the adaptability of the economy to various kinds of disruptions should be taken as the basis of the concept. Freedom of action, then, is defined in terms of the costs of switching from one option to another. In some cases those costs may be prohibitive. One example might be an immediate switch from nuclear-based energy production to a system based on solar energy.

We have shown, then, that our conceptual framework focuses on how well the economy adapts if disruptions occur. That capacity for adjustment depends on a large number of factors. The disruptions may come in the form of quantitative restrictions on fuels or rapid and unexpected price changes. In order to minimise vulnerability, power plants and other installations might be designed in such a way as to permit the use of alternative fuels; at the same time stockpiles could be built up in order to supply our energy needs if other sources became unavailable. Above all, however, much could be gained by distributing the risks more widely than we do today, that is, by investing in different fuels and kinds of energy. Thus a disruption in trade involving one sort of fuel or a sharp rise in the price of a given kind of energy would have less devastating effects. In that case, however, one would consciously abstain from minimising one's costs at present prices.

In order to reduce vulnerability and enhance freedom of action it is necessary to increase our capacity to substitute one production factor for another. One example is to design combustion installations in such a way as to allow the use of various fuels. Furthermore water-transmitted heating systems provide a relatively high degree of flexibility, since they can be connected to different kinds of energy sources. A substitution of capital for energy can be achieved through improved insulation and the installation of thermostats. Labour can be substituted for energy by improving the servicing of equipment and thus increasing its efficiency, by more careful monitoring of processes, and so forth.

However, the most crucial opportunity to increase the possibilities for substitution lies in the selection of new technology. That technology is embodied in fixed capital, objects designed for use over a long period of time. Hence a strategy for energy policy implies a systematic effort to guide the selection of new technologies in a direction that will enhance future possibilities for substitution.

Is there any reason why one should formulate goals for energy policy on the basis of such concepts as vulnerability and freedom of action? Are not power companies, industrial energy users and ordinary consumers already adjusting their behaviour to the possible risks associated with future energy supplies? Thus does not the market mechanism automatically steer systems for energy conversion in a direction that ensures a good balance between our degree of vulnerability and other social goals? Our answer is no. We believe that it would be possible to design a market system that would strike that happy balance. But existing institutional structures render such a solution impossible, primarily for the following reasons. In the first place, a market solution presupposes the existence of perfect capital markets that permit an equitable balance to be struck between present and future. Furthermore it assumes that all risks can be insured. Unless those conditions are met individuals and companies that acquire fuel stockpiles, for instance, will carry most of the risk involved in such an investment. As long as the market system cannot guarantee reasonable distribution of risk by means of various kinds of insurance it will never manage to achieve a desirable balance between vulnerability and the costs of avoiding it. There is the additional problem that information on potential future developments is very unevenly distributed among individuals and organisations; hence it is incumbent on the state authorities to increase the flow of information.

A Model for the Simulation of Energy Policy in Relation to the Economy

The model that has been used for the simulations presented below is a multisectoral growth model of the general equilibrium type.[5] Prices and quantities produced are arranged in such a way as to have equilibrium in all product markets, as well as full utilisation of available capital and labour. This means that energy policies never result in layoffs or unemployment. Instead their effects can be studied through such variables as factor prices and margins for consumption. The model is thus designed to illuminate long-term economic trends. This purpose is also reflected in the treatment of external factors: in the model economy currency rates are constantly adjusted so as to maintain equilibrium in the balance of payments. On the basis of certain assumptions about net capital formation, the development of labour supply, changes in productivity, as well as the evolution of volumes and prices in world trade, the model generates projections of a number of macroeconomic variables for the next ten to twenty years. In the following discussion we shall concentrate on the predictions made with regard to the scope for consumption and to factor prices, given various sets of assumptions about energy policy and developments in the international oil market.

The model contains an aggregate energy sector whose output of various energy products is held to fixed proportions. Hence the model is unsuitable for analysing problems related to the choice of energy sources or technology for energy production. However, it is able to shed light on macroeconomic decision-making problems related to total energy use and the efforts to control it. Nevertheless one reservation is called for in this respect. The assumptions about net capital formation and changes in productivity are made 'outside' the model. In real life, however, those phenomena are also determined by such factors as profitability and production growth – that is, factors that are usually affected by energy policies. Thus the model is unable to demonstrate how energy policy affects economic development through changes in capital formation and technological development. This means that the model tends to underestimate the effects of energy policy on economic development.

In all industrial sectors in the model, as well as in the public sector, total output is a function of inputs of capital, labour, energy and various intermediary inputs. Different combinations of inputs can lead to the same amount of output – in other words, there is a measure of interchangeability among the inputs that is best described by the term 'substitution elasticity'. The ration of substitution elasticity between two inputs is a measure of how 'easily' one input can be substituted for another. A single example will make this clear. Suppose the price of energy rises by 10 per cent in relation to the cost of capital utilisation. If it then becomes profitable to decrease energy input by 5 per cent in relation to capital input per unit of output, substitution elasticity between capital and energy is 0·5. If on the other hand the profitability of energy savings is only 2 per cent in relation to capital input per unit of output, substitution elasticity is 0·2

Together with price elasticity in the energy demands of private households, substitution elasticity between energy and other inputs is a measure of flexibility in the use of energy. When these elasticity ratios increase, the costs of a given reduction in energy use decline, as does the economy's vulnerability to disruptions in the energy supply.

In recent years a number of attempts have been made to calculate the substitution elasticity between energy and other inputs. The results are strongly contradictory, but they still provide a basis for educated guesses. Thus a reasonable estimate would be that the substitution elasticity between energy on the one hand and capital and labour on the other is not lower than 0·1 and probably not higher than 1·0.[6] Lacking studies of our own in this area, for the purposes of our simulation we have assumed a ratio of 0·15 for all sectors of production. We have opted, then, for a very conservative assessment of flexibility in the use of energy.

For the remaining assumptions our primary source has been the report of the 1975 Commission on Long-Term Economic Growth. On that basis we have assumed that the supply of labour, as measured by working hours, will gradually decrease over the remaining years of this century. The annual growth rate of the public sector is put at 2·5 per cent, given constant prices, which is somewhat slower than the rate assumed by the commission. The volume of world trade is presumed to grow at an annual rate of 4 per cent, while world market prices – with the exception of oil – are taken to be constant in real terms. We assume that real oil prices will grow by 2 per cent annually between 1980 and 1990. After that, each of the simulations makes different assumptions about oil prices.

A Few Model Calculations

The model calculations were focused on an attempt to estimate the vulnerability of the Swedish economy to increased oil prices. For the period 1980–2000 we designed two scenarios for the development of oil prices and two strategies for energy policy. Hence, just as in our introductory example, four cases can be discerned. A model calculation was made for each of those cases in accordance with the schema in Table 11.3.

Table 11.3

Strategy	Scenario 1	Scenario 2
A	calculation I	calculation III
B	calculation II	calculation IV

The following definitions of scenarios and strategies were used:

Scenario 1   The world market price of oil rises by 2 per cent annually[7] between 1980 and 1990, and by 5 per cent annually between 1990 and 2000 (thus annual increases in the average price level of energy amount to 0·1 and 0·8 per cent respectively).

Scenario 2   The world market price of oil rises by 2 per cent annually between 1980 and 1990. Between 1990 and 1995 oil prices become five times higher, then remain at that level till the turn of the century.

Strategy A   No special measures are taken to affect the volume or flexibility of energy use.

Strategy B   In the 1980s resources are invested in an effort to increase the flexibility of energy use; 20 per cent of industrial investments are devoted to that purpose, and so the substitution elasticity between energy and capital/labour inputs increases from 0·15 to 0·25 in the early 1990s.[8]

Calculation I has much in common with the 1975 commission's assessments of the factors determining economic developments between 1980 and 2000. It can therefore be used as a 'basic calculation' in our analysis.

In calculation I the average annual growth of GNP is 2·4 per cent. This implies a considerable slowdown in economic growth; between 1950 and 1972, for example, the GNP's average annual growth rate was 3·6 per cent. This is bound to affect the growth of energy consumption. However, our calculation also shows a slowdown in the growth of energy consumption per unit of GNP. In the period 1950–72 the consumption of energy increased by an average of 5 per cent each year, while the corresponding figure in our basic calculation is 2·8 per cent. In calculation I, then, the annual growth rate in the consumption of energy per unit of GNP is roughly 0·4 per cent, as opposed to 2·4 per cent during the period 1950–72.

A possible explanation can be found in the development of energy prices. Between 1950 and 1972 the real energy price level dropped by almost 3 per cent annually. In our calculation, however, it increases by a few decimal points each year. Another explanation is the relatively slow growth of production in the energy-intensive basic industries. Despite the fact that calculation I implies a substantial slowdown in the growth of energy consumption, that growth rate is nevertheless higher than the goal set by the 1975 Energy Policy Bill. According to the Bill, the growth of energy consumption was to be limited to 2 per cent annually between 1974 and 1985, while zero growth in the use of energy should be our target by 1990.

In Table 11.4 we present the figures obtained for the volume of total consumption in the various calculations. The results are given in the form of an index for 1990 and 1995.

Table 11.4 *Index for Total Consumption, 1990 and 1995, Using Different Assumptions Regarding the Development of Oil Prices and Strategies of Energy Policy (1980 = 100).*

	Scenario 1	Scenario 2	Vulnerability
Strategy A	140; 160	140; 133	0; 27
Strategy B	138; 159	138; 136	0; 23
Difference between A and B (A − B)	2; 1	2; −3	

Regardless of the strategy chosen the assumed rise in oil prices at the beginning of the 1990s will have a considerable effect on the development of the scope for total consumption. This conclusion contradicts our experience in 1973–4 but it may still be perfectly plausible. One possible explanation is that the increase in oil prices assumed here has no effect on the world market prices of other products.[9] Swedish exports of goods and services are probably more energy-intensive than Swedish imports, with the exception of oil products. Thus, given our assumption, the model tends to over-estimate the deterioration in our country's terms of trade. Another explanation is that the impact of the oil crisis of 1973–4 was cushioned by the fact that the higher oil prices were allowed to result in a balance-of-payments deficit, thus permitting the adjustment to be made over a longer period of time. In the model economy, however, that adjustment is made immediately, while maintaining external equilibrium. Finally, the costs of oil in 1973 represented a very small part of total production costs; thus even a relatively sharp increase in the price of oil had less impact. But in our calculation for 1990 oil costs – reflecting earlier price increases – account for a considerably higher proportion of total costs.

We have already mentioned that total capital formation, the supply of labour and the development of productivity are all determined 'outside' the model. This means that changes in oil

Table 11.5   *Index for the Development of Factor Prices 1990 and
1995, Using Different Assumptions Regarding Oil Prices and Energy
Policy (1980 = 100)*

		Scenario 1	Scenario 2
	Wage index	134; 154	134; 136
Strategy A	profitability index	97; 89	97; 79
	wage index	133; 149	133; 135
Strategy B	profitability index	103; 93	103; 85

prices primarily affect the terms of trade and the distribution of
resources among the different sectors, while the development of
GNP is largely a function of assumptions about the growth of
resources. As is shown in Table 11.5, the increase in oil prices
would have a negative effect on GNP as well, so that the
implications for total consumption will be even larger than those
indicated by Table 11.4. It is interesting to note that with strategy B
the effect on factor prices will be considerably lower than with
strategy A, which underlines the importance of investing primarily
in increased flexibility and adaptability.

Strategy B, according to Table 11.4, manages to reduce the
vulnerability of the economy from 27 to 23. The cost of achieving
this can be expressed as 2 index points of total consumption. It
should be noted, however, that the assumptions behind strategy B
are relatively pessimistic: over a ten-year period 20 per cent of total
investment will go to R and D projects aimed at increasing our
flexibility in the use of energy. This is an incredibly grandiose effort.
If it were possible to engage in a more modest effort, yet still
increase the substitution elasticity between energy and capital/
labour inputs from 0·15 to 0·25, strategy B would appear in a more
favourable light.

Conclusions

The conclusions that can be drawn from our discussion may be
summarised as follows:

(1)   If a rational discussion of energy policy is to take place, it
appears necessary to arrive at a working definition of such
concepts as freedom of action and vulnerability. There is no
guarantee that the definitions we have introduced are the best
for all purposes. We believe, however, that they possess a
sound intuitive basis and provide an essential link to economic
theory.

(2) In public debate it is frequently asserted that a marked reduction in the rate of growth of Sweden's energy consumption would lessen our vulnerability and increase our freedom of action. We have tried to demonstrate that efforts to achieve increased flexibility or adaptability can be more important. The government must try to strike a desirable balance between energy conservation, measures to increase flexibility and the costs of these policies. Unfortunately, there is no serious cost-benefit analysis available to facilitate that choice. It may be noted, however, that much has been done to reduce the growth rate of our energy consumption and to find new sources of energy, but almost nothing has been done to increase the adaptability of the economy.

(3) Public debate on energy issues has for the most part been based on a limited number of scenarios and still fewer alternatives for action. The options considered have generally focused on the growth rate of our energy consumption and our preferred system of energy supply. We wish to state, first, that the number of case studies is too small and, secondly, that both the analysis and the debate have been too narrow in scope. In our opinion the analysis of energy problems and strategies in the 1980s should focus on how the Swedish economy reacts to changes in the price and availability of various kinds of energy. This might provide a realistic idea of how the policies of the 1980s will affect our freedom of action in terms of energy through the 1990s and beyond.

(4) A big push is necessary in the field of systems analyses of energy economics. At present there is only one economic model in Sweden for the study of the questions we have discussed. Contrast this situation with that of the US Department of Energy, whose employees routinely use their computer terminals to evaluate alternative energy policy; nevertheless, to the extent that they are built on central economic theories they do provide an excellent frame of reference and facilitate a consistent analysis. By means of a research effort in this area, superstitions and preconceived ideas may be replaced by a rational utilisation of society's intellectual capital.

Notes: Chapter 11

1   For a more general discussion see P. Bohm, *Samhällsekonomisk effektivitet* (SNS, 1976). For a more detailed analysis similar to ours see Allen V. Kneese, 'Natural Resource Policy 1975–1985', *Journal of Environmental Economics and Management*, vol. 3, no. 4 (December 1975).

2   For a discussion of the effects of energy policies on income distribution see Bo Diczfalusy, *Energi och inkomstfördelning* (Sekretariatet för Framtidsstudier,

Rapport 408–76, 1976). Diczfalusy's results indicate that energy policies affecting prices have a relatively insignificant impact on the cost of living, at given patterns of expenditures, of three household categories defined with regard to the size of their disposable income.

3 This becomes particularly relevant in so far as energy-saving measures are warranted from a global point of view.

4 It should be noted that we entirely disregard any growth taking place during the period.

5 See L. Bergman, *Energy Policy in a Small Open Economy: The Case of Sweden* (International Institute for Applied Systems Analysis, Laxenburg, Austria), Research Report 1978–16. The model comprises seven industrial sectors (energy, area-based production, processing industry, manufacturing, transportation, trade and private services, and housing), one aggregate public sector and a household sector. Exports are determined by the relationship between domestic and world market prices for each product group, and the growth of world trade. The import element of the domestic supply of various product groups is determined by the relationship between domestic and world market prices.

6 As concerns the relevance of assumptions regarding substitution elasticity, see W. W. Hogan and A. S. Manne, 'Energy-economy interactions: the fable of the elephant and the rabbit, in Hitch (ed.), *Modeling Energy-Economy Interactions: Five Approaches.* (Washington DC, Resources for the Future, 1977). For a survey of various attempts at a quantification, see Lennart Hjalmarsson, 'Substitutions-möjligheter mellan energi och andra produktionsfaktorer', in L. Hjalmarsson (ed.), *Energi och samhällsekonomi* (Lund, Liber Läromodel, 1979).

7 Please note that we are referring to real price changes; the price of oil rises by 2 per cent annually over and above the general price level.

8 It should be stressed that this is merely an assumption. However, our assessment is likely to be conservative.

9 Unfortunately we have been unable to include in our model the changes in relative world market prices as a result of the oil price increases.

12

Wages, Prices and Taxes in the 1980s

KARL-OLOF FAXÉN

Over the last decade the international inflation rate has risen to levels unprecedented in peacetime. Sweden is not the only country to have been plagued by soaring prices during the 1970s: the same is true of most OECD members. What lies behind this phenomenon? Is it simply a matter of coincidence – the by-product of certain errors in economic policy, particularly in the United States during the Vietnam War and the early 1970s? Or is there a systematic pattern here, possibly related to the international system of payments or growing inertia in the labour market, not just in Sweden but throughout the OECD area? What role does the expansion of the public sector play in all this?

How one proposes to deal with the problem depends very much on how one tends to answer those questions. The reply offered by the McCracken Report[1] is that the inflation of the 1970s was due to a combination of pure chance and political errors. Thus, with a little luck and some improvements in policy, in the 1980s the OECD area should be able to return to the norms of the 1960s: an unemployment rate of 2·5 per cent, an inflation rate of 3 per cent and an annual increase of 5 per cent in production per working hour in manufacturing industry. In the two years since the report was published, however, its optimistic predictions have not been borne out by experience. There is more reason than ever to discuss structural causes and to find solutions that involve changes in the system, not just more efficient implementation of traditional conventional modes of economic policy. The systemic change that we will discuss here concerns wage policy and its co-ordination with fiscal policy and public spending. Is it conceivable that a different approach to wage policy might hold back inflation and unemployment, that is, enhance stability?

How Stable Is our Economic System?

During the 1970s inflation, unemployment and currency rates have fluctuated so unpredictably and uncontrollably that the very structure of the international economic system has been called into question. Does a disruption in the system – such as the oil price increase of 1973–4 – automatically trigger mechanisms that restore equilibrium? Or could a disruption set off a long-term spiral of increasing unemployment, accelerating price increases and ever more unstable currency rates, a process that cannot be controlled via the conventional economic policies that have hitherto been accepted as 'part of the system'?

According to the neoclassical economic theory that epitomised liberal tradition, the answer to the first question is an unqualified yes. This is largely due to the fact that neoclassical theorists lacked both the perspective and the tools necessary for analysing the conditions under which instability occurs, that is, those processes that deviate systematically from equilibrium. The development of a theory of control in the postwar period has encouraged a more systematic analysis of the stability of economic processes. In much the same way as one observes how an automatic pilot keeps an aeroplane on course despite external turbulence it is possible to study how economic policy can maintain constant prices and full employment in spite of such economic shockwaves as the oil price increase. Obviously it is dangerous to carry this kind of analogy too far; nevertheless it does point up the need for a more precise discussion based on the following questions.

What do we mean by stability? Even if a system eventually finds its way back to equilibrium (and can thus be considered stable in that sense), it may take a long and circuitous route that is far from desirable. No definition of stability can be of any practical use unless it takes that into account. A stable system is one that can be restored to equilibrium (stable prices and full employment) reasonably quickly through conventional economic policies and which will not immediately slip out of balance again. The entire process of adjustment, then, must take place under conditions of decreasing inflation and unemployment. But we still need a way of applying this theoretical analysis to the practical situation, and the proper formulation for doing so has not yet been found.

What are our standards for an 'acceptable' level of disruption, both qualitatively and quantitatively? A system may adjust well to small disruptions, yet a major crisis will send it into violent and prolonged fluctuations. An automatic pilot may be able to cope with any normal gusts of wind and maintain the aeroplane on a stable course. Nevertheless there will be situations that warrant the intervention of a human pilot. Thus the disruption exceeds acceptable limits, the system of aeroplane-plus-automatic-pilot is no longer stable. Stabilisation requires intervention from outside the system. One particular difficulty in discussing external disruptions of stability is that conventional mathematical theory is geared to minor disruptions only – it focuses on the area immediately adjacent to the point of equilibrium. In order to deal with stability in relation to large-scale disruptions more complex mathematics are necessary.

The practical problems facing us in the 1980s may be said to involve two aspects of stability: on the one hand the internal stability of a closed economy (the entire OECD area, for example, or a large country like the United States); on the other the stability of a single (small) country and the adjustments it must make (currency rates, capital movements) to the fluctuations of the international economy. As far as I know, there has not yet been an analysis of the latter problem. The former, however, has been the subject of an ongoing debate in the *Scandinavian Journal of Economics*[2] and my own discussion is drawn largely from that source.

The debate is centred on a very simple model comprising three kinds of variables: prices, wages and money. The rate of change of prices and wages is determined by the balance of supply and demand in the markets for goods and labour. The objective is to show, through theoretical analysis, how relations of stability depend on the relative inertia of different markets. Although a constant and desirable state of equilibrium (stable prices and full employment) is assumed in all models it can be demonstrated that stability some-times tends to be suboptimal under quite tolerable conditions of inertia. Under other equally tolerable conditions of inertia, however, there are good prospects for stability. It is therefore impossible to make any generalisation about stability that would be valid in all cases.

So much for theoretical analysis. Quite clearly we must question the assumption that economic policy should be discussed on the basis of models of general equilibrium. Such limitations, founded on the notion of a stable, clearly consistent world, have no basis in reality. Rather, the international economic system we inhabit is quite likely to be either far from full employment (as was the case before the Second World War) or, however slowly, drifting into an inflationary spiral (as the experience of the last three decades seems to indicate). Although the system does not lack the capacity to restore equilibrium, the equilibrium it achieves is not very stable. Even though the system will eventually return to full employment and a stable currency after a disruption, it may take a long time. In the process of adjustment, both inflation and unemployment are quite likely to increase, as has been the case during the late 1970s. According to the model cited above this is due to the relative inertia of the markets for goods and services. This problem of stability cannot be overcome simply by improved methods of analysis or prognosis, nor by the more sophisticated fiscal or mone-tary policies. Instead the solution must be sought through a change in the very conditions of inertia – a change in the system itself.

It should be noted that the change envisioned here is to eliminate merely the *inertia* of the markets, not to abandon the market economy as such. Prices and wages will be established through the market, as before. The difference lies in the attempt to influence the relation between the rate of change in prices and wages, on the one hand, and supply and demand in various markets, on the other. This, indeed, is the objective of the incomes policies undertaken by various countries: to alter certain conditions of inertia that affect the relationship between wage formation and supply and demand on the labour market, but without jeopardising the market itself. While it is certainly true that incomes policies have proved ephemeral and marginal in their effect – when they have had any effect at all – their purpose has nevertheless been clear.

In our country instead of a government incomes policy we have had a system of centralised wage negotiations. In accordance with the EFO report,[3] the attitudes of the contracting parties have been determined largely by the market. The contracting parties have tried to keep wages close to the 'mainstream', which in turn is determined by productivity in the sector exposed to foreign competition and international price developments. This is the full extent of the active intervention undertaken during the EFO era. Since the late 1970s, however, the international context has shifted and Sweden now requires a more active wage and salary policy. No abandonment of the market is implied. The collective agreements would continue to serve as the main instruments of wage and salary policy, with sanctions available in cases of non-compliance.

A more active wage policy in Sweden must be adapted to the global environment of the 1980s – for example, to the mobility of currency rates and varying rates of inflation in different countries. Swedish incomes policies should also be designed to enhance the overall stability of the OECD system. Before narrowing our perspective to the framework of the national economy, therefore, we should first consider the general dimensions of the problem.

Inflation and Unemployment in the OECD Area

Since there is no theoretical analysis of stability in this context we shall have to proceed on the basis of statistics on unemployment, prices, wages and productivity in the OECD area.

The standard solution to the problem indicated by Table 12.1 is to try and hold back inflation over a sufficient period by means of a highly restrictive monetary and fiscal policy, even at the price of increased unemployment. If one could count on the same gains in productivity as in the 1960s it should be enough to slow down wage

Table 12.1   *Developments in the OECD Area: 1965–78*[4]

	1965–8	1969–72	1973–5	1976–8
Unemployment (%)	2·5	3·0	3·9	5·1
Consumer prices (% annual increase)	3·3	5·1	11·3	8·9
Labour cost per hour (% annual increase)	7·3	10·2	15·0	9·7
Productivity in industry (% annual increase)	5·1	4·8	2·0	4·2

Note: annual increases adjusted for GNP.

increases by some 3 percentage points a year, that is, from about 10 to 7 per cent. Inflation as a result would be limited to roughly 3 per cent. To achieve this one would have to tolerate an unemployment rate of 6–7 per cent for a few years.

But the real question about these restrictive policies is how much they would hamper gains in productivity, causing dwindling investments and prolonging the underutilisation of industrial capacity. If the effect exceeds 3 percentage points a year, thus restricting the OECD area to an increase in productivity no higher than in 1973–5 (2 per cent annually) then the lower wage increases and restrictive policies will have no appreciable impact. Although it is quite unlikely that productivity would suffer as much as that – 1–2 percentage points is a more reasonable assumption than 3 – there would still be considerable losses. It is tempting, then, to try and reduce inflation by using the productivity effect in the opposite direction, that is, by pursuing an expansionary fiscal and monetary policy in order to increase investments and promote full utilisation of industrial capacity. This more expansive policy is known to have many advocates, at least among those countries with a balance-of-payments surplus. As for OECD as a whole, greater demand could be expected to have a more striking effect on productivity than on the rate of wage increases, and inflation within the area would not increase.

But this is true only under conditions of high unemployment, about 5 per cent. At a level of 2–3 per cent it is the other way around. When unemployment is low, the rate of wage increases is affected more than productivity. Moreover with a policy designed to stimulate demand there is necessarily a time lag (a year or two) and this only compounds the uncertainty of its effects. It is crucial, therefore, to switch from expansionary to restrictive policies without delay when the moment comes. One must always plan ahead, beginning to prepare the necessary restrictive measures long before one reaches full utilisation of capacity and an acceptable level of unemployment.

It is not easy to have such complex relationships as a basis for economic policy. Admittedly the system can be considered stable in some sense of the word. It is not, however, a satisfactory sort of stability, which accounts for many of the difficulties encountered since 1971. It becomes all the more interesting then to search for an alternative economic policy that does not require such delicate timing. As an illustration let us imagine a one-time decrease of costs and prices through a tax cut – perhaps a reduction in payroll taxes by 5 percentage points.[5] This would affect the development of prices and costs through a kind of shock – a mirror image of the oil-price increase, if you like. The rationale for such a measure can be traced back to the conditions of inertia, particularly in the area of wage formation. A sharp, non-recurrent decrease in labour costs seems a promising way of trying to break the inflationary spiral, as well as the unacceptably high unemployment rate and underutilised productive capacity that go along with it. This implies a fiscal policy that is initially expansionary, but which gradually becomes more restrictive as public revenues increase and one draws closer to the goal: full utilisation of capacity and an acceptable level of unemployment. From the point of view of economic policy-making, the dynamics of such a process are simpler and easier to master than the strategy cited above. It requires fewer refinements of foresight and timing. Provided that public expenditure is stable, such a fiscal policy can be incorporated quite smoothly into the normal flow of government budgetary arrangements.

If such a policy could be facilitated by a change in the system, greater stability would be the result.

A Longer-Term Wage Policy

Wage formation in Sweden, while very much affected by collective agreements, is not entirely determined by them. The wage drift plays a highly significant role. Collective agreements do not eliminate the influence of market forces; they merely modify inertia in the relationship between market factors and real wage developments. In the 1980s we can expect rapid fluctuations of international prices and exchange rates – hardly the best of conditions for forecasting demand for single products and hence continuing problems of economic policy for a small country like Sweden. With a firmer, more consistent policy of collective agreements as the basis, can we develop a monetary and fiscal policy capable of lifting the Swedish economy above the OECD average in the pursuit of such goals as full employment, stable currency rates, high investments and strong growth? And, in so doing, can we help bring increased stability to the OECD area as a whole?

The wage agreement for 1978–9 can be seen as a step in that

direction. It recognises that we must slow down inflation and reduce our relative costs in order to give Swedish exports a much-needed boost. To begin with, there were reserves of unused industrial capacity. Productivity was considerably lower than it might have been, primarily because demand for our exports was too low. Due to the relative cost situation, market shares to the tune of 20 per cent had been lost. There was plenty of productive capacity to spare. To both sides in the wage agreement the mobilisation of those reserves was more important than any differences over how the benefits would be distributed. As for the methods of mobilisation, they had to be compatible with the dynamics of the international economic system, as it was understood by the contracting parties. It was a matter of maintaining equilibrium in the midst of a highly turbulent environment. The cautious policy recommended by the McCracken Report – the 'narrow path' – did not garner much support. Moreover the 'narrow path' policy seemed to be at odds with the prevailing conception of the forces at work within the OECD system today. Yet an alternative policy – one that would achieve full-capacity utilisation more quickly than the 'narrow path' – implied considerable risks (see Figure 12.1).

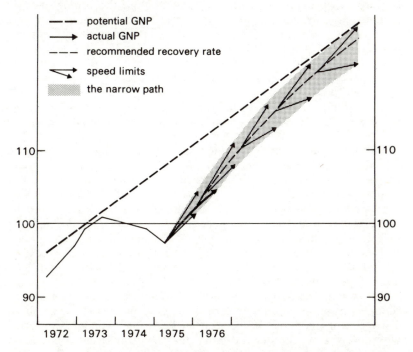

Figure 12.1   *The 'narrow path' towards full employment and price stability (GNP for OECD area 1973 = 100, logarithmic scale*

From an international point of view, the basic problem of a small country that depends heavily on foreign trade is that overblown fiscal policies are detrimental to its competitive position, saddling it with large balance-of-payments deficits. Those deficits in turn undermine the value of the currency; the rate goes down while prices, in terms of one's own currency, go up. This makes it all the more difficult to pursue an aggressive economic policy. Indeed there is enormous risk of being trapped in a vicious circle of rising inflation, growing balance-of-payments deficits and, in the long run, high unemployment rates. These risks can be reduced if wage formation is kept under control through long-term centralised agreements. Under those circumstances expansionary fiscal policies would be more acceptable.

In the wage agreement of 1978–9, then, the contracting parties felt they were making a contribution by holding back the rate of cost increases. In return they expected a more expansionary fiscal policy that would reduce unemployment. The guarantee clause was the vehicle they used to pressure the government into a more expansionary fiscal policy. That clause was designed to ensure that certain fiscal measures, for example a cut in payroll taxes, would be required to prevent prices from going through the ceiling. This in turn would stimulate an increase in private consumption, at a rate selected by the contracting parties, and thus provide some impetus for economic growth.

The principal weakness of the plan may have been that two years simply was not long enough. The inertia of the economy is so great that it will take at least three years to register the full effects of any stabilisation agreement. As it is, however, the government has had to face a new round of negotiations since the agreement expired at the end of 1979.

The liberal minority government didn't play ball when the second oil shock hit the Swedish economy. Nothing was done to keep prices below the 1979 ceiling. After an extra round of negotiations, 1·5 per cent wage compensation was agreed in December 1979. The May 1980 general strike and lockout in the SAF-LO area could not be ended without a substantial increase. The policy of decelerating inflation was, however, resumed in 1981–2 agreements with LO and PTK (the salaried unions). The 1982 rate of price increase is expected to be around 6 per cent against around 13 per cent in 1980 and 11 per cent in 1981.

The wage drift constitutes another weakness. True, it has been reduced from an annual rate of 6–7 per cent in 1974–6 to about 3 per cent in 1978 and 3·5 per cent in 1979. One wonders, however, whether this represents a victory for the Employers' Federation campaign against unacceptable wage drifts, or whether it merely reflects changing conditions in the labour market and deteriorating profit margins. In other words, if profitability and employment are restored to normal levels will the wage drift remain at 3 per cent or will it rise, whatever the campaigns being waged against it? It is obvious that a wage drift of 6 or 7 per cent in the early 1980s would crush any hope of stabilisation and undermine any fiscal policy aimed at maximising both utilisation of capacity and growth in productivity.

Such a wage drift would have immediate repercussions for the balance of payments and the international value of the Swedish crown. This would further jeopardise our efforts to stabilise the situation. We would slip into yet another vicious circle. Figure 12.1[6] illustrates the problems that confront economic policy in its attempt to bring about a sustained recovery. Under present conditions, with the existing heritage of pessimism regarding growth and inflation, the rate of expansion must move between very narrow limits – high enough to encourage investments, but not so high as to set off a new spiral of inflation. That requires a policy of cautious activism. Once optimism revives, however, the system's own built-in stabilisers should be sufficient to correct minor deviations from the desired trend.

Figure 12.1 shows the actual development of GNP in the OECD area up to and including 1976. But the curves and symbols representing potential GNP, recommended recovery rate and speed limits are qualitative rather than quantitative in nature, indicating the strength and duration of the recovery.

Capital Movements and Purchasing-Power Parities in the 1980s

In the international economic system of the 1980s we can expect the exchange rates of major currencies, the American dollar, the Japanese yen, the German mark, and so forth, to be determined in the short run by financial factors and immediate expectations. Hence it will not be the relative wage costs of the countries concerned – the purchasing power parities, to use Gustaf Cassel's term – that will determine short-term developments within the system of floating exchange rates that was imposed on us, willy-nilly, in the 1970s and is likely to stay with us in the foreseeable future.

What does this mean for a country whose currency rate is rising, owing to such financial factors as interest rates, capital movements, and the like? Costs will be held down and inflation kept back, but at the same time its competitive position in world markets will be weakened. Switzerland is perhaps the most extreme example, but West Germany and Austria might also be mentioned. Conversely if a given currency is faced with unfavourable financial conditions it will be difficult to limit inflation and keep wages under control.

Take the US dollar, for example: its weakness is due mainly to the financial problems created by the accumulation of very large and liquid dollar reserves outside the United States. The situation is further aggravated by the effects of an increasing demand for imported oil.

It is particularly vital for a small country to avoid a disadvantageous position *vis-à-vis* international capital movements and other financial factors. For if one tries to pursue a more expansionary fiscal policy than is feasible under the current external balance, one is apt to stumble into a series of depreciations – and that in turn will breed expectations of further depreciations. Above all, short-term international factors must not be allowed to disrupt wage formation.

Do Centralised, Longer-Term Agreements Enhance Stability?

Is it desirable for centralised labour market organisations – the Employers' Federation, the Confederation of Trade Unions and the Cartel of Salaried Employees in the Private Sector – to negotiate general agreements that have a strong influence on overall costs? Does this have a stabilising or a destabilising effect in terms of inflation and the external balance of payments? How is our system doing in comparison with, say, the German or American system?

The German system seems to work well in the sense that wage negotiations are capable of adapting to situations in which external factors, primarily the exchange rate of the German mark, tend to restrict the growth of domestic costs and prices. There is no independent resistance so collective agreements can be made at a level that more or less reflects external economic conditions. On the other hand the German system of collective negotiations, with its regional branch agreements, may not give contracting parties sufficient scope for the independent action that is sometimes required by the international position of the domestic economy. Can wage policy play an active role not just a passive one? Can it do more than simply avoid interfering with developments determined by a combination of international factors and domestic economic policy?

The same might be said of the American system. There, too, wage formation has been adapted to international conditions. The international position of the dollar has weakened, not because of purchasing-power parities but as a consequence of other factors, including capital movements and the oil situation. Wages are increasing at a substantially higher rate than in West Germany.

With respect to the American case, perhaps it is worth noting that while a certain inertia in wage formation may be an advantage in one situation, it can be a handicap in another. The large, oligopolistic USA corporations often have long-term contracts with built-in automatic cost-of-living clauses. These agreements do not expire at the same time but are layered, so to speak, over time. Under such conditions any anti-inflationary policy that seeks to limit the money supply will also, in the short run, cause unemployment. Only slowly and gradually can such a policy reduce inflation. This inertia allows inflationary expectations to persist, thus prolonging the United States' problems with its external balance of payments.

As for the Swedish system, its troubles seemed to begin in 1975. Overcentralisation led to 'overshooting'; it is unlikely that the same thing could have happened under the German or American system of negotiations. When price developments in 1974 produced strongly inflationary expectations, the contracting parties over-reacted during negotiations in the autumn of 1974 and spring of 1975. Even if the external conditions were similar this probably would not have occurred in decentralised negotiations of the German or American sort.

On the other hand it is important to emphasise that the Swedish system – centralised collective agreements based on international conditions – worked relatively well for twenty years, until 1974. In other words it was effective as long as international conditions were reasonably stable and predictable. It was fairly successful in adapting wage developments to those of prices and productivity in the sector exposed to foreign competition, as described in the EFO model. But in the turbulence stirred up by the oil crisis these guide-lines became blurred or, to put it another way, the margins of prognostical error became too large.

The crisis in costs and profitability was not just created by inflationary wage agreements; a number of increases in payroll taxes in the years 1973–7 also played a significant role. But if higher taxes were needed to finance the ever-growing public sector, why choose the payroll tax rather than the value added tax? This was a consequence of the parliamentary situation in the early 1970s: with the bourgeois parties and the Communists united in their opposition to an increased value added tax, the Social Democrats were forced to opt for the payroll tax instead. There was no long-term strategy behind the choice; it was simply the most expedient route in parliamentary terms. Later on, higher payroll taxes were justified on the grounds that they could be deducted from the room allowed for wage increases, thus hypothetically ensuring that labour costs would rise at a slower rate.

As it turned out, however, the impact of higher payroll taxes was complicated by the effects of the wage drift and the negotiated wage increases. Their deduction from the room allowed for higher wages was largely a formality. In calculating that room for the years 1975–6 it was all but impossible to predict international price and productivity developments in the sector exposed to foreign competition. And if these underlying assumptions were inaccurate, then the estimated room could scarcely be credible, nor could the deduction. In fact the actual room proved to be dramatically lower than the estimate, and it is most unlikely that the estimate would have been so high if it had not been for the payroll tax.

Since the two-year agreement of 1975–6, however, there has been a striking reduction in the growth of wage costs. The parties have gradually worked their way down to lower figures both for wage increases and for price increases. Once it got past the crisis of 1975 the system of centralised negotiations proved capable of rational adaptation to the external conditions for wage formation. At the same time, though, this adjustment has meant that the contracting parties are no longer continuously trying to adapt domestic wage formation to international factors. Instead the domestic situation has become the chief frame of reference: an attempt to reduce inflation and influence fiscal policies in the direction of fuller employment was the main thrust of the agreements for 1978–9.

The Relationship between Taxes and Wages

Although we voted in a non-socialist government in 1976, public expenditure continued to grow at the same high rate. Today it is still running riot, and this is particularly true of local governments. In Sweden there is a multitude of relatively autonomous local governments, each with its own income tax – a system that really has no parallel in any other country. One foreign visitor, shocked by this arrangement, is said to have called it the closest approximation to anarchy to be found in the real world.

The fiscal problems our country can expect in the 1980s will largely be determined by a kind of reverse decentralisation. Although a great many regional and local assemblies will be able to make decisions involving public expenditure, they will not necessarily have to bear full responsibility for covering the costs. They always have the option of joining with other regional or local governments to extract subsidies from central government. If such alliances just maintain a reasonable degree of unity they will be able to withstand any political challenge – as local politicians are well aware. Thus although the central government does not set the priorities for local expenditure it will have to underwrite it, if only to prevent local governments from imposing excessive tax increases. In such cases an increase in the central government's subsidies to the locality, financed by growing indirect taxation, may seem preferable to letting the total public deficit rise. After all this expenditure is a *fait accompli*, and increased local taxes are hardly a realistic alternative. In the 1970s, when our GNP seemed stalled at a low growth rate, the big loser was the private sector, which declined in absolute terms.

Figure 12.2 shows the scope for increasing private expenditure out of factor incomes between 1950 and 1990. In 1950–60 and 1960–70 the private sector in Sweden was still capable of expansion, despite higher public expenditure. Income from labour and capital still offered some scope for increasing private expenditure. During the 1970s, however, the slowdown in economic growth was almost entirely at the expense of the private sector, which declined in proportion to other sectors throughout the decade.

As far as the wage policies of the 1980s are concerned it is particularly interesting to note that even though GNP may return to a more normal rate of growth (we have assumed 3 per cent a year) the margin for growth in the private sector will still be negative. Even if our total growth in GNP were devoted to public expenditure it still could not cover it – assuming public expenditure continues to rise at the present rate.

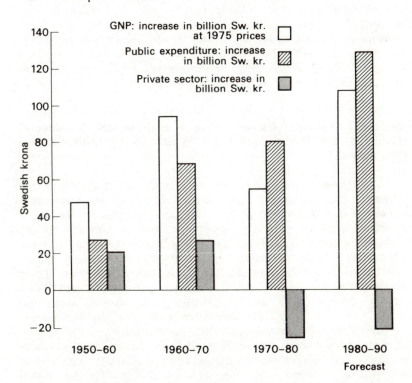

Figure 12.2 *Scope for increasing private expenditure out of factor income, 1950–90*

As illustrated in the graph for the 1980s in Figure 12.2, the expansion of the public sector has reached a point where the margin for private expenditure is shrinking, despite the fact that production in private industry has made substantial gains. Unless effective brakes are applied, the increased fiscal appetite of the public sector will condemn wage-earners to a whole decade of declining real standards of living. This will occur even if productivity reaches a higher level of development, and obviously it will create grave difficulties in the area of wage policy.

It is this problem rather than the task of gradually adjusting income-tax rates to inflation that represents the main challenge. Formerly annual adjustments in tax rates were necessary in order to make possible some real measure of wage increases; since the introduction of indexed marginal rates for income taxes levied by the central government, this is no longer the case. This does not mean it would not be highly desirable to lower marginal income-tax rates – that is a different matter altogether. Such a tax cut would be most attractive to the contracting parties in wage negotiations, although there could be a problem, namely, that the effects of lower marginal tax rates would be used as a political argument for higher indirect taxation, which is easier to sell than the expansion of public expenditure as such. Still, weighed against the ever-increasing rate of public expenditure, lower marginal income taxes would scarcely have any impact at all on public finances.

Can the Contracting Parties Continue to Limit the Freedom of Action of the Public Sector by Means of Centralised Wage Agreements?

One drawback of longer-term wage agreements is the difficulty of predicting changes in prices and productivity. Formerly it may have seemed reasonable to make the contracting parties in the labour market bear the brunt of that uncertainty; in the future, however, it might make better sense for this responsibility to be taken on by the public sector. It already comprises over 60 per cent of the economy, and that share can be expected to increase during the 1980s. Over the next decade, then, it seems incumbent on the 40 percenters to band together against the 60 percenters in order to settle the question of who, given the unpredictability of external economic conditions for wage formation, will bear the risks.

In accordance with this strategy the contracting parties in the private labour market might put most of their efforts into increasing real private consumption after taxes and ensuring the lowest possible inflation rate. There is no reason to press wage demands to an extreme if it is possible to obtain a guaranteed rate of increase in real private consumption after taxes for active wage-earners over a given period. The size of corporate profits is determined not by wage negotiations but by fiscal policies. There are indications of such a development both in the report of the Royal Commission of 1978 on Long-Term Economic Trends and in the revised budget of April 1979. Given the scale of expenditures we can expect in the 1980s, even a marginal change in the public sector will have a considerable impact on corporate profitability and growth potential. Hence the contracting parties will develop more interest in exerting pressure on the public sector than in trying to influence the ratio of wages and profits.

Local tax rates are not under any kind of central control, which does present a problem. From another point of view, however, it may well be an advantage. If local expenditures by smaller communities are seen as a form of private consumption, they can be considered part and parcel of the guaranteed increases in that sphere. If the inhabitants of one municipality want to pay for boating marinas and riding facilities with their own taxes, while those in another prefer vacations abroad to higher taxes at home, then both kinds of expenditure – boating and riding as well as travelling – can be put in the category of private consumption. There is no problem, then, in the lack of central influence on local taxes. Difficulties do arise, however, when local governments *en masse* commit themselves to expenditure that their own constituencies are unwilling to pay for, and then try to blackmail central government into bailing them out. That sort of tactic is less likely to succeed if central government is unable to finance higher subsidies to the municipalities – by increasing indirect taxation, for example – because the contracting parties in wage agreements have set limits on its freedom of action.

One obvious weakness in this strategy – possibly a fatal one – is that the limits on governmental freedom of action will have to be set in terms of public income, not public expenditure. In 1978–9, when productivity was lagging, it made perfectly good sense to pursue an expansionary fiscal policy, including public borrowing on a vast scale. But in the 1980s, as more normal conditions are restored, this will no longer be the case. Indeed if collective agreements are hedged with clauses aimed at a guaranteed increase in real private consumption for the active labour force, the result could well be a deep crisis in our international balance of payments, not a slowdown in the activities of the public sector. And in a situation where public expenditure is allowed to rise, yet a ceiling is imposed on taxation, the resulting growth in public deficits will certainly lead to difficulties at the international level.

Despite such complications, the imbalance in the shares commanded by various components of the national economy will probably tend to unite wage-earners against the public sector, not against corporate profits. This might imply the consolidation of capital and public needs within a common pool. First, a certain proportion would be set aside for the real private consumption of the active workforce; then other groups – old age pensioners, capital-owners, public servants, and so on, would divide the remainder among themselves. As for the long-term effect of this development on relations between the contracting parties in the labour market, it is scarcely desirable for discussions on the distribution between wages and profits to take place outside this exclusive bargaining relationship, that is, to be shifted to the public sector, where the issues will inevitably become politicised. Even if employers and employees are in agreement, therefore, the only way they can influence the public sector is by appearing to be in conflict. This is bound to have a detrimental impact on social development in general.

Yet this situation does have the important effect of rendering central government more powerful in relation to local governments. If central government yields to the local governments it will have to resort to tax increases – at the expense of wage agreements. If the contracting parties adopt long-term stabilisation agreements, however, they will have a better chance of exerting pressure on the public sector.

The Wage Policy of the 1980s

Several factors suggest that long-term stabilisation agreements will become more and more common during the 1980s. First and foremost is the change in the international situation. Such a wage policy is crucial in order to ensure full employment and stable prices in a milieu characterised by unemployment and inflation, as well as by highly variable exchange rates whose primary causes, in the short run, are international financial factors and expectations. Secondly, the proportions among the major components of the economy – public services, corporate profits and the real private consumption of the active labour force – will shift in the 1980s, making it necessary for wage-earners to turn against the public sector in order to maintain their present level of real private consumption. A decline in the annual growth rate of local government consumption – from 4 to 2 per cent – will give wage-earners in the 1980s a much larger increase in private consumption than they had in the 1960s.

As far as we can see, the contracting parties in centralised negotiations are the only factor that can counteract the rampant growth of the public sector. But a one-year contract will not do: there simply is not enough time to exert any effective influence. This is yet another reason to expect long-term stabilisation agreements to become the trend of the future.

Notes: Chapter 12

1 *Towards Full Employment and Price Stability* (Paris, OECD, June 1977). An eight-member group of independent economists chaired by Paul McCracken (and including Assar Lindbeck) was responsible for the report.
2 The debate began with an article by A. Leijonhufvud, 'Effective demand failures', *Scandinavian Journal of Economics*, March 1973, and a comment on that article by H. Grossman, ibid., September 1973. Two more recent articles, 'The limits to stability of a full-employment equilibrium' (P. Hovitt, September 1978) and 'The corridor and local stability of the effective excess demand hypothesis: a result' (K.-G. Lövgren, March 1979), contain the analysis I have used.
3 G. Edgren, K.-O. Faxén and C. Odhner, *Wage Formation and the Economy* (London, Allen & Unwin, 1973).
4 Sources for the unemployment figures are: *Towards Full Employment and Price Stability* (Paris, OECD, 1977), p. 339, and *Economic Outlook* (Paris, OECD, December 1978); for consumer prices, *Economic Outlook* (OECD, December 1978), pp. 37 and 127. Labour costs and productivity figures were provided by the US Bureau of Labor Statistics for eleven countries, adjusted for GNP.
5 In the US context this idea has been presented by Arthur M. Okun in 'Efficient disinflationary policies', *American Economic Review*, Papers and Proceedings of the Ninetieth Annual Meeting of the American Economic Association, May 1978, pp. 348–52.
6 The source of Figure 12.1 is *The Road to Full Employment and Price Stability*, summary of the McCracken Report (Paris, OECD, June 1977), p. 191. See note 1, above.

13

Income Formation in a Mixed Economy

BENGT-CHRISTER YSANDER

Sweden's mixed economy has sometimes been described as an attempt to combine capitalism and socialism. And indeed it does express both a desire to reap the benefits of a productive system geared toward the market and international trade and a commitment to distribute these benefits in accordance with rather ambitious ideas of solidarity and justice. The only way a capitalistic allocation of resources and a socialistically inspired distribution of benefits can be combined and co-ordinated is through income formation. Ideally, this process should not only promote better living standards among various groups in society but also encourage higher levels of efficiency and industrial adaptability. If Sweden's mixed economy is to achieve a balanced development in the 1980s it is vital that income formation continues to serve this dual purpose. Well, can it?

Swedish economic development in the 1970s has been taken as proof that the mixed economy is on the verge of a breakdown. The escalation of egalitarian expectations as mirrored, for example, by increasing tax pressures, growing intervention in income formation and far-reaching proposals for changes in the structure of industrial ownership, is said to have delivered a crippling blow to unfettered income formation and the kind of incentive structure necessary for efficiency in decentralised labour and capital markets. Even if such harsh conclusions do not seem quite justified, it is none the less obvious that the developments of the 1970s have bared a number of problems and conflicting objectives in the realm of income formation. And in so doing they have also raised the question of how fast and by what means social transformations can be effected within the framework of a mixed economy.

These are great and decisive issues for the Swedish economy. They can be approached from various angles – I will try to indicate a few of them here – but the crux of the matter, as far as a mixed economy is concerned, is to recognise that policies of redistribution

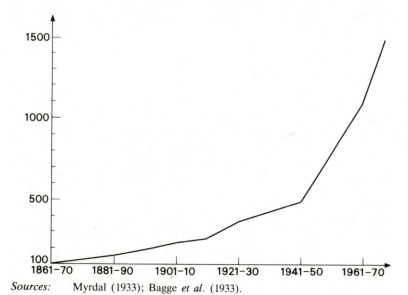

Sources: Myrdal (1933); Bagge *et al.* (1933).

Figure 13.1 *Real wages for adult male industrial workers (1861–70 = 100; the index figures refer to ten-year averages)*

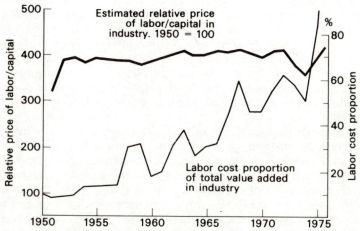

Sources: SNR (Swedish National Accounting), SCB (National Central Bureau of Statistics), Bergström (1976), Edgren *et al.* (1970).

Figure 13.2 *Relative price and cost share of labour in Swedish manufacturing, 1950–76.*

are subject to certain limiting factors. I shall discuss this problem in terms of the distribution between capital and labour, among various kinds of labour and among different categories of wage-earners.

The Rising Cost of Labour

One way of illustrating our economic development is to measure the real wages of industrial workers over the last 100 years (see Figure 13.1). The graph shows a continuous increase in real wages, with a marked acceleration after the Second World War. However, it tends to understate the rise of living standards, particularly with regard to the postwar years. Real wages do not tell us about redistribution by way of the public budget, nor do they reflect the value of the social insurance benefits that are being paid for by wage-sum taxes.

The increased well-being of wage-earners is paralleled by increased corporate labour costs, including various wage-related taxes. How has the higher cost of labour affected corporate options with regard to technology and investments? In order to offer any useful answers to that question, we must first study how hourly labour costs have developed in relation to the price of capital. Figure 13.2 shows the postwar development of the relative price of labour/capital. It is an attempt to quantify the relative cost development of labour as compared to real capital – to reconstruct the situation faced by a company contemplating an investment decision. Here the price of real capital utilisation can be expected to reflect not only the cost of machines and buildings, but also the minimum net yields stipulated by creditors, allowances for future depreciation, and the structure of corporate taxation. Yield requirements have been calculated in terms of the average effective return on industrial stocks and bonds, adjusted for the proportions of capital borrowed and capital owned (for a more detailed discussion of this capital cost concept, see Bergström, 1976, and Bergström and Södersten, 1979).

The dramatic increase in relative labour price as shown by Figure 13.2 may be attributed both to the development of real wages and at the same time to shifts in the various determinants of capital cost. Labour's relative share in industry underwent a sharp decline over the last few years of the period covered in the graph, largely owing to the intervention of measures to relieve corporate taxation, which in turn have substantially reduced the companies' capital costs.

With the relative price of labour on the rise, it is reasonable to assume that companies will replace human labour with machines. Over this period total working hours in industry were in fact reduced by about a seventh, while the value of capital equipment per working hour continued to rise. However, Figure 13.2 makes it clear that this trend toward capital-intensive methods was not strong enough to counteract increased wage costs. Indeed the wage proportion of the total value added industry remained fairly stable for much of the postwar era; only in the last few years have there been any marked changes. Not surprisingly we also find that, from 1960 on, short-term variations in relative price are reflected to some extent by changes in the proportion taken up by wage costs.

Figure 13.2 presents us with a reality that can be described or interpreted in many ways. It is frequently taken as proof that the scope for increased mechanisation does have limits after all; to some extent, however, this is offset by the fact that technological development tends to move in labour-saving directions (cf. Bentzel, 1978; Bergström and Melander, 1978; Jungenfelt, 1966; Åberg, 1969).

Another approach to the graph is to address the limitations of its way of measuring. Although the cost of a working hour has risen very high in relation to capital costs, this does not necessarily mean that the same drastic cost increase applies to comparable labour inputs. Conditions have improved in various respects – in particular through a higher educational level in schools as well as better on-the-job training – and there is greater efficiency in the distribution and management of work. It is not unlikely, therefore, that the qualitative returns on an average working hour have been substantially increased.

What Determines the Price of Capital?

To what extent can an 'explanation' based on economic models really account for the relative pricing of labour and capital? And is it possible for this relative price to be influenced and altered without undermining the very foundations of the mixed economy? These questions, crucial as they are to the current political debate, have another role as well: in the realm of economic theory they have set off what is known as the capital controversy,[1] one of the fiercest debates of the postwar era. A highly simplified illustration of the problem is provided by Figure 13.3, in which a system of co-ordinates indicates the movement of factor prices – real wages and real capital interest – over time. Here the economic development is interpreted in terms of equilibrium, against the background of a secure world in which all change is predictable. We also need to be able to compare labour and capital inputs at different times in order to 'explain' the prices of labour and capital in terms of their respective productivity.

Economic development is a continuum of technological choices, new combinations of machinery and human knowledge, and hence new sets of prices.[2] Does this mean that political measures would have no effect on the long-term relative price of labour/capital?

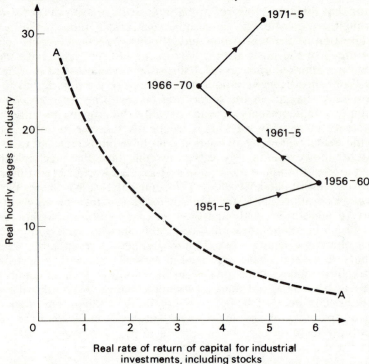

Sources: SCB (National Central Bureau of Statistics), SNR (Swedish National
Accounting), Bergström and Södersten (1979b).

Figure 13.3   *Real wages and real rate of return of capital in industry; theory
versus reality*

Such a conclusion would be warranted only if we made the further
assumption that prices are determined entirely by costs, irrespective
of demand. Otherwise the relative price would be affected by such
factors as the conditions of ownership and the distribution of
wealth. Therefore the political implications of this particular, rather
specialised model are somewhat anticlimactic. Although the relative
price of labour/capital in the model is not determined directly by
distribution policies, it can be influenced by measures to redistribute
wealth. Even in the abstract world of economic models the
problems of distribution persist – here one simply resorts to more
fundamental institutional changes in order to solve them. It is not
just that the model's specific assumptions about economic
development are suspect; we also know that the stable world it
portrays is quite remote from the real world of the mixed economy
with its uncertainties and disequilibria, its public sector and
government price regulations. We have no right to assume that the

actual development of the relationship between wages and capital yields, as shown by the five-year averages in Figure 13.3, can be interpreted in terms of a single unique path from one point of equilibrium to the next.

Hence in order to interpret and analyse postwar developments in Sweden we are forced to abandon the idea of explaining the long-term development of wages and yield of capital rents in terms of economic theory. Instead, for the purposes of long-term analysis, we must assume either wages or capital rents to be 'externally' given. For a number of reasons it is preferable to make the yield of capital the exogenous factor, with the wage level simply reflecting the surplus generated at a particular choice of production. In this case, what will determine long-term capital yield or an 'acceptable' level of profitability? Will that question be decided at political party caucuses or centralised wage negotiations? Can the Swedish Riksdag steer the long-term conditions of profitability in a certain direction – by changes in corporate taxation, for example – and expect the market economy to switch over smoothly to a growth track corresponding to the new relative price of labour/capital? Such notions seem implicit in many of the proposals put forth in recent political debate.

It is quite clear that corporate capital costs can be influenced by corporate taxation. But it is not at all clear whether the government and the Riksdag, through measures affecting the domestic capital market, will be able to alter the long-term profit expectations of private lenders regardless of developments in the outside world. Indeed most economists tend to believe that in a decentralised, open economy like ours long-term capital yield requirements are determined primarily by the investment opportunities available in the outside world. The choice of investing in one country or another is assessed largely in terms of the relative political and financial risks involved. This hypothesis seems very much in line with the more or less parallel development of profitability displayed by industrial countries during the postwar years.

From this point of view Sweden's gradual reduction of effective corporate taxation can be interpreted as an effort on the part of the government to satisfy external profit requirements, thus providing some compensation for dwindling gross profits. However, one must be extremely cautious about using this hypothesis to explain shorter-term developments in the capital market. Today Sweden's capital market is segmented, regulated and, consequently, inert. Industrial investments are financed not only through internal savings and other corporate resources, but also by households, the public sector and foreign lenders. Among these sources of capital there may be marked differences in motives for saving, investment opportunities and sensitivity to changes in interest rates.

Even with such reservations, however, the probable conclusion must be that in the long run developments in international capital markets make it impossible for the relative price of labour/capital to be a purely autonomous matter. This relative price is undeniably a decisive element in the choice of technology, the rate of growth and the allocation of resources. It is debatable, however, whether it is equally decisive in the area of income distribution. After all, the dividends and capital gains yielded by industrial investment represent only a tiny proportion of the nation's total personal wealth.

Major economic policy decisions may be influenced by one's conception of how capital yield requirements are determined. One recent example comes from the area of taxation, where it has been proposed that a general tax should be levelled on factors – that is, that value added tax be extended to cover investment goods as well. Increasing investment costs are meant to reduce the income of capital-owners. But since long-term profit requirements depend primarily on the outside world, as discussed above, such attempts to reduce capital yields may ultimately affect not the owners but the employees, whose jobs and living standards could be compromised by dwindling investments and slower economic growth.

Capital Formation and Capital Prices in the 1980s

If the profit requirements of the outside world determine our chances of affecting the distribution between labour and capital in an open, decentralised economy how does that affect the problems of capital formation that seem to dominate the current debate over long-term economic prospects?

The point of departure for the debate is the contention that the Swedish economy has a built-in savings shortage. According to that theory, even in the long run and at full productive capacity our spending and saving pattern causes industrial investments to become inadequate, our growth too slow and our foreign debt too large. Against this background compulsory funds are sometimes presented as a necessary complement to existing capital markets and opportunities for self-financing (cf. SOU, 1978, and Ysander, 1979b).

It is difficult, if not impossible, to predict precisely what rate of return on capital will be required in the 1980s to achieve an adequate long-term increase in investment level. It is often argued, albeit indirectly, that there will be a long-term increase in profit requirements. Under conditions of greater instability and commercial risk companies will no longer be able to accept the liquidity risks inherent in a low solidity ratio and will thus be forced to lower their debt ratio by means of increased profits and a higher proportion of self-financing. So this argument brings us right back to the question of what risks are in prospect on Sweden's capital market. The same question arises when we consider various proposals to complement the existing capital market by means of new, collective forms of finance. How will such measures affect industrial investments and the profit expectations of private lenders? That may depend primarily on whether they are designed to increase risk-taking or to reduce it.

Thus the government and the Riksdag can act, if only indirectly, to steer developments in the proper direction. Above all, economic policies can be used both to minimise the risks borne by individual investors and, at the same time, to help make the capital market better able to adjust quickly and smoothly to such changes.

Wage Differentiation versus Profit Differentiation

Although the relative price of labour/capital in industry is crucial to investments and the allocation of resources, it does not have much of an immediate impact on income distribution. In the realm of distribution, wage formation becomes the decisive element. A persistent goal of postwar wage policies and wage formation has been the achievement and maintenance of long-term equilibrium wages – equal pay for equal work – for each sector of the labour force.

A long-term equilibrium wage for a given profession or category of employees refers to the smooth wage development that would occur if all adjustments to the needs of the business cycle and all structural adaptations could be made without temporary variations in pay among different companies, sectors, regions, and so forth. In concrete terms such a principle means that all employees in a given professional category should be entitled to the same wages, no matter where they work – in profitable or unprofitable enterprises, in expanding or stagnating sectors, in a region of rapid growth or an underdeveloped one. The individual wage-earner should not have to bear the risks implied by technological and economic uncertainties.

In this fundamental sense wage solidarity is hardly a controversial principle. On the contrary it can even be viewed as a prerequisite for the central contracting organisations, making possible a successful co-ordination of the demands and interests of their members (see Grassman *et al.*, 1978, ch. 5). From the trade unions' point of view the principle seems to complement their desire to limit the role played by local agreements and to minimise the wage drift. From the corporations' point of view it seems very much in line with their pursuit of long-term wage stability or regulation – a goal established by the very documents that ratified the Swedish Employers' Confederation at the turn of the century.

There is a natural congruence between the organisational

structure of the labour market and this version of the principle of wage solidarity. The very fact that the unions are organised along sectoral lines, for instance, makes it logical to start with a sectoral application of the basic tenet of equal wages for equal work. With mergers between unions and the formation of centralised negotiating cartels, there is a tendency to apply the principle to increasingly larger sectors of the total area covered by collective agreements.

At the same time the principle implies a redistribution of risk-taking within the economy. When variations in profitability among individual companies are no longer reflected in wage differentials, then profit differentiation tends to become sharper, corporate risk-taking increases, and profits play a larger role in determining structural adjustments. This, after all, was exactly what the trade unions were aiming for when they conceived their programme of solidarity back in the 1950s. Moreover the role of profits as major determinants of the allocation of resources has been further enhanced by tax policies that proved more advantageous to profitable, expanding companies than to more marginal ones.

To wage-earners the principle of solidarity has meant a sort of trade-off: wage risks go down only to be replaced – at least in part – by employment risks. In the policies of the last few years there has been a notable effort not only to equalise those local employment risks but also to diminish their overall effect. Such attempts, however, are bound to create a political dilemma. Public job guarantees imply, more often than not, that the government will take over part of the risk faced by capital-owners. And that in turn raises questions about income distribution: ought not such risk-taking be paid for out of the owners' projected profits? However, proposals of this sort imply a socialisation of capital that may in the long run be incompatible with the desire to maintain a decentralised capital market.

How Are Equilibrium Wages Determined?

What determines how much a university lecturer should earn as compared to a worker in a steel foundry or a refuse collector? We know that short-term variations in relative wages can be explained by market conditions. But can the theory of the market economy also help us understand the relative development of long-term equilibrium wages? Can our earlier arguments regarding the relative price of labour/capital now be used as a basis for generalisations about a situation characterised by a multitude of labour inputs and, accordingly, by a wide variation in wages?

One way to generalise might be to imagine a world in perfect equilibrium: technological and organisational development would follow a single pattern, no matter what the politicians or the parties in the labour market may decide; each new technological choice, moreover, would be precisely correlated with a given set of relative wages and capital rents. Those sets of factor prices, therefore, would change continually, in accordance with the economic 'script'. In such a model even long-term wage formation could be described as endogenous. And in the long run, too, the wages of a given group of employees would be equivalent to its marginal product. We can simplify even further by treating the skills of various kinds of labour as just varying amounts of measurable homogeneous units – a sort of human capital. Wages in that case would be seen as the interest earned by such capital – the return on an investment of education and talent. Given our earlier assumption of a chiefly exogenous profit requirement for capital, it would follow that wages – as well as the distribution of wages under conditions of equilibrium – are determined mainly by developments in the outside world, though our own human capital resources also play a part.

With this application of the human capital theory, then, one would be inclined to dismantle the government's whole arsenal of policies and regulations. It would be futile to attempt any manipulation of wage formation for the purposes of distribution. Such measures would only create new 'market failures' and these in turn would be reflected in new problems of employment and under-utilisation of resources. In short the only way of influencing wage formation would be by indirect means: by equalising educational opportunities among individuals through an improved system of loans or a redistribution of wealth (Schultz, 1963, and Becker, 1964; cf. Lindbeck, 1974).

What if one is reluctant to interpret developments in terms of the equilibrium model and is sceptical about the theoretical assumptions cited above? Then one must look elsewhere – among the social factors – for an explanation of long-term relative wages. From this point of view relative wages are a matter of political and social convention. One major consideration in such conventions is the standards, both quantitative and qualitative, of formal education. International surveys, such as those of the OECD, suggest that in Sweden, compared with most other industrial countries, children from middle- and upper-class families are still substantially over-represented in institutions of higher education. Moreover it is more probable here than elsewhere that such an educational background will lead to a correspondingly privileged situation in terms of professional position and salary (OECD, 1973 and 1974; Sohlman, 1976). According to Nam's OECD study (OECD, 1973), the over-representation of upper social strata in university enrolment during the 1960s was higher in Sweden than in all other OECD countries except Spain, Portugal and Italy. In this sense wage formation can be said to express social classification even across generational lines.

Nevertheless during the 1960s and 1970s Sweden has also shown marked tendencies towards the equalisation of wages among various categories of employees. The most noticeable elements in that equalisation have been the diminishing wage gap between men and women in the same professional position, and between white- and blue-collar workers.

The latter trend – at least as it applies to the area covered by the Swedish Employers' Confederation – is illustrated in Figure 13.4. In both cases the equalisation has been in accordance with contemporary changes in the labour market. The expansion of such public sectors as health, welfare and education has created a larger demand for female labour and must have had an impact on women's wages in industry as well. Furthermore the employment situation has been considerably less favourable to white-collar workers than to blue-collar workers during the past decade. At the same time, with the achievement of some equalisation within trade union membership, pressure has been growing for an acceleration of that process and for a radically different wage structure as well. Hence tensions among various wage-earning groups have increased and their cumulative demands for compensation may add to the risk of cost inflation and labour conflicts (Faxén, 1976).

Source: SAF (Swedish Employers Federation), Faxén (1976).

Figure 13.4 *Cumulative wage-cost difference between white- and blue-collar workers, 1963–75*

During the 1970s the central contracting parties in the labour market have been intensifying their pursuit of the solidarity policy, with the ultimate goal of narrowing existing wage differences not only within individual companies but across the board. This endeavour has led not only to conflict with the employers but also to tensions within the trade unions – as expressed, for example, in the growing number of wildcat strikes and in the tendency for local agreements and wage drift to have a greater relative impact.

To what extent do centralised wage negotiations determine long-term relative wages? In the wage structure of countries whose labour market is significantly less organised and centralised than Sweden's there has been a similar tendency toward equal pay and an equalisation within wage-earners associations. Thus we cannot rule out the possibility that the major role of centralised negotiations, as far as the long-term wage structure is concerned, is simply an *ex post facto* codification and legitimation of certain shifts in social values and attitudes that tend to occur more or less simultaneously in most industrial countries.

Wage Equalisation in the 1980s

Many of the problems associated with wage formation in the 1970s can be interpreted as a lack of co-ordination between structural changes in the technological and social spheres. Disequilibria and conflicts in the labour market seem to express collision between two wage principles: 'power of the purse' and 'quality of work'. Economic history, including the postwar era in Sweden, overflows with examples of structural, technology-induced changes that have subjected wage-earners to difficult and conflict-ridden adjustment processes; they may face not only a decline in their relative position on the labour market, but the loss of their jobs.

However, the labour market of the 1970s has also exemplified conflicts of a different sort. Rising egalitarian ambitions and quick shifts in attitude regarding the relative quality of different jobs – coinciding, among other things, with a higher and more uniform educational level among younger workers – have raised demands for radically different wage structure. There is every reason to expect such demands for equality to be just as vocal during the 1980s, as the labour market begins to feel the full effect of the educational boom of the 1960s and 1970s. In order to satisfy those demands without loss of jobs or of profits we will obviously need sufficient economic growth, rapid technological change and consistently high mobility in the labour market. A different wage structure presupposes fresh technological alternatives and a revised pattern of production; generally speaking this can be achieved only by the acquisition of new equipment and successful adjustment to a new sectoral and regional structure. As far as wage formation is concerned, then, it is growth – and the conditions determining it – that dictates the scope for distribution policies.

In public debate, however, a different relationship between growth and wage equalisation has frequently been emphasised. Mobility in the labour market requires a wage structure flexible enough to offer workers strong economic incentives for changing jobs. In the long run, of course, such requirements will be diametrically opposed to the trade unions' demands for equalisation of short-term and local wage variations. But even if one accepts the far from self-evident assumption that wage incentives are vital for mobility, our practical experience so far seems to indicate that progressive tax scales play a significantly larger role than wage equalisation in reducing those incentives.

Taxes and Transfers

So far we have discussed only the pricing mechanism of factor markets. In Sweden's mixed economy, however, factor prices are not decisive for the distribution of real incomes and living standards. Instead that distribution is increasingly being determined by public decisions on taxes and subsidies. The subsidies affect the real price paid for production factors either directly, or indirectly, by determining how much can be bought for a given nominal income. In this sense, most of the public budgets – the main exceptions being expenditures for public utilities and certain transfers unrelated to income – can be considered instruments of a public price policy. Through various factor taxes and factor subsidies – from income taxes and energy taxes to the twenty-five crown subsidy for vocational training and regional financial aid – the market price and use of production factors are affected. By means of product-related taxes and subsidies politicians also influence consumer markets for tobacco, alcoholic beverages, food, medicine, housing and, above all, various kinds of social services and insurance.

A summary of the redistributive effect of such public price regulation is presented in Figure 13.5, which shows the development of tax and subsidy ratios in the postwar period. The tax ratio measures what proportion of the aggregate gross income of the private sector (excluding capital depreciation) goes to taxes and levies. The subsidy ratio tells us what proportion of that income consists of transfers from the public sector, including social insurance compensation. The graph shows that taxes and levies took slightly more than 23 per cent of disposable private income in 1950 while by 1976 their share had risen to 60 per cent. Only 8 per cent of

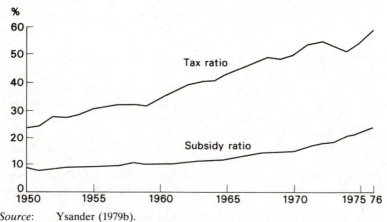

Source: Ysander (1979b).

Figure 13.5   *Tax and subsidy rates, 1950–76*

disposable income in 1950 was made up of transfers and social insurance payments; in 1976 a fourth of that income was dependent on such sources (see Ysander, 1979b).

Is it possible for this ever-larger public price regulation – whose chief motivation is a concern for redistribution – to go on without causing undesirable distortions of factor price formation and hence of resource allocation throughout the economy?

The Breach of Neutrality in Tax Policies

Taxes and subsidies ought to be neutral – that is, they should not affect or alter the conditions for individual decisions on resource allocation except in so far as this is part of an explicit political objective. Furthermore market decisions must be independent of political decisions on taxes and subsidies. In other words the public price regulation brought about by taxes and subsidies should be viewed as externally given, not as a matter for negotiation by individuals, households and enterprises.

Unless these conditions are met public authorities will take on more and more of the responsibility for the allocation of resources in the various markets. If taxes and subsidies have a significant impact on the relative prices of various production factors this in turn will affect jobs and profits in individual companies and sectors. In short, measures aimed at redistribution can inadvertently create a whole industrial policy that gets in through the back door, via income formation. Profitability crises and employment problems may in turn put pressure on the state to correct the situation through appropriate policies in the spheres of employment and industry.

All this is nothing new; it has long since been recognised. Over the last few decades there has been a concerted effort to keep taxes as neutral as possible, despite mounting pressures in this area. Different tax regulations were integrated within the framework of a consistent income tax system and a switch was made from turnover tax to value added tax, to name just two major examples of this policy. The trend towards more comprehensive tax legislation may also be interpreted as expressing a desire to maintain the independence of taxation.

During the last few years, however, owing to a combination of high taxes, inflation, and internationally induced disruptions of the business cycle, it has become increasingly difficult to maintain even the illusion of neutrality and independence with regard to taxes and subsidies. It is a well-known fact that even when gross capital yields are identical, net yields will vary widely because of tax differences. This is due in part to the difficulties involved in finding equitable and efficient methods of taxing capital gains within the framework of income taxation (Johansson, 1977, and Hansson, 1978). As far as wages or salaries are concerned, individual choices of job or profession, working hours and forms of compensation have been determined increasingly by the design of the tax system (see Ysander, 1979b). Thus policies of redistribution have made it harder to maintain an efficient system of resource allocation. At the same time, because households and businesses have been given opportunities and incentives to adjust their resource allocation so as to draw maximum benefit from the public sector, there are growing inequities in the distribution of income and wealth. Today the living standard of a given household often depends more on how much one expects to make in the form of tax-favoured capital income than it does on the size of the wage-earner's pay packet. Similarly, some professional and income categories have far greater access than others to legal tax deductions, subsidies and various methods of tax avoidance. Thus while the formal tax system has become increasingly comprehensive and consistent, the actual situation is marked by growing injustice and inequality. In so far as changes in the tax system are inspired by ambitious plans for the redistribution of income and wealth, such policies now tend to be counterproductive.

Wage Agreements versus Tax Agreements

The lack of independence in recent tax policy has had an especially noticeable effect on wage formation. Taxes and government subsidies have made it more difficult to conclude labour agreements and have exacerbated tensions and demands for compensation among different categories of wage-earners. High levels of taxation and steeply progressive formal tax scales which vary from one group of employees to another, in addition to a rapid rate of inflation, have forced the government to take an increasingly active role in centralised wage negotiations.[3] Those gross wage increases that are compatible with the maintenance of relative price stability and a favourable competitive position may imply a level and distribution of net wages that is unacceptable. At this point one of two things will happen. The government may adjust income tax rates in an effort to counteract the effect of inflation and establish a more acceptable level of net wage distribution. During the 1970s most of the improvements in net earnings among low-income groups have been generated in this way. Unless adequate adjustments of this kind are made compensatory wage claims may well trigger an inflationary cost push, raising the spectre of problems in sales and employment. As a result the government may then be forced to balance out the impact of the wage agreements by such *ex post facto* measures as employment subsidies or labour legislation.

In both cases the influence of the government and the Riksdag becomes dominant, not only in overall wage negotiations but also in specific agreements concerning individual categories of employees. The central organisations in the labour market thus have less and less power to affect the outcome of the negotiations.

Alternatives for the 1980s

We can expect growing difficulties in our attempt to combine state-sponsored redistribution with independent price formation and an efficient, stable system of resource allocation. Ultimately we may be forced to choose between two radically different alternatives.

The first alternative would be an ever more comprehensive income policy with the major responsibility for distributing the resources available for wages being turned over to the government and the Riksdag. Such regulation, particularly with the added support of publicly guaranteed real wages or other minimum wage guarantees, would facilitate long-term wage stabilisation. But this course of action would take us farther and farther away from the mixed economy that now prevails. It is difficult to imagine that a comprehensive incomes policy would not eventually affect capital incomes as well as wages. To regulate factor prices is to regulate corporate profits. Thus it scarcely seems likely that a centrally regulated process of income formation would be compatible with a decentralised system of resource allocation.

The second alternative would be an attempt to re-establish the neutrality and independence of taxation through a radical restructuring of the tax system. This, presumably, is one of the main purposes of the various proposals currently making the rounds – taxes on expenditure rather than income, for example, or expanded social insurance and new forms of indirect taxation that would gradually take on a larger share of the tax burden. Our chances of re-establishing autonomous income formation will probably depend largely on the future rate of inflation. All the above-mentioned risks of distortion and injustice will be multiplied if inflation is high. A low rate of inflation, therefore, is a prerequisite for keeping problems to a minimum and for creating a negotiating climate that facilitates long-term readjustments.

But Sweden's present tax system has a destabilising effect; it increases the sensitivity of the economy to external inflationary trends. This is yet another reason for the requisite changes in the tax system to be discussed as soon as possible, so that they can be undertaken in a situation that still offers relatively favourable external conditions for price and wage stability.

One of the most crucial problems today is that redistribution policy defeats its own purposes by distorting resource allocation in individual markets and thus providing strong incentives for 'tax adjusting' behaviour. We are fast approaching a situation in which the formal system of taxes and subsidies bears little resemblance to its actual impact. Though formal tax scales are steeply progressive, for example, they may already be having the opposite effect among certain high-income groups, since the real tax burden – as measured in terms of living standards – tends to decline as incomes rise. In this way distortions of allocation combine with undesirable effects on income distribution into a truly unholy alliance.

In practice the two alternatives I have outlined may not be wholly incompatible. It is possible – perhaps even probable – that far-reaching changes in the system of taxes and subsidies will require a more active government incomes policy over the next few years. This would be true if a tax on expenditure were introduced, for instance. And it would certainly apply to the more utopian idea of a gradual shift to net wage negotiations, which would obviously require special government measures during the transitional period. In order to avoid imbalances in the various sectoral labour markets, for example, the relative wage costs of various groups of employees would have to be kept at a more or less constant level. This could be accomplished via some sort of wage tax that is not directly related to income – a differentiated tax on education, perhaps.

The Limits of Redistribution Policies

My original question about the conditions of income formation in a mixed economy was above all concerned with the factors that determine the scope for a policy of redistribution. Let me briefly summarise the conclusions suggested by the previous discussion.

In a small, open economy like ours the chief determinant of domestic capital costs will be private capital yield requirements, which in turn are based on alternative investment options available abroad. Hence there are limits on the power of political decisions to bring about quick and radical changes in capital income's share of total income. Though such changes are intended to alter the distribution of income they are more likely to affect investments instead.

Policies aimed at an accelerated equalisation of wages may in a similar manner end up by creating unemployment rather than improving income distribution. Looking ahead to the end of the decade, will it be possible to satisfy demands for equalisation while still maintaining a balanced course of development? That will depend very much on our rate of economic growth. In this respect there is already a clear conflict between demands for lower mobility and increased local job security, on the one hand, and hopes for a radical transformation of the wage structure, on the other.

One of the key issues of the 1980s will be whether free wage formation will have sufficient scope to survive, despite the expectation of further increases in the demand for public services and the related needs of tax finance. The situation is far from hopeless. But one prerequisite of any long-term solution is a willingness to start out from an unbiased analysis of the actual functioning of the present system and to consider radical changes in the whole structure of public finance.

Notes: Chapter 13

1   For a general review of the capital controversy, see Bliss (1975) and Harcourt and Laing (1971).
2   For an account of cross-sectoral studies of the return on investments in education and an analysis of how wage differences can be interpreted in terms of human capital, see Klevmarken (1974) and Ysander (1978).
3   On the question of how and why marginal taxes affect negotiations a brief explanation may be in order. Perhaps the easiest way to approach the problem is to measure tax progression by comparing net average after-tax wages (as a percentage of gross wages) with the net additional income produced by a marginal wage increase. In the absence of a generally accepted term, let us call this the 'progression ratio'. If that ratio is 3 it means that in order to obtain a given increase in one's net wages one must demand a gross wage increase that is three times as high. If, for instance, a wage-earner is to be compensated for an inflation rate of 10 per cent and achieve a 3 per cent real after-tax increase, he or she must demand a gross wage increase of $3 \times 13 = 39$ per cent. The average progression ratio today (including subsidies as well as taxes) is likely to be about 2, but it varies widely – from a low of 1·25 to a high of 5 – among different groups of wage-earners and salaried employees. The highest progression ratio is usually found among low-income workers.

216 Sweden: Economic and Social Policy

References: Chapter 13

Åberg, Y. (1969), *Produktion och produktivitet i Sverige 1861–1965* (Stockholm, The Industrial Institute for Economic and Social Research).

Bagge, G., Lundberg, E., Svennilson, I. (1935), *Wages in Sweden 1860–1930* (London, P. S. King & Son), I–II.

Becker, G. (1964), *Human Capital* (New York, National Bureau of Economic Research).

Bentzel, R. (1978), 'A Vintage Model of Swedish Economic Growth from 1970 to 1975', in *The Importance of Technology and the Permanence of Structure in Industrial Growth*, (eds B. Carlsson, G. Eliasson and I. Nadiri) (Stockholm, The Industrial Institute for Economic and Social Research).

Bergström, V. (1976), 'Approaches to the Theory of Capital Cost', *Scandinavian Journal of Economics*, no. 3.

Bergström, V., and Melander, H. (1978), *Production Function and Factor Demand Functions in Post War Swedish Industry* (Stockholm, Arbetslivscentrum (Work Life Center)), Working Paper W 1978:8.

Bergström, V., and Södersten, J. (1979a), *Inflation, Taxation and Capital Cost*, Working Paper no. 19, (Stockholm, The Industrial Institute for Economic and Social Research).

Bergström, V., and Södersten, J. (1979b), 'Nominal and Real Profit in Swedish Industry', *Skandinaviska Enskilda Banken Quarterly Review*, no. 1–2.

Bliss, C. J. (1975), *Capital Theory and the Distribution of Income* (Amsterdam, North-Holland).

Edgren, G., Faxén, K.-O., and Odhner, C. E. (1973), *Wage Formation and the Economy* (London, Allen & Unwin).

Faxén, K.-O. (1977), 'Wage Policy and Attitudes of Industrial Relation Parties in Sweden', *Labor and Society*, vol. 2, no. 1.

Grassman, S., *et al.* (1978), *Blandekonomi i kris?* (Mixed Economy in Crisis) (Stockholm, Business and Social Research Institute).

Hansson, I. (1978), 'Skattesystemet, inflationen och investeringarna', *Ekonomisk debatt*, no. 4.

Harcourt, G. C. and Laing, N. F. (eds) (1971), *Capital and Growth* (Harmondsworth, Penguin Education).

Johansson, S.-E. (1977), 'Lönsamhetsbedömning under inflation', *Skandinaviska Enskilda Banken Quarterly Review*, no. 3–4.

Jungenfelt, K. G. (1966), *Löneandelen och den ekonomiska utvecklingen* (Stockholm, The Industrial Institute for Economic and Social Research).

Klevmarken, A., *et al.* (1974), *Industritjänstemännens lönestruktur*, (Stockholm, The Industrial Institute for Economic and Social Research).

Lindbeck, A. (1974), *Inequality and Distribution Policy Issues*, (Paris, The Directorate of Scientific Affairs, OECD).

Myrdal, G. (1933), *The Cost of Living in Sweden 1830–1930* (London, P. S. King & Son).

OECD (1973), *Mass Higher Education* (Paris).

OECD (1974), *Towards Mass Higher Education* (Paris).

Schultz, T. W. (1971), *Investment in Human Capital* (New York, The Free Press).

Sohlman, Å. (1981), *Education, Labor Market and Human Capital Models* (Stockholm, University of Stockholm).

SOU (1978), *Kapitalmarknaden i svensk ekonomi* (The Swedish Capital Market), Government Commission Reports (SOU) 1978:11 (Stockholm, Government Printer).

Ysander, B.-C. *et al.* (1978), *Earning and Learning* (Stockholm, National Board of Universities and Colleges).

Ysander, B.-C. (1979a), 'Våra skatter 1950–2000', in *Svensk Skatteforskning* (Stockholm, Humanistisk-samhällsvetenskapliga forskningsrådet).

Ysander, B.-C. (1979b), 'Postskriptum till fondfrågan', in N. Lundgret (ed.), *Sju socialdemokrater om löntagarfonderna* (Stockholm, Tiden).

14

Perspectives on the Future of the Swedish Economy – Two Extreme Alternatives

ERIK LUNDBERG

The Experience of the 1970s

The path taken by Sweden's economic development over the last decade offers some valuable guidelines for a discussion of our prospects for development in the 1980s. The main points can be summarised as follows:

- The low *growth rate* of GNP between 1969 and 1979 – 1·5–2 per cent a year, compared with 4–5 per cent in the 1950s and 1960s. The difference is so great that it is no exaggeration to call it a break with the past. This is a global phenomenon: world trade is increasingly unstable; the growth of productive capacity is lagging behind; exchange rates are fluctuating. All these are very much of the new international conditions for economic development in Sweden.
- A significantly higher *rate of inflation* – 8–14 per cent annually instead of 4 per cent – and, in addition, stronger price fluctuations. The combination of these two tendencies is what we call 'stagflation'.
- Lower *employment* is a feature of post-1974 developments. Some 8–10 per cent of the actual and potential labour supply in the market has no regular employment.
- Expenditure by *the public sector* (including transfers) has expanded from about 40 per cent of GNP to 65 per cent. Since its income has not increased as rapidly the net result has been a drop in public finances – from +10 per cent of GNP to −4 in 1978.
- *Investment and savings ratios* have declined, while the structure of investments and savings has undergone significant changes.

- Since the mid-1960s, our *balance-of-payments* position has tended to become weaker, especially in 1973–7. A mounting foreign debt is a new feature of our economy.
- A number of *structural disequilibria* have emerged in various sectors of the Swedish economy. They are chiefly the result of international structural crises, which in turn have been exacerbated by a lower rate of growth in world production and foreign trade. Our country has been hit particularly hard by the crises, since many of them have concerned such basic Swedish industries as iron ore, iron, forestry and shipping. Swedish industry seems to have lost a good many of its comparative advantages in the international distribution of labour.
- The 'British disease' that afflicted the Swedish economy in the 1970s has brought about a change in economic policy. We have had much more of an active wage policy in terms of taxation; a strongly selective element has also been introduced into labour market and industrial policies. In part this may be seen as a response to uneven economic development, particularly since 1974, but it is also a consequence of rising expectations with respect to employment and regional parity. Hence political interference in industrial decision-making has become more and more prevalent. Admittedly we may still be too close to the 1970s to make valid generalisations, and it may be premature to speak of trends. After all the decade was severely fragmented by the boom of 1973–4 and the deep recession of 1975–7. Nevertheless my general remarks may provide a useful starting point for a discussion of our prospects for the 1980s.

Moreover one finds that visions of the future are sometimes prefigured by the current goals of government economic policy as well as by the attitudes of various social groups toward the ends and means of economic development. Again let me summarise the situation, outlining some of the recent changes that have occurred.

- For a variety of reasons *growth objectives* have been cut back. There seems to be a consensus that conditions for growth are deteriorating, partly because of long-term international trends toward decline, but also because of reduced domestic capacity for adjustment. The 1978 analysis of the Royal Commission on Long-Term Economic Trends has resigned us to the prospect of a 2–3 per cent annual growth rate in GNP. General attitudes toward growth are scarcely as self-evident as they were in the 1960s. More and more voices are being raised to question the intrinsic value of a rising material standard of living. Economic growth has been downgraded; it is now seen chiefly as a vehicle for other goals – such as full employment, the minimisation of social frictions in the process of income redistribution, and the optimisation of the mixed economy system.

- Professions of faith in *stable currency* are still a consistent feature of government Bills. But that target is given a very flexible interpretation, based on the current inflation rate. What people are talking about here is keeping the price level as stable as possible. The goal of price stability has thus become a means of preventing, within the framework of stable currency rates, a decline in the competitive position of Swedish industry, thereby defending certain objectives with respect to our balance-of-payments situation. In a number of other countries an excessively high rate of price increases has been met with strong protests; in Sweden, however, people still believe that the goal of full employment is far more important than that of price stabilisation. Nevertheless a double-digit annual inflation rate is considered highly undesirable.
- *Employment objectives* have been made sharper and more precise in the 1970s. New slogans have emerged ('jobs for everybody'); new demands have been advanced for job security and full employment at the regional level. Furthermore, employment policies have been broadened: they seek not only matter to combat existing unemployment but also to facilitate the entry of new groups into the labour market, thus raising the total level of employment. Then, too, the scope has widened in the sense that we must now face employment problems in the workplace, before actual layoffs have occurred. At the same time there is greater urgency among the public with regard to employment goals – quite a contrast to the general resignation as far as price stability is concerned. Sweden's bad employment record during the 1970s has not led people in our country, as opposed to those in several others, to accept more modest objectives. On the contrary they are now demanding employment near the areas where they live, a minimum of relocation and maximum job security and, on top of all that, meaningful work under conditions that meet certain qualitative standards.
- Aspirations and attitudes with regard to the *public sector* are complex and highly contradictory. On the one hand there is a vast demand for public services, which are considered more important than a wider choice of the products supplied by private industry ('gadgets'). Social needs, the inexorable demands of the pension system and increased claims for income equalisation have been the driving force behind the massive explosion of transfer expenditure in the 1970s. As far as needs are concerned there is virtually no limit on how high public expenditure could go. But the rising pressure of the tax squeeze has also engendered criticisms of the public sector's inefficiency

in pursuing social goals, including the somewhat ill-defined objective of income distribution.

As a matter of fact, public attitudes towards income equalisation have not emerged very clearly during the 1970s. Instead they seem trapped in a set of vague assumptions that make certain rational economic policies – which would make things worse for low-income groups and, apparently, benefit high-income groups – seem politically unacceptable. Although people offer no explicit demands for income distribution (in all its dimensions), they seem to feel that now, as the decade ends, we are farther away than ever from achieving 'satisfactory goals'.

With regard to national objectives for *capital formation*, there is unanimity on the importance of raising the savings ratio from the low level of 1977–8, principally as a means of reaching other goals – for example, industrial expansion to eliminate the current balance-of-payments deficit. As for the *balance-of-payments* objective itself – now apparently postponed till the end of the 1980s – the broad support it has mustered seems partly due to mistaken attitudes or preferences. People may believe it is unnatural, or even immoral, for a rich country like Sweden to become dependent on foreign loans to cover its savings deficit, especially if, in doing so, we make it harder for poor countries to fulfil their own more legitimate borrowing needs. In addition there is the worry that increasing reliance on international financial resources may jeopardise our autonomy – that at the end of the 1980s we will be invaded by officials of the International Monetary Fund eager to prescribe drastic cuts in public welfare expenditures. It scarcely seems probable, however, that the mismanagement of public finances and foreign payments will become severe enough to bring current trends to such a climax.

There is a great deal of disagreement over what public policy on capital formation should be. To what degree should we rely on the operation of free market forces, to what extent on collective savings in various forms? The crux of the matter is the minimum profit level that can be tolerated. It seems generally accepted that some improvement in the profitability of private enterprise is necessary in order to re-establish our economy as a functioning system. But attitudes begin to diverge when it comes to questions of power and income distribution, and this complicates the situation. Various forms of collective savings offer no real alternative. There, we are moving into the terrain of objectives and attitudes that concern the viability of the economic system itself, and demands for its transformation.

• The post-1974 period of deep recession and stagnation,

combined with a number of severe structural crises, can be said to have made the *viability economy* a more pressing issue in a number of respects. The signals given by prices and profits are often misleading. Inflation and 'superprofits' in 1973–4 prompted overinvestment (even on an international scale), leading to overproduction and structural crises in a number of sectors. These problems can only be overcome very slowly. The dynamics of economic development have been deficient in the 1970s, in the sense of both 'destruction' and 'creation', to use Schumpeter's terms. Unprofitable lines of production disappear too slowly, or not at all. And even when resources are made available they are not always used to advantage by expanding enterprises or sectors. There are too few new investments and areas of expansion in private industry.

- One new feature of the 1970s in the *uncertainty* of future prospects, so that there are greater risks associated with investment. As a result, investments have increasingly been geared toward rationalisation rather than expansion. The prevailing uncertainty can be traced back to the great disruptions of the 1970s: the oscillation of international exchange rates, fluctuations in the rate of inflation, structural crises, and so forth. In addition there is general uneasiness about such matters as prices, energy supplies, growing protectionism and threats of wage-earners' investment funds.

These negative experiences with the performance of private industry in the 1970s, and the fear of future hardships, have brought about two diametrically opposed attitudes. According to the first, the troubles we experienced during the 1970s were not due primarily to deficiencies in the market economy. Rather, the blame rests squarely on bad government policies, in Sweden and elsewhere. Those policies have caused inflation, stagnation, disruptions in the balance of payments and shaky currency rates. As for government intervention when breakdowns occur, such tampering with the market system has only undermined confidence still further. Above all, it is the huge public sector, with its disruptive system of taxes and social welfare, that is responsible for dysfunctions in the market economy.

The opposite opinion can be expressed in equally strong terms. The price mechanism of the market is too shortsighted to provide the guidance needed to deal with long-term structural disruptions. Large investments involving expansion into new technology and markets are too risky to be assumed by individual companies with limited financial resources. Corporate cost-benefit analyses are incompatible with basic socioeconomic/macroeconomic principles in several crucial respects: they express excessive profit expectations and too-high an aversion to risk; environmental and other external costs are not usually taken into account; wage costs fail to reflect the real social costs in the case of corporate liquidations, and so on. A relatively free market system is unstable; furthermore, even if it does operate in a dynamic, expensive manner it tends to hasten the growth of intolerable inequities in income and wealth.

What can we conclude from such arguments? Either that the market system can be made to function reasonably well, as in the 1950s and 1960s, with a limited amount of government intervention, taxation and stabilising measures, or, on the other hand, that our problems during the 1970s and our anxieties about future hardships in the 1980s warrant an interventionist economic policy – perhaps even a radical reappraisal of the rules of the game of the mixed economy. In order to clarify the problems I shall now develop two extreme alternatives. The first proposes a socialistic planning system based on wage-earners' funds as a natural reaction to the difficulties of the 1970s. In contrast to such a development, I shall also indicate a radically different way out of the dilemma.

Roads Leading to a System of 'Fund Socialism'

Obviously, radical changes in the economic system are not simply going to be legislated by the Riksdag or the government. But let us say there is a series of severe crises combined with a rash of economic policies which, while fully understandable and justifiable, prove disastrous. In that case it would be quite possible for us to slide into a system of plans and regulations in which the market economy would be reduced to a very marginal role. This is how it might happen.

The simplest scenario would begin with a profound energy crisis. A serious disruption in our supply of oil and a subsequent price rise, combined with severely limited sources of nuclear power (a maximum of five plants during a brief transitional period), would force a rapid transition to a society of 'coal and firewood'. Major changes in production and transportation would result. There would be mounting demands for investment in new power plants and the conversion of old ones, as well as pressure to shut down highly energy-intensive, timber-consuming installations. This would cause a decline in productivity, but it would also yield improved possibilities for full employment. It is easy to imagine other consequences that would have important implicatons for companies and individuals alike: rationing of electricity and fuel consumption; the planning and regulation of new investment; restrictions on imports and foreign travel to keep the balance of payments under control. Obviously the energy crisis would affect all industrial countries to some degree. Our import restrictions would thus be part and parcel of a crisis in international trade that could involve a virtual epidemic of protectionism and bilateral trade agreements. In addition there will be the cumbersome task of relieving economic hardships. A declining or stagnating GNP will trigger problems of income distribution, and while these can be coped with over a short crisis they will prove burdensome to any government if the situation becomes permanent.

There is no need to attempt any further variations on this theme, although certain parallels might be drawn with the period of the Second World War (1941–5) when we did experience a 'coal and firewood society'. But we were far better equipped, both politically and economically, to deal with it then. I shall therefore restrict my comments to a more typical sort of extreme alternative. Even in this case, however, we must bear in mind the risk of external disruption brought on by faltering oil supplies.

The major option presented by the Royal Commission of 1978 on Long-Term Economic Trends expresses the possibility that economic development will follow a rather favourable course up to 1983 and even beyond. Many people have challenged the optimistic assumptions on which that prognosis rests. For example, its critics have questioned the commission's assessment of our ability to mobilise sufficient amounts of unused productivity reserves; to promote adequate investments in the manufacturing industry despite dwindling corporate solidity and low profitability; and to bring about the requisite expansion of exports. In particular, the favourable trend projected by the commission presupposes effective, consistent economic policies that could cope with any disruptions that might occur during that period.

I find the current debate less than illuminating, particularly on that last point. The real question is how the Swedish economy will make the transition from the recession of 1977–8 to the stable course of growth assumed by the commission. This is where things can easily go wrong. I am especially concerned with 1980–1, and the dangers posed by inflation and balance-of-payments difficulties.

The cash deficit of the public budget has reached absurd proportions (nearly 50 billion crowns in 1979, that is, about 12 per cent of GNP), and it is likely to remain at that level for the next few years; hence the problems caused by this situation will be difficult to correct. It is inevitable that the deficit will be highly – and increasingly – liquid. Even if you assume a maximum of public borrowing outside the banking system and abroad, the share carried by the banking system is still so significant that the total money supply will increase by nearly 20 per cent in 1978–9, and perhaps at much the same rate over the following years. Thanks to the restrictive monetary policy of 1977, the liquidity ratio of the economy as a whole (M3/GNP) did not reach its peak until 1980. In the past, however, this kind of situation has always led to accelerating inflation. And during 1980–1 the stockpile of inflationary 'explosives' has been growing.

It should be obvious that purely mechanistic calculations have no place here. Rather, the following elements must be taken into account.

The size of the budget deficit is not permanently fixed. One might think that the rapid growth in GNP (5 per cent in actual volume up to 1980, and more than 11 per cent nominally) would have automatically reduced the deficit by increasing tax revenues and decreasing the need for subsidies. But this effect has already been taken into account in the Treasury's calculations, and its weakness is due largely to the relatively high proportion of profits – which do not give much of a boost to tax revenues – in the total value added. The liquidity of the budget deficit could be limited by a sharp rise in interest rates, thereby encouraging companies and households to increase their holdings of long-term public bonds. However, since the rise in interest rates would presumably have to be steep, it would also have negative effects on corporate investments. Moreover such a marked deviation from international interest rates would be difficult to enforce without tighter regulations.

Higher liquidity may work in various ways to reduce capital imports and increase capital exports. In so doing it may create growing deficits in the balance of payments which would give the government greater scope for further borrowing. But since these loans would be from foreign sources they would imply no expansion in the money supply and hence no increase in liquidity on a domestic level. This would let some of the air out of the inflation balloon.

- The alternative is a higher rate of price increases. There is no simple, mechanistic cause-and-effect relationship between an abnormal swelling of the money supply and soaring prices. But there are some good empirical reasons for believing that the two phenomena are connected. Business enterprises are the chief beneficiaries of increased liquidity; the budget deficit is reborn in the 'higher' form of corporate profits. Corporate resistance to wage demands tends to weaken with rising liquidity and purchasing power. Tensions in the labour market heighten with an improvement in the business cycle; supply and demand for labour seem disjointed from one region to the next. From labour's point of view the development of real wages has been unsatisfactory over the last few years, especially since profits have been rising rapidly, in absolute as well as relative terms. At the same time there is growing anxiety about future price rises, particularly because of the worrisome build-up of excess liquidity in Sweden and the accelerating rate of inflation in other countries as well. It is quite easy to imagine, therefore, that the growth of Sweden's wage costs will increase to perhaps 12 per cent (rather than the 8 per cent predicted by the commission) and that our rate of inflation will approach the 10–11 per cent figure that was common over much of the 1970s.

My extreme alternative also presupposes a weak government whose anti-inflationary policies prove a complete failure. The two-pronged threat of balance-of-payments deficiencies and accelerated growth in prices and wages is apt to trigger a tough credit policy (as in 1969–70, but even tougher) and a tax squeeze. As a result, future upswings in the business cycle might be stopped short, causing a marked slowdown in production growth. All this might be further intensified by international down swings. These problems will be compounded by a mounting budgetary crisis. It was unreasonable enough that the budget remained weak even during the economic upswing. But a new recession, bringing a heavier demand for public expenditure and slackening in tax revenues, may well carry the deficit to absurd proportions (15 per cent or more of GNP, as in Italy or Iceland).

This would mean that until 1982 the stagflation of the 1970s will not only continue but even become worse. Industrial investments, lacking the time to pick up any sustained momentum, will have fallen below the already too-low level of 1969. Productivity reserves, then, will not have been mobilised to the degree assumed by official forecasts; indeed, industrial capacity will have grown weak and inefficient. Employment goals, however, will have been managed somewhat better, partly through an increase in selective employment subsidies, partly by means of a strong continued expansion in the public sector. The rate of public spending will have been driven up by the recession. As a result of deteriorating balance of payments and cost inflation, further depreciation of the crown may have become necessary.

Do we need further proof that the mixed economy of the 1970s does not work? The grim process of stagflation, according to my extreme scenario, will make radical changes in the system seem all but inevitable. The scenario assumes that private enterprise will not have used the healthy profits of 1979–80 for the purpose of long-term productive investments. Instead the profit will have been eaten up by short-term rationalisation projects, purchases of public bonds and wage increases. In reaction to this failure to bring about industrial capital formation by means of a decentralised profit system, there will be a vigorous campaign for collective savings in various forms. This will 'solve' a number of the dilemmas encountered by a market system that depends on private profits:

- Goals for improved distribution of income and wealth are less likely to be undermined by the inequities that accompany high, uneven profits in a privately owned economy. In certain expanding industrial sectors, however, high profits may be tolerated if wage-earners or the state, through collective funds, are given a 'full' share of the proceeds.

- Wage-earners' funds and state-owned funds for restructuring can provide a reasonable solution to problems of power-sharing.
- Decisions on the rate of capital formation, for example, through a tax on the *wage sum*, can be arrived at more democratically than is possible under the present system.
- Investment decisions can be made more responsive to social goals. Corporate profitability standards may be lowered in order to accommodate such social needs as full employment.

The conclusion, then, is that the government – via restructuring funds, as well as sectoral and project planning – must be the great innovator: with the help of corporate managements and employees it will identify and invest in certain key areas of expansion. Clearly the rate of investment can be vastly improved by pouring money into a number of large sectoral projects distributed fairly evenly among various regions of the country. This would make it possible to limit profit requirements, eliminate the aversion to risk and make full employment the highest priority. It would not be feasible, of course, to undertake such large-scale ventures in production and exports amid the sort of chaotic subsidy conditions that prevail today. Rather, they must be co-ordinated within the framework of a global, long-term, rolling investment plan.

Perhaps I should stop here to deliver a few stirring phrases – such as those offered by Social Democratic Party motions on industrial policy, or the Commission on Employment – on the possibilities of organising and promoting industrial expansion. But I shall resist the temptation to duplicate such documents and refer the reader back to the originals.

As usual the corporations will pose little actual resistance to the various co-operation projects though they will make strong objections in principle. The temptation is overwhelming when the government offers financing and guarantees at advantageous terms, primarily to the smaller companies, for development projects on an almost awesome scale. But these ventures will require the systematic development of an 'economy of negotiation' – a symbiosis between corporate management and the representatives of trade unions, restructuring funds and planning institutions. Corporate managers will gradually adapt their skills to the new demands for negotiating ability and drive, which they will put to good use in defending the interests of the trade union, the general workforce and the geographic region.

Probably no more than a dozen large investment projects

(roughly 0·5–5 billion crowns each) will be needed. They may be tied in with large-scale export projects and supported by state-owned trading companies or bilateral agreements. It may be said that investment policies aim at *creating* new comparative advantages to replace those that have been lost. Vast public purchasing programmes and development projects may be undertaken to cover the basic needs of private consumption. As in all planning systems the government will try to guard against any blatant failures. Fortunately in this kind of fund-socialist economy the odds are much better that potential disasters can be turned into success stories, in terms of volume and employment (in contrast to the Steelworks 80 fiasco of the early 1970s). In any case it will be hard for outside observers to identify mistaken investments.

Thus we can anticipate the development of an extensive framework for selective subsidies of wage and capital costs on the one hand and price regulations on the other. Both will be part of a whole system of selective economic policies whose criteria of profitability for the most part will no longer be based on price signals provided by the market. Such a system might be viewed as a generalisation and enhancement of the sort of policies currently being applied to housing and agriculture. Obviously some remnants of a 'pure' market economy – comprising small and medium-sized enterprises in trade and industry – are bound to persist. Most of these enterprises will serve the large corporations, governed by collective funds, as subcontractors and buyers. The new development funds will help finance the expansion of such small and medium-sized companies.

In the process of developing this fund-socialist system it is quite conceivable that the contradiction between capital and labour in terms of income distribution will be relegated to a fairly minor role. Profit analysis will become a kind of shadow calculation with no real effect on distribution. As a consequence there will be less need for free wage negotiations; instead we will have a long-term incomes policy, designed in relation to the central planning of production and investments. Negotiations will have to shift their focus to wage relations in the context of various kinds of qualitative job assessments.

There are various dangers associated with a fund-socialist system of this sort. Some, though not all, are economic. Understandably there are bound to be a great many errors in investment, perhaps on an even larger scale than in the 1970s. Protection against competition and a dysfunctioning price mechanism will allow efficiency to remain low. But such problems should be measured against those of the 1970s which, according to this scenario, are bound to be intensified. The point of departure, after all, was a mixed economy on the verge of collapse.

The primary risks of the new system are in fact of a political and moral sort. A confusion between political corporate decision-making is being created. Our political system is not constructed for the kind of long-term decisions required in a fund-socialist system, and I am not very optimistic about the chances of establishing viable decentralised fund-and-sector systems where decisions can be made without strong political interference. There will be an epidemic of political wheeling and dealing; where it will lead is anyone's guess, though we can try to extrapolate on the basis of our experience during the 1970s.

We are bound to lose much of the pluralism inherent in the old system. This will be a society of negotiations behind closed doors, in which the major prerequisite for success is no longer one's ability to make good deals on market terms. Responsibilities will automatically be hidden and confused. To the outside observer it will become virtually impossible to understand and identify causes and effects amid this tangle of political understandings, this mishmash of subsidies and licences. A number of works on political economy – from Adam Smith to Assar Lindbeck – describe just how bad things can become.

The Public Sector and the Second Extreme Alternative

My contention is simply that Sweden's mixed economy in its present state is totally vulnerable to disruptions of the kind that took place in 1974–6 and seem to be recurring in 1980–2. I believe that this sensitivity to disruption is related to malfunctioning markets. These in turn are due primarily to an oversized public sector, which has a crippling effect on the self-healing forces of the market. In fact there are cumulative tendencies toward snowballing inefficiency in the capital and labour markets alike.

Both the Commission on Capital Markets and the Bjurel Committee have shown how absurdly distorted the pricing of savings and credit has become as a consequence of the combined effects of inflation and progressive income tax. There is too wide a gap between what the saver actually receives in real, after-tax terms, and the cost to the company, particularly of risk capital. The deficiencies of this system tend to lead household and corporate savings into unproductive channels. Regulations and subsidies then become necessary.

The corresponding gap in the labour market is the difference between corporate labour costs and the real after-tax income of the employees. Here too we have serious consequences in the form of miscalculations and inequitable distributions of resources. It can be argued that our persistently high level of underemployment is largely a result of the fact that wage costs are excessive in comparison to the cost of borrowed capital, leading to unnecessarily high rates of labour-saving rationalisation and automation. The combination of high marginal income tax and wage-sum taxes are pushing wage costs upward, while inflation and subsidies keep the cost of (borrowed) capital down. Because of the high marginal costs of hiring younger workers, the unemployment rate among this age group is particularly pronounced.

If these distortions become cumulative it is not due to the markets themselves but to the response of the Riksdag and the government. Employment rates are declining in private industry and trade; efforts toward rationalisation reinforce that trend. It is really only in the public sector that employment has continued to expand and even accelerate during recessions. In order to finance that expansion, however, tax increases must continue. To the extent that the increases affect income tax and wage-sum taxes, they produce a cumulative tendency towards ever-higher revenue and expenditure in the public sector, leading to further disruptions in the functioning of the market economy.

In the first alternative it was thought that this process would die a natural death in the post-1979 stagflation crisis, thus providing a sort of point of departure for new directions. The second alternative, however, will relate to the prospects and recommendations hinted at by the Advisory Board of SNS and the Bjurel Committee (the Special Delegation on Industrial Policy) in the winter of 1978–9. The method aims at a radical reordering of the public sector and its finances – for the purpose, among other things, of making the capital and labour markets work more effectively.

We have already shed some light on the obvious risks of sliding into a fund-socialist system. Minor changes in taxation will not suffice to ward off the risk of a deepening crisis. In my second scenario, therefore, I shall imagine a radical thrust that combines the clean-up of public finances with a strongly stabilising incomes policy. I do not intend to present a precise programme, but rather to indicate what kind of goals should be fulfilled. The public deficit should be trimmed to a maximum of 10 billion crowns – 2–3 per cent of GNP – through a combination of tax increases and reduced transfer expenditure. Subsidies for enterprises, food and housing must be cut back by about 10–20 billion crowns a year. Many public services and welfare benefits could be partly or totally financed by the payment of fees; they could also be decentralised, as the SNS Economic Policy Group, among others, has suggested. Such proposals need not be seen as reactionary. The enormous transfer payments and subsidies being paid out today are the crudest possible methods of approaching income equalisation, and they impose an unreasonably heavy burden on public finances.

A radical clean-up of the public budget as indicated above will also provide wider scope for the expansion of public consumption and for higher levels of employment. However, increased indirect taxation, among other things, will be needed to facilitate an effective cut in income taxes. A reordering of public finances along these lines will produce a non-recurrent rise in prices – a minimum of about 5 per cent. That is the inevitable cost of a thorough clean-up. But this last gasp of inflation should be compared to the current rate discussed above – perhaps 10 per cent annually – if fiscal policies remain 'stable'. Now how can that non-recurrent inflation be held at bay by means of a planned incomes policy? One obvious requirement is that wage-earners be guaranteed a real growth in income and that the real standard of living of low-income groups be protected. It would make sense for such a policy to cover a three-year period. Thus stresses inevitably created during the first year by the once-only surge in price would be made tolerable by improved prospects for a real wage increase during the following years.

Under such an incomes policy, wage formation must be regulated by means of taxation. But a non-recurrent increase of over 10 per cent in the consumer price index can only be partially offset by income tax cuts. Nominal wage increases must be strictly limited to a maximum of 8 per cent, with lower increases for those with higher incomes. During the 'clean-up' limited reduction in real wages must be tolerated in order to ward off an extra cost push.

As a matter of fact, as a result of such a policy we should see a sharp upswing in the financial position of the public sector, a correspondingly strong improvement in our balance of payments, and increased margins for investment. And after that successful fiscal and incomes policies will have prepared the way for precisely the kind of balanced expansion projected by the Commission on Long-Term Trends. But why, then, should we tolerate prices that rise at an annual rate of 6 per cent? In this extreme scenario the goal should be much bolder – say, 3 per cent, as suggested by the SNS Economic Policy Group. The improved budget and balance of payments should provide the basis and credibility for the higher valuation of the crown such a price stabilisation goal would presumably require.

It is far from easy to spell out the implications of this extreme alternative and its clean sweep of public finances. One cannot allow oneself to become nostalgic about the successes of the 1960s, for instance, and dream of going back to the conditions that prevailed in those days. That era will never return; history moves in only one direction. And besides, the triumphs of the 1960s already contained the seeds of the tensions that later erupted in the grim stagflation crisis of the 1970s.

The purpose of the extreme alternative I have just outlined is to show that it is possible to combat the trend toward a fund-socialist society. Its concrete purpose, therefore, is to prevent us from sliding into the kind of development I described in the first scenario. In this respect it is primarily a matter of trimming the total public sector to reasonable proportions – say, a gross proportion of GNP of some 45–50 per cent (the same as in other comparable countries). But it is considerably harder to be precise about what else this second scenario would mean to different social groups. One might hope, for example, that a sharp decline in marginal tax rates would stimulate a decisively larger measure of individual initiative in trade and production, improve mobility and increase the propensity to work and save. There would be a reversal of the trend towards transactions concluded outside the market and tax system, and that in itself would help clean up public finances.

Another crucial effect would be that the system of wages and prices would more accurately reflect the value of a given labour input and the cost of public services. With drastic cuts in direct taxes and the elimination of most subsidies, individual choices between work and leisure would be based on more rational premises. When the costs of various public services begin to have a more immediate impact – that is, if a household is affected each time it uses these services – decisions will increasingly be based on individual preferences.

Nobody can offer quantitative predictions about what the positive effects on job satisfaction and productivity are likely to be. It is equally impossible to be specific about how this scenario would affect the distribution of income among different households and social groups. In this latter case we shall have to cut our way through a jungle of taboo concepts about the goals of income distribution. It will be necessary to compare the increased inequality of wages and incomes that would be produced by a combination of direct tax cuts and increasing but unevenly distributed work inputs, on the one hand, with the inequities prevailing today as a consequence of rampant tax evasion and high capital gains (due to soaring inflation), on the other.

It is impossible to say that one type of income distribution is 'better' than the other. The difference is rather that the real, after-tax inequities that would arise in the second of my scenarios are closely related to positive, socially desirable effects on productivity, while this is less true of the first alternative I have outlined. Income distribution policy must focus primarily on guaranteeing an acceptable standard of living for the least affluent groups in society. According to this philosophy one need not be too concerned about the distributive effects among the gainfully employed; one should concentrate on lifetime incomes rather than the ups and downs of yearly incomes. Above all such a policy would limit the role played in income formation by certain elements – inflation and tax evasion, for example – that are far more objectionable, macroeconomically speaking, than a few inequities.

Conclusion

As far as I can see, the second scenario is considerably less realistic than the first. Indeed I think it quite probable that we will be impelled, via a grave stagflation crisis, into a fund-socialist system. One prerequisite for such a development is the prevalence of weak governments that emphasise short-term, ineffective solutions to current problems. Such solutions are quite likely to be inflationary, since they are the product of compromise and represent the easiest way out in situations of conflict. Regulations and subsidies of various kinds are the most forceful measures these weak governments can muster.

I have intentionally given an abbreviated, dramatised version of how fund socialism and a planned economy might emerge. It is more likely to be a process of gradual backsliding plagued by many mistakes and diversions – due to changes of government, for example. A substantial number of restructuring funds and government-backed industrial ventures may be expected in the 1980s, and this can be viewed as a necessary and desirable development under present conditions. Corporate uncertainty about the rules of the game is what restrains private investment initiatives and this, in turn, is reflected in a rather erratic policy of state ventures, combined with an increasing rate of expansion in the public sector. There will be no catastrophe – just slow growth (or no growth at all), a too-high inflation rate and no satisfactory solutions to employment problems on a nationwide or regional scale.

A strong governmental coalition would be needed to bring about the clean-up in public finances prescribed by the second, more 'liberal' of my extreme alternatives – but such an authority will probably never come into being. Not even a stagflation crisis in 1980–2, as outlined above, would be sufficient. It is possible that a severe oil crisis and the resulting 'coal-and-firewood' society might inspire the formation of a forceful government – but only for the purpose of overseeing the necessary regulation of a planned economy.

I have posited these two extremes in the hope that the isolation of ideal types will clarify certain problems of policy. They are not meant to be a forecast: real developments as determined by the less-than-ideal economic policies of a succession of governments are likely to fall somewhere between the two alternatives – though probably closer to the fund-socialist, planned economy extreme than to its opposite.

My discussion of the first alternative is based on my *fears* of serious external and internal disruptions, combined with inadequate economic policies – much the same sort of thing we experienced in the 1970s. But my *hope* is that the disruptions will turn out to be minor and that the governments will be lucky with their stabilisation policies. In that case we will not just slide into a new system but will be free to choose one, after due consideration. I must admit, however, that 'hope is pleasant company but a bad adviser'.

15

Sweden's Role in the World

OLOF PALME

Armament and Détente

It is now over thirty years since the end of the Second World War. Europe has been rebuilt. The memories of the landscape of ruins left by the war have faded. The peoples victimised by the war have with enormous efforts built a new life for themselves. In Eastern as well as in Western Europe people continue their endeavours to improve their societies and their living conditions. Despite great differences in their political and economic circumstances they share a common dream of the future: a better society based on the conviction that all human beings have equal value, on co-operation in the face of common problems and on freedom from fear.

But peace is not definitively secured. Huge military forces guard each side of the frontier between East and West. Ever since the end of the Second World War the peoples of Eastern and Western Europe have been tied to the two military superpowers, the USA and the Soviet Union. Both sides threaten to use nuclear weapons against each other in the event of war. Between the USA and the Soviet Union, once united in a victorious struggle against Nazism, deepest mistrust and tension have prevailed. They have each armed their half of Europe in the conviction that if they did not, the adversary would quickly move his positions forward. Every change in the perception of the world has been considered a threat to their own security. In every local conflict they have sensed the plottings of imperialism or communism.

By the end of the 1950s the nuclear armament race of the superpowers had led to a balance of terror. Neither side could any longer start a nuclear war without risking a devastating blow of retaliation against its own population or its allies in Europe. Still, both camps continued a policy of challenge and threat against each other. Both East and West pursued a policy of brinkmanship. They wanted to make their adversary believe that they were prepared to use nuclear weapons to pursue their interests. They went as far as to the brink of disaster.

In the early 1960s mankind witnessed how the two military giants were close to becoming the victims of their own adventurous policies. The peak was reached during the Cuban crisis when the superpowers were brought to see for themselves what it meant to face the precipice of nuclear war. Both sides began to sober up. Attempts were made towards détente. In the summer of 1963 a treaty was concluded to stop all nuclear bomb tests in the atmosphere. Shortly afterwards our then foreign minister, Torsten Nilsson, welcomed the treaty with the following words: "By this token of goodwill and ability to agree the atmosphere has lightened. A beam of sunlight has pierced through the clouds of grinding uncertainty and dismal fear that have been pressing the minds of men. We breathe more easily and feel new hope that a great war can be avoided, a war which would surely mean the annihilation of millions of people and maybe entail the destruction of our whole civilization." Torsten Nilsson interpreted the sombre mood of the times as well as the hope that was ignited by the new policy of the superpowers.

But many years passed before the will to reach agreement made a real breakthrough in the relations between East and West. Only in the late 1960s did the present period of détente begin. In the 1970s the policy of détente has resulted in two SALT agreements between the superpowers on a limitation of the nuclear armament race, the European Conference on Security and Co-operation, negotiations between NATO and the Warsaw Pact on the reduction of troops in Central Europe, and wider co-operation between East and West in all areas. Agreements have been reached on improved human contacts across frontiers and better access to information from the other side.

It may be said that the contours of a more peaceful world are becoming visible. But at this very moment, as we begin to hope that the era of the cold war is finally behind us, we have recently witnessed how easily the climate between the superpowers can deteriorate. And so the armament race is gaining momentum once more. This tends to increase the mutual mistrust and undermine the very basis of détente. Postwar experience has taught us that the emotional atmosphere in the relationship between the superpowers plays a decisive role in the danger of war. During periods of mistrust and aggressiveness between the great powers there are greater risks that an incident which is by itself insignificant could trigger a series of measures and countermeasures which could escalate into a confrontation between the superpowers. Conversely, in a situation where the desire for détente is prevalent, there is more scope for peaceful solutions to conflicts and the avoidance of miscalculations and fatal mistakes, however large the arsenals on both sides.

For Sweden as well as the other states of Europe it is vital that the policy of détente should be continued. Our policy of neutrality contributed to keeping us out of the Second World War. It has kept us out of the bloc politics of the superpowers. Our day-to-day foreign policy decisions – based on the policy of non-alignment – have confirmed and strengthened the credibility of our will and ability to stay neutral in the event of war. Our territory is not of decisive strategic importance to the superpowers. But that does not mean that we can count on avoiding the effects of a conflict between the superpowers in Europe. Once a war has broken out, reason has been rebuked.

It is therefore a central task for Swedish foreign policy to seek to contribute to easing the conflicts between East and West and to maintain and strengthen the process of détente in Europe and the world.

Nordic Co-operation

We work together with the other Nordic countries for détente and security. Every single Nordic country has a policy of safeguarding the stable and peaceful situation in Northern Europe. The superpowers share this interest. They know that any attempt to change the security pattern to their own advantage would immediately meet with actions from the other side to restore the balance of power. The Nordic zone of stability with its low degree of tension would then be lost. It has always been a fundamental task for the Swedish policy of neutrality to work with vigilance and care for stability in the Nordic area. This task will not be less important during the 1980s.

One essential factor of stability and security in the Nordic area is Nordic co-operation. Its depth and extension are unique. The basis for this intimate and growing co-operation is a community of language, culture, tradition and cohesion. The Nordic countries' different choices of security solutions have not prevented this development. Nordic co-operation embraces most sectors of social activity. It has long comprised a common Nordic labour market and important cultural co-operation. But it goes much further than that. A harmonisation of legislation in the five countries is continuously taking place. Programmes of co-operation have been developed in a number of areas: social policies, regional policies, education, research, environment protection, work environment, consumer policy and transportation. Economic co-operation between the Nordic countries is of particular importance. In the 1980s industrial development and energy supply will be in the spotlight. The Nordic Investment Bank, established a few years ago, will have an important role to play. The common fund for technology and industrial development can provide essential contributions to an expanding Nordic economic co-operation. I foresee that such an expansion will take place during the 1980s.

Sweden's Role in Promoting International Détente

In Europe, Sweden has long endeavoured, on the basis of its policy of neutrality, to help overcome the contradictions between the superpower blocs. Our policy of neutrality has given us the possibility and therefore the responsibility for contributing actively to building bridges between East and West. During the cold war period our foreign minister, Östen Undén, tried to play down the contradictions and strove for co-operation in an era of confrontation. His was a voice of reason in those hard times. In his capacity as executive secretary to the UN Economic Commission for Europe, Gunnar Myrdal made an active contribution to the efforts to promote co-operation between East and West during the worst storms and stresses of the cold war.

We have continued these policies. During the 1970s Sweden has participated actively in the efforts to bring the European Conference of Security and Co-operation (ECSC) to a successful conclusion. We have focused our efforts particularly on such measures as can increase confidence between states in the military field: commitments to give prior notice of military manoeuvres and invitations to send observers. We have also proposed a more open accounting of military expenditures. It seems natural to continue in the 1980s with our active participation in the follow-up on the ECSC, in order to gradually bring about the putting into effect of the various parts of the final declaration of Helsinki.

The Helsinki Declaration implied a vitalisation of East–West co-operation within the framework of the UN Economic Commission for Europe. Concretely, this has so far led to preparations for a high-level pan-European meeting to decide on intensified co-operation to improve the human environment in Europe. In the 1980s we should participate in that process and work actively for extended co-operation in the areas that fall within the mandate of the commission. East–West co-operation in these substantial areas, with the purpose of harmonising and co-ordinating national measures, will teach us to speak in the same terms and thus dispense with the language of confrontation created in the days of the cold war.

Another possibility for furthering the process of détente which we should test is the establishment of a Swedish institute for the study of détente. Such an institute, with researchers from East and West, could be given the task of contributing to more subtle, less rigid views of reality than the current ones. The clichés about the adversary which have dominated in the East and in the West have often constituted an obstacle to the process of détente. Such an institute could monitor the short- and long-term trends of détente seek more knowledge of the strategic, political, economic and social preconditions for further détente. The role played by the Stockholm International Peace Research Institute in the field of disarmament shows that such an initiative has a chance of making an impact internationally.

Economic and Political Change in Europe

One of the reasons for tension and conflicts between states is the fact that crises and problems exist within states. They create the insecurity, anguish and fear on which tension-mongers thrive. And, conversely, the foremost resistance to tension is offered by societies marked by their citizens' trust in them and faith in their stability and development potential.

In the communist states of Eastern Europe the social systems now face ever-increasing demands for reform. As is most clearly illustrated by the developments in Poland, people react against oppression and lack of respect for human rights and freedoms. The Eastern European economies are confronted with a new situation: development and industrialisation with scarce resources. Thorough changes in economic decision-making are becoming necessary. This cannot be brought about in isolation but implies, as the Polish experience shows, reforms in all sectors of social activity. This development follows its own laws. One thing is clear, however: it requires the withering of paralysing, bureaucratic centralism. Power and influence have to be decentralised. The change is laborious and difficult since it tends to meet stubborn resistance from an unbending, encrusted power structure.

The progress that can be made in this regard during the 1980s will be essential for the peoples of the Soviet Union and the rest of Eastern Europe. Such progress will also contribute to the process of détente. It can lead to a stable long-term expansion of East–West trade by raising the capacity of the East to diversify exports and finance the extensive imports from the West necessary to facilitate and expedite the restructuring of the Eastern European economies. For us such a development would mean a chance to further an important objective of long standing in Swedish foreign policy, namely, to expand our export markets.

In the West the last few years have entailed extensive unemployment, economic stagnation and inflation. A mood of despair and pessimism has gained ground in Western industrialised countries. There are conservative groups that nourish such moods with a view to sharpening their own demands for wage controls and cuts in social security. They are against trade union demands for co-determination and economic democracy. They threaten to move their companies to countries with low wages and taxes in the Third World. This is irresponsible not only from a social but also from an economic point of view. For the logical consequences of such demands and threats are shrinking markets, economic depression and protectionism, which would lead to joblessness, a lower standard of living and worries for the future.

It is urgent that we fight against these moods. It is important to recreate the faith of people in Western Europe in the future. Developments of the 1970s may not have shown spectacular progress of the kind produced by the 1960s, when so great expectations for the 1970s were aroused. But instead we have had day-to-day reforms which may provide a good basis for long-term progress. The first steps have been taken on the road towards economic democracy, with all its possibilities for increased capital accumulation and increased co-determination which make for secure jobs and stable growth. Similar developments seem to be under way in other European countries. The re-establishment of democracy in previous dictatorships has increased the chances for an extension of the public service sector, which provides not only more security but also new job opportunities and growing markets. The ever stronger demands for national independence and economic liberation in the countries of the Third World have led to progress in the creation of autonomous national economies with enormous needs for investment and consumption increases in order to raise the low standard of living. This means huge future markets for a Western Europe prepared to open its markets to the exports of autonomous developing countries. And Western Europe has a staggering production potential in its well-trained labour force, its high industrial productivity and its advanced technology.

Higher growth on a worldwide scale will lead to increased pressure on the earth's natural resources and raw materials. It will be necessary to develop technologies and social patterns that are more economic in terms of resources and energy. And we should not just stand there, watching passively. The slowdown of the late 1970s must not lure us into delaying action; changes in technology and social patterns are long-term processes. Therefore the 1980s must be a decade when we intensify the construction of a society which is able to economise on resources and yet achieve balanced growth and social progress.

It will be an important task for us in the Europe of the 1980s to vie for expansive policies, with full employment and a just distribution of income as our main objectives. The fact that Sweden has not adhered to the European Community obviously does not mean that we want to isolate ourselves from Western Europe where our major markets are. Nor does it mean, contrary to what was asserted by the advocates of Swedish membership in the Community, that our staying out has deprived us of all possibilities of influencing developments. Sweden is an autonomous partner of the European Community. And we have sought new ways and means to participate in the efforts to solve the present economic problems.

Swedish Policies of National Security

The endeavours to strengthen the process of détente are an important part of Sweden's policy of national security. That policy is being formed by the interplay between foreign policy, defence policy, policy for international disarmament, trade policy and aid policy. Lately public debate on the importance to be accorded to defence policy within the wider context of national security has been intensified once again. Impatience with the slow pace of disarmament negotiations and worries over the worsened situation of poor countries have sometimes led to the erroneous conclusion that Sweden would make its best contribution to world peace by unilateral disarmament. In this context it is important to keep in mind the role played by Sweden's defence in the military stability and balance of Europe.

Drastic cuts in Swedish defence could lead to increased pressure from the superpowers on our Nordic neighbours. The conclusion we should draw from present international trends is that we must strengthen our contributions to peace within the framework of our foreign policy rather than by unilateral disarmament. At the same time, however, it is important that we should have a realistic and constructive public debate on defence issues. The commission charged with the preparation of the defence decisions to be taken in 1982 has been instructed to analyse, against the background of cost trends, how to establish a reasonable balance between the tasks and resources of our defence. This implies a thorough analysis of the international situation and the prospects for détente. We must also carefully study what role the risk of a conventional large-scale attack in the context of an armed conflict between the great power blocs should play in our defence planning for the future.

The struggle for international agreements on disarmament has traditionally been an important element in Sweden's policy of peace and security. We still have every reason to pursue our efforts for disarmament, patiently and energetically, within the UN and in the disarmament commission at Geneva. We must make the fullest possible use of the possibilities offered by our position of non-alignment and our technological knowhow. An important task for our disarmament policy in the 1980s will be to seek a gradual withdrawal of the nuclear weapons stationed in Europe or designed to be used against it. Even though no immediate risks of war are at hand in Europe, the presence of tens of thousands of nuclear weapons here constitutes a latent threat to our security.

The superpowers have reached approximate equality in the strategic nuclear arms race. Negotiations are going on in Vienna on a reduction of conventional forces in Central Europe. At a future stage of the SALT negotiations it is expected that they will include a discussion of so-called tactical nuclear weapons in Europe. This being so, it is a common interest for all the peoples of Europe to demand that the superpowers establish as an objective that Europe shall be freed from nuclear weapons. Sweden must also direct attention to such military doctrines as imply that limited nuclear wars can be pursued and won. That attitude leads, *inter alia*, to investments in smaller nuclear weapons such as the neutron bomb. This weapon lowers the nuclear threshold, increases the risk of war and also expresses a frighteningly inhuman way of thinking; it must be severely condemned.

Our efforts must also continue to mobilise strong public opinion for a gradual transfer of the enormous resources now being wasted on the armament race to peaceful purposes. Above all we must free resources in order to establish a more just economic order in the relations between industrialised and developing countries. The huge gaps between rich and poor countries not only run counter to the need for international solidarity. They also constitute a direct threat to peace. A conflict stemming from the economic injustices between North and South may in its extreme consequence lead to a global conflagration.

The Liberation of the Third World

During the last few decades the struggle in the Third World for national liberation has been an important element in world politics. National liberation movements have demanded the right for their peoples to decide on their own future. Frequently they have been forced to defend that right in an armed struggle. Their endeavours have been successful. Autonomous states are being built on the ruins of colonial oppression.

In Sweden we have approved of these endeavours for a long time. We have not looked on passively but rather tried to offer our support in various ways to the national liberation process in the Third World. In the course of the 1960s and 1970s this political and economic support was developed and extended to become an important link in Swedish foreign policy. The process was sometimes controversial; some people criticised this part of our foreign policy. It was said to run counter to our basic security interests. It was said to be irreconcilable with our policy of neutrality. It was criticised for doing alleged harm to our economy by hurting Swedish commercial interests. Some of us still remember the mendacious campaign about supposedly lost export orders because of our assistance to Vietnam. We should not devote ourselves to the problems of the Third World, said our critics; it was only a marginal concern to us. Swedish foreign policy should rather be limited to activities of relevance to our own geographic area.

In other countries as well, criticism was voiced in certain circles against Sweden's active support for the liberation movements. This was easier to understand. After all, the demands of national liberation movements for self-determination were directed against strong economic interests in Western industrial countries. Those capital interests created instruments for themselves to maintain the economies of colonisation even after the colonies had become autonomous states. The 1960s and 1970s have given us some understanding of the application of such instruments; the Vietnam War and the Chilean *coup* have provided brutal and bloody examples. A central role has been played by the collaborators of the colonial era. Military juntas have been provided with new, immensely cruel weapons specially devised to terrorise civilian populations.

New motives have been advanced to justify interventions by the great powers. There are modern successors to the themes of old-style imperialism such as 'the white man's burden', 'the mission of civilisation', or the gunboat diplomacy 'right' of intervention – often confirmed by treaty – to protect one's own economic interest. Nowadays the interventions have been made 'in the pursuit of democracy, freedom and human rights'. However, they have been carried out with the brutal violence of oppression. The new themes have stimulated the development of new instruments of intervention. We should not forget the destabilisation measures used to overthrow a democratically elected president in Chile, nor the so-called urbanisation programme in South Vietnam, which meant that age-old traditions of Vietnamese villages were blown to pieces and the social roots of the peasant population cut off.

Nor is it difficult to identify with the demands for national independence raised by national liberation movements. This support for the liberation struggle did not imply total identification with the liberation movements or uncritical acceptance of their programme or future social system. Obviously one did not assume responsibility for what a movement in another country would do once it came to power. The liberation movements never promised they would build their societies after the victory according to our wishes. They did not make a revolution to please us. We have reasons – in some cases – to criticise developments in these new states, but we must not hold them responsible for our own broken illusions. Not even the excesses of a revolution can justify imperialism or colonialism.

Swedish popular movements have sided with the liberation movements. The young people of Sweden and their organisations have played a central role. First the Southern Africa solidarity movement was formed. Then the Vietnam solidarity movement grew to be a powerful moulder of public opinion in Sweden.

We must of course not exaggerate the importance of our contributions. They were modest, seen in an international perspective. But we did protest against oppression and cruelty. We participated in an international public opinion campaign against those who opposed the demands for freedom. We maintained that it was illusory to believe that demands for social justice could be held back by violence and military might. We stressed that one cannot freeze the social situation in the world and that national, economic and social liberation was a precondition for durable détente and peace. We upheld the rights of the small peoples in the world of the superpowers.

The Swedish arsenal of foreign policy measures was given new forms of political and diplomatic support for the liberation struggle in the Third World. Our UN policy was developed. Humanitarian assistance to the national liberation movements was introduced, at first indirectly through popular movements and humanitarian organisations such as the Red Cross and the Save the Children Fund. After some time, direct assistance to the liberation movements grew to be an important part of the Swedish programme for development assistance. Once the movements had won their national freedom, we focused on a fairly extensive programme of development co-operation with the new states in support of their endeavours to build autonomous economies and societies. We must not forget that the absence of outside help or outright isolation makes it more difficult for the new states to defend their independence against the superpowers.

The struggle for national self-determination was an attack on an international system of relations between states marked by the division of the Third World into colonial realms and spheres of power. The peoples of the Third World were dependent objects in the world of the superpowers; the issue of their liberation was a function of relations between superpowers. In this perspective the struggle for self-determination was treated primarily as action liable to bring about changes in the balance between the great powers. The struggle was viewed as another factor of tension. It was said to constitute a threat against world peace. Overall strategic interests and a desire to maintain world peace were thus advanced as arguments for the resistance to liberation.

This superpower view of the Third World's liberation did not die with the dissolution of colonial realms. It was sharpened and developed. They said that national liberation entailed political power vacuums which in the name of the balance of power had to be filled by superpower presence. The former American secretary of state, Henry Kissinger, tried to establish a status quo guaranteed by the superpowers in the Third World. By agreement between the two superpowers to show restraint in cases of conflict within the other's sphere of influence, the basis was to be laid for a new 'legitimacy' in a world divided between the two blocs. This superpower 'legitimacy' was to be the guarantee of stability and peace.

The establishment of a dialogue and co-operation between the superpowers in the interest of disarmament and peace is a very positive development. It is a necessary element in a global process of détente. This, however, can never be an argument for a division of the world between two opposing blocs. Such a division does not lead to peace and stability. Instead the result would be a dangerous and insecure world. Internal conflicts in the countries of the Third World as well as conflicts between those countries would be deepened by being drawn into the struggle between East and West. They would be more difficult to solve. To incorporate the states of the Third World into the global balance of power would be to increase the risks of spreading the conflicts to other regions where the superpowers stand opposed to each other. An intensified struggle between superpowers for spheres of power and influence in the Third World would lead to increased tension and risks of dangerous confrontation.

It was to prevent such a development that a number of Third World states in 1961 initiated co-operation within the non-aligned movement. Its members did not want to be drawn into the superpower relationship with its conflicts and contradictions. As an alternative to a world divided into blocs, the non-aligned advocated a world where the national right to self-determination is fully respected, a world free from interventions by superpowers or other great powers in the internal affairs of small states. The non-aligned group includes states with extremely different social systems and values, with a wide variety of opinion even on central foreign policy issues. The very fact that this heterogeneous group has been able to stay together so far bears witness to the strong cohesive force inherent in the struggle for autonomy *vis-à-vis* the superpowers. Let us hope this cohesion will remain.

The endeavours of the non-aligned states are consistent with the traditional goal of Swedish foreign policy: to secure, in all situations and in the ways we choose ourselves, our national freedom of action in order to preserve and develop our society within our frontiers and according to our values, politically, economically, socially and culturally; and in that context to strive for international détente and a peaceful development. The realisation that durable peace and détente are impossible as long as small states are subjected to the Realpolitik of great powers is a concept fundamental to social democratic foreign policy since the beginning of the 1920s. Branting (the then leader of the Social Democratic Party) appeared in the League of Nations as a spokesman for the small states and took the role of opposition on issues where a combination of great powers was directed against the interests of small states. Östen Undén later gave eloquent expression to this same consciousness when in 1940 he criticised the German Nazi doctrine for a new order in the international system, the so-called *Lebensraum* doctrine. He made the following point: 'A durable peace can never be built on such a division of the dwellings of the earth that the smaller peoples are reduced to being mere squatters in the *Lebensraum* of some great power.'

The same concept has guided us as we have shaped our foreign policy with regard to the Third World in the 1960s and 1970s. We have taken a stand for nationa. freedom and independence. We have condemned intervention and interference in the internal affairs of other states – such actions must never be met by passive silence in the international system of relations between states; that would be interpreted as acceptance. As a small state, we have as our goal a world in which the principles of sovereignty and non-intervention are fully respected. This has also made it possible for Sweden, albeit to a modest extent, to build bridges between South and North in a period marked by crises and the risk of polarisation. This is not a result of having taken a neutral stand in conflicts relating to international economic liberation. Rather, it is a consequence of relations with countries of the Third World having been built up by our foreign policy. Sweden, which is a part of the industrialised world, has gained the confidence of the Third World to a certain degree. The policy of neutrality is a precondition for our credibility. At the same time our support for national liberation in the Third World has constituted an integral and important part of the totality of foreign policy actions by which we assert our will and ability to be neutral in wars on the basis of non-alignment.

It is important for every Swedish citizen to act in such a way as to keep the confidence of the Third World. This means that we must continue to give consistent support to the struggle for liberation. Fearful passiveness and reluctance to criticise and condemn those who defend the exploitation of the countries of the Third World will be taken by those countries as support for the forces that strive to preserve colonial structures. If the role as a bridge-builder is seen as a chance for us to press the Third World into concessions in their struggle for freedom and independence, then the capital of confidence we have built up will soon be eroded. Our international profile is written by our actions. It is shaped by the vision of the world continuously reflected in our foreign policy. And when they read our profile in the Third World they will be looking for the analysis of the international situation which determines our foreign policy positions. Our credibility cannot be upheld merely by using a few harsh words of criticism or general expressions of support for liberation which over the years have been incorporated in our foreign policy vocabulary. The words must be supported by an explicit analysis and vision of the world.

The liberation of the Third World has not been fully achieved. In important respects it will mark world politics of the 1980s as well. In Southern Africa colonialism has brought about the apartheid regime of South Africa and the illegal South African occupation of Namibia. This regime is internationally isolated. But it disposes of a gigantic machine of oppression. It is armed to the teeth. The decisive question facing Southern Africa in the 1980s is whether a negotiated solution for peaceful transition to majority rule in Namibia and a peaceful dismantling of the apartheid system remain possible, a dismantling which makes possible a peaceful, multiracial society. The case of Zimbabwe shows that majority rule works well and that several decades of racial conflict and oppression can be overcome. The alternative is that the liberation process in Southern Africa turns into a devastating racial war with immense sacrifices in terms of human suffering and considerable risks of a conflict between the superpowers.

The answer to the question depends to a large degree on the position of the Western great powers. The day they decide to support fully, and adhere to, UN sanctions in order to press South Africa into accepting majority rule in Namibia and a gradual dismantling of the apartheid regime, South Africa will not be able to resist the pressure. However, as long as the Western powers limit themselves to verbal criticism and exhortations to negotiate but refuse effective sanctions, South Africa will resist peaceful solutions. The tendency will then be towards a racial war. Manoeuvres in order to play for time will not solve the contradictions. Attempts to establish black puppet regimes in Namibia 'legitimised' by 'elections' directed by the white racists will not stop the struggle for liberation.

Why then do the Western great powers seem reluctant to accept the liberation of Southern Africa? Why do they not withdraw their *de facto* support for the apartheid regimes?

We know that the great Western industrial countries have vast economic interests in Southern Africa, particularly in the form of private investment. And it is understandable that the exploitation of raw materials and underpaid black labour in the well-endowed South Africa and Namibia must make these investments extraordinarily profitable. But it is difficult to see that this can be of such vital interest in the long run for some of the most wealthy and mighty states of the world that they should be prepared to destroy their relations with Africa and the entire Third World, act against the fundamental values on which their own societies have been built and accept a development which would lead to serious risks for world peace. Another motive advanced by the Western powers against accepting the liberation of Southern Africa is the fact that the liberation movements receive arms from the Soviet Union and Eastern Europe. This means, they say, that the strategically important Southern Africa will fall into the arms of the Russians and leave the Western sphere of influence for the Eastern sphere if the liberation movements come to power.

This argument represents the same superpower perspective on the liberation of the Third World that we encountered during the Vietnam War, and once more as a motive for intervention, via South Africa, in Angola, as rich in raw materials as its neighbour Namibia. It is an irrational argument because it presupposes that the peoples who have fought for freedom and independence are ready to give up that independence in return for arms and political and economic support. The peoples of Africa want support on their own conditions because they seek their liberation and because they want to defend their human dignity. They will surely prove to be very eager to defend their self-determination even against those who have given them military assistance. Experience has already proved the point.

What should Sweden do to support the liberation of the Third World in the 1980s? Briefly, we should consistently maintain our political and economic support for that liberation begun during the 1960s and 1970s and shape this support according to the conditions prevailing in the world of the 1980s.

A concrete contribution is the recent legislation initiated by the Social Democrats prohibiting investment in South Africa. At the same time it is essential that we continue to work within the UN for increased pressure by stronger sanctions against the apartheid regime and, generally, extend our political support in other forms to the liberation struggle in Southern Africa as well as our economic support for the liberation movements and the victims of apartheid. It is particularly important that we should in every conceivable way seek to make the great Western industrial countries support effective UN sanctions against South Africa.

Conditions for a New International Economic Order

Swedish development assistance and our participation in the normative process of the UN system in support of the development of developing countries must be extended to include even more support for the liberation of the Third World. The main objectives of our development assistance policy already correspond well to the demands that can be made on it: support for national and economic independence and a development marked by economic and social equality and democratisation.

It is now more than five years since the developing countries together formulated their demands for a change in the distribution of resources and power in the world. The headline was impressive and challenging: a new international economic order. It was done against the background of the dramatic action of oil-producing countries that had hurt the economies of industrial countries. The food crisis and increasing inflation had strengthened the feeling of many developing countries that the time was ripe for profound changes in the world's economy.

The great industrial countries in particular saw this as confrontation politics. They warned the developing countries against ganging up together and demanding changes in the economic system: it had served everybody well and would continue to do so. Some of them even refused to accept the expression 'a new international economic order'. Hardly anything has happened in terms of putting the new world order into effect. The relations of dependence they wanted to break up have been sharpened drastically for many developing countries, not least by the drastic increase in their debt to the major international banks. Industrialised countries have had enough of their own problems: their inability to provide jobs for people, social conflicts, inflation, the crisis of the international currency system. For these countries as well dependence on the major capital centres has increased.

But it is not the persistent and increasing inequality between countries – and within countries – that is in the focus of current international debate. The key words today are 'interdependence' and 'mutual advantage'. The international exchange of goods and not least the tremendous capital expansion after 1973 have tied East and West as well as North and South together in relations of dependence which to a large extent lack political direction and functional institutional frameworks. The rather confused debate on the rules of the game of economic exchange between countries – I suppose this is how the concept of 'international order' can be defined in this context – might be easier to come to grips with if one could separate two things. First, it is evident that the rules of the game have to be adapted to current international economic realities. To a great extent governments lack the means of control in relation to the multinational corporations. The international credit market and the currency system have not kept pace with the huge financial redistribution between oil-producing countries and industrialised countries. The position of the dollar as a reserve currency has been questioned while reserve asset creation through international decision in the form of special drawing rights, SDRs, remains underdeveloped. There are no rules to provide at the same time for the industrial export interests of low-income countries and the needs of industrialised countries for supplies of raw materials, employment and structural adaptation. Secondly, it is a question of how to devise the rules of the game in a way that not only passively adapts them to the reality of the day but consistently seeks to provide for fundamental demands for a more just distribution of resources and influence between poor and rich countries. This is what the initiatives of developing countries in the UN five years ago were all about, but international negotiations have gradually pushed this aspect to one side. The two aspects condition one another. Unless the international economic system is brought to function better, there will be no preconditions for international reforms to enhance equality. Between nations as well as within them a redistribution of wealth and decision-making powers is facilitated by balanced economic growth. Conversely, it is only such redistributive reforms that will in the long term create a basis for well-being, social justice and peace between nations.

The discussion on the new international economic order has primarily dealt with macroeconomic questions, the overall relationship between industrialised market economies and developing countries. A number of proposals for reform have been presented at international conferences within the framework of the so-called dialogue. But at the last moment industrial countries have opposed a stubborn 'no' to all reforms, which has led to a growing desperation among developing countries. The industrial countries have very consistently defended their economic superiority.

At the same time there is a growing consciousness that the reforms being discussed within the framework of the new international economic order will primarily benefit the countries who are a bit more advanced in their development. The poorer countries have little to gain. Besides, precious little is known about how the reforms would affect the majority of people in the various countries. A system for more stable commodity prices, which is a central demand of the developing countries, may lead to increased resources being channelled to commodity-producing developing countries. But who stands to gain from such improvements? Will they raise the miserably low wages of, say, the miners who bring the raw material out of the mountain, or the dockers who struggle from dawn to dusk for a few crowns to unload the cargoes. Will resources be used to give them, their children and their wives, access to better food, health and education? Or will it be the rich élite that enriches itself even more? Or maybe multinational corporations, who by means of various pricing tricks see to it that the profits disappear to some tax haven? The same questions can be addressed to practically all proposals for change or reform of the international economic system.

Against this background many people have begun to advocate a link between demands for a new international economic order and national strategies to provide for the elementary needs of individual citizens for employment, food, housing, health care and education – so-called basic needs.

Many developing countries regard it as interference in their internal affairs when demands for certain national policies are made a condition for international agreements. Such demands have been voiced in particular by industrialised countries which in their own internal policies give little scope for redistribution in favour of the poor and in their international policies have been modest donors. The demands for redistribution of wealth within developing countries are then easily conceived as mere excuses of the unrepentant. There is a risk, then, that those of the rich world who defend their privileges more strongly than anyone else use conditions within developing countries as an argument against an international redistribution of wealth. By the same token the rich countries are accused of trying to avoid a new international economic order by offering 'lollipop' aid in favour of the poorest. It appears to be a method of keeping them poor. The aim is simply to increase the markets for the products of industrialised countries instead of building up the production capacity of the poor countries. But such difficulties must not prevent us from trying to clarify, to the extent of our ability, the interplay between national endeavours to improve the situation of the majority, and international reform.

The international debate on development issues thus presents a fragmented picture today. The driving force of the message conveyed by developing countries to the rest of the world in 1974 resided to a large extent in their keeping together the destitute underdeveloped, the half-industrialised and the oil-rich. The shift of emphasis in the present picture of international negotiations has certainly to do not only with the altered position of industrialised countries. Within the large group of developing countries developments have gone in different directions. The oil-producing surplus countries have got an ever-increasing community of interest with the industrialised countries where they invest their surplus. Within the group of so-called middle-income countries are a number of states which are in a stage of rapid industrial expansion and have a primary interest in access to markets and credit in the rich countries. The least developed countries have been the hardest hit by the world economic situation; their scarce export incomes have covered an ever-shrinking share of their imports.

This fragmented picture, however, must not for a moment be

allowed to obscure the imperative necessity of reaching quick and concrete results in the so-called North–South dialogue. For the growing gap between rich and poor countries, and the conditions under which poor people live, are not only something inhuman and intolerable but also a growing threat to world peace. I am convinced that constructive solutions to the problems presuppose a balanced economic growth with a view to achieving full employment and social justice in industrial as well as developing countries. If the latter are to fight their way into shrinking markets in the industrial countries, the consequences will only be further increased unemployment, even more serious structural problems and ever stronger protectionist tendencies. Growing markets and increased employment create quite different preconditions for openness and generosity in relations between states.

It is quite clear that the pressure exerted on the economy of Sweden and other industrial countries by industrial products from developing countries will increase. A number of countries, particularly in Latin America and Asia, have the infrastructural conditions for an increased industrial production. The debt burden they have incurred can now only be done away with through a rapid expansion of exports. The fact that the very debt burden forces developing countries to adopt a development model with large deficiencies (exports to industrialised countries rather than a gradual build-up of purchasing power and national markets as well as trade between developing countries) makes it even more urgent to reach international agreements on writing off their debts. We may think that a development strategy that had done more for the basic needs of the broad layers of population would have been preferable. We have the right to maintain that in the international debate, as well as to point to the potential of increased economic co-operation between developing countries. But we shall not be able to avoid the demands for increased access to our markets and a gradual restructuring of our production. The guiding principle of Swedish policies must be openness and participation in this readaptation. It is the only way consistent with our view of the relationship between rich and poor countries. It is also the way that, in the long run, will provide the Swedish economy with development opportunities. For we must not forget the large markets, not least for investment, which open up in advanced developing countries.

But openness is not the same thing as *laissez-faire*. It implies a reasonably fair distribution of the burden of readaptation between the rich countries. Otherwise the pressure from low-priced imports will be so strong that Swedish industry cannot even manage the production level necessary to our contingency needs, let alone the smooth adaptation which is a precondition for our labour market policy being able to help people find new employment. This is what has happened within the garments sector, where a regulation of imports has been found necessary. Those who condemn measures of protection in this kind of extreme situation choose to forget the realities of contingency planning and employment policies in our country. The passive trade policy they advocate would soon undermine the foundations of a long-term, solidarity-oriented policy in relation to developing countries.

Increased scope for the exports of industrial products from developing countries, stabilisation of commodity prices, debt consolidations – we must be part of the work for international solutions in all these fields. But at the same time we must retain the possibility of discussing how they should be devised in order to provide as much support as possible for the countries and peoples most in need of support. To treat all countries categorised as developing countries in the same way would amount to a rather reckless discrimination against the poorest, as well as against those countries who have taken on the responsibility of a profound policy of social justice. On the whole we must dedicate ourselves to increasingly wide co-operation with developing countries. Trade, industrial co-operation and technological transfers will be in the forefront. There are already a number of tools for stimulating the interest of private industry; things like agreements on investment protection, export credit support, support for consultants, and so forth. In addition there is a need for new measures in order to extend our co-operation with developing countries in a way consistent with our goals of solidarity. In the future the government must play a more active role in our industrial co-operation with the Third World. In the Labour Movement and a New International Economic Order Programme, concrete suggestions have been put forward for *inter alia* agreements of co-operation with countries that struggle for national independence and social and economic justice.

What I have just said amounts to an endorsement of the ideas in favour of putting mutual interests in the forefront of the North–South dialogue. They reflect a reality. The endeavour to defend the peace, to use the advantages of the international division of labour, to further development in such a way as to favour everyone – all this must have the capacity to unite the nations of the world. If only the political will is there, I am convinced that it is possible to translate these objectives into a series of reforms and concrete measures in the field of international economic co-operation of great importance for a balanced economic development. It does not mean that one would do away with the market system at the international level – which has been the slogan used to mobilise resistance in rich countries. But it does mean fairly strong regulation of the market system with a view to creating a larger measure of justice for poor countries.

It is correct to assess common interests between rich and poor countries, and to present the possibilities of mutual advantage. But one must not forget that many countries will not be drawn into such a development. There are no multinational corporations lining up to invest in Mali or any other of the extremely poor countries of the Sahel cruelly hit by natural disasters. Not many people talk of the mutual advantage to be gained from co-operation with the most destitute. It is convenient to forget this if you wish to condone the egotistic tendency of industrialised countries in considering that development assistance has lost its importance or if you want to conceal the fact that the economic great powers, the USA, Japan and Western Germany, have neglected their international pledges of assistance, in itself a great scandal. But those destitute countries are on the map and will remain there. They will for a long time depend on assistance. Two demands are involved: that the great industrialised countries, after more than a decade of demonstrated lack of political will, should at last assume their responsibility to build up their assistance to a level corresponding to that of Sweden, the Netherlands and Norway. And, secondly, that the large international aid institutions should use the major part of their resource flow to support the development efforts of those countries which are not favoured by industrial co-operation or trade concessions within the framework of demands put forward in the negotiations for a new international economic order.

Between now and the year 2000 it should be possible to eliminate hunger and what is called absolute poverty in the world. It is a matter of drive and political will. Once, in the United States of America, they decided to reach the moon in a given year. It was a matter of mobilising technology and putting it to use. If you decide to do away with famine and poverty it is a matter of changing political and social conditions. And that is far more difficult. But there is no other action that would be more important in our times for the defence of peace in the world.

The 1970s, despite all disenchantments, was the decade when we began to find avenues to a dialogue and a détente in the conflict between East and West. It remains crucial to peace that we should vindicate détente. Sweden will always support that effort.

The 1980s will be the decade when the dialogue and the efforts to devise constructive co-operation between North and South will come to the foreground for those who want to defend peace. It is a matter of peace and mutual dependence. And in the last resort it is a matter of solidarity with other people in their struggle for social and economic justice.

Index

References in **bold characters** denote chapters or sections that are wholly concerned with the subjects to which they refer.